THE INC

THE INCANDESCENT

Michel Serres

Translated by Randolph Burks

BLOOMSBURY ACADEMIC
LONDON • NEW YORK • OXFORD • NEW DELHI • SYDNEY

BLOOMSBURY ACADEMIC
Bloomsbury Publishing Plc
50 Bedford Square, London, WC1B 3DP, UK

BLOOMSBURY, BLOOMSBURY ACADEMIC and the Diana logo are trademarks
of Bloomsbury Publishing Plc

First published as *L'Incandescent*, Michel Serres, © Editions Le Pommier, 2003

English language translation © Bloomsbury Publishing Plc, 2018

Randolph Burks has asserted his right under the Copyright, Designs and
Patents Act, 1988, to be identified as Translator of this work.

Bloomsbury Publishing Plc does not have any control over, or responsibility for,
any third-party websites referred to or in this book. All internet addresses given
in this book were correct at the time of going to press. The author and publisher
regret any inconvenience caused if addresses have changed or sites have ceased
to exist, but can accept no responsibility for any such changes.

A catalogue record for this book is available from the British Library.

A catalog record for this book is available from the Library of Congress.

ISBN: HB: 978-1-4742-9741-7
PB: 978-1-4742-9740-0
ePDF: 978-1-4742-9742-4
ePub: 978-1-4742-9743-1

Typeset by Deanta Global Publishing Services, Chennai, India
Printed and bound in India

To find out more about our authors and books visit www.bloomsbury.com
and sign up for our newsletters.

For e. marguerite.

CONTENTS

1 MEMORY AND FORGETFULNESS

THE GRAND NARRATIVE[1]

At the end of the lane rising through the forest, positioned on a tall grassy hillock, surrounded by a torrent descending from the mountain, a farm and its annexes overlook a cirque dominated by glaciers. Beneath the morning sun and the motionless air, this view, this landscape, this scene reveal to me, in an ecstatic epiphany, the quiet presence of the things in their exact place. Transparent and wide, space here seems to swallow up time, suspended.

Descent into duration

In front of the door of the house built at the foot of alpine pastures, a little girl of three is playing; as a birthday gift yesterday, she received a cream pink doll with green pants. Behind her, the calm facade with stone lintels still shines with the ochre paint applied with a great deal of effort back when the hay harvest abounded seven years ago. Her grandfather built the metal shed to the left of the main building, itself constructed at the beginning of the last century on the ruins of an old windmill erected in the location of an ancient monastery set up long ago on the premises of a temple – whether Roman or Gallic, we have forgotten – in front of rocks moved by a thousand-year-old flood on the part of this dancing and malicious torrent whose course is dug into the Jurassic strata of the mountains enclosing the semicircular horizon beneath snows said to be eternal.

The toy comes from a store; the little girl no longer babbles and already talks; the paint job dates from recent years, with a mild climate, the new building from before the warm years when the glaciers began to recede, the windmill from the last century, the monastery from the Early Middle Ages, the old stones from before Jesus Christ, the flood from more than a thousand years ago, the mountain from the Tertiary ... As though by steps or degrees, I distinguish the fragile toy in front of the frail child leaping and running in front of the open door, the light shed in front of the heavy rocks, the house in front of the river and the river in front of the high black wall, a millionaire in years, beneath the dazzling Sun, a billionaire star.

How long has the little girl played with the doll? When did her father paint the facade? I easily remember. When did the first occupants of this place erect those stones? This requires more expertise. How long has the torrent flowed, the glacier descended from its bergschrund, the mountain risen to three thousand metres? How long has the sun shone? With datings that are now exact, knowledge answers these questions concerning my perception, then feeds and lastly reverses it: from the depths of the mountains and from the height of the sky, a temporal scale falls onto my shoulders, a scale that flows like a cascade towards me, an old man close to his death.[2]

Little balconies of space-time

In a few days the doll, in torn clothes, will be missing an arm, soon pulled off; in two years the child will have to leave for school in the morning. These walls will still be standing; she will believe them to be immobile her entire life, at least lasting. Her father who coated them because he saw them wearing away has, ever since his own childhood, thought that the mountain was stable. Leaning back against rocks he believed to be unchanging, he noticed that the stones come loose with time and stabilized their rickety breaches with rubble stone extracted from the nearby mountain wall; he built with the hard immobile, drawn from a quarry dug out in width, height and depth. In front of the farm she believes to be eternal, the little girl already regrets having damaged the toy she is holding in her hand and sometimes lifts to her mouth.

Behind the child, the wall; behind the father, the mountain: each of them perceives, twice, something stable. In front of them, the little torn clothes or the denuded facade: each of them perceives, twice, something moving. So daughter and parent believe they are bustling about on a kind of balcony, on a small step of space – behind them, upstream – and of time – in front of them, downstream.

The rose and the gardener

On their narrow and respective terraces, each one, with their backs to space and looking at time, could say with Fontenelle that as far as any rose can remember, no gardener has ever been seen to die. The latter sees the former be born, open, wilt and then disappear with the passing of time, but if the flower could see or feel, it would admire the ever so slow movements of its cultivator, stable and immune to wear, in space. For the little girl, the farm doesn't budge, and her father in his turn knows, like his entire line, that mountains are not moved. Upstream from these two lives, fast like roses, devoted to wear and decline, we find spatial stability, the house and mountain playing, let's say, the role of the gardener; here are two levels composed, as I have risked saying, of a space and a time. Sitting on a solid riverbank, parent and child watch a river flow. In front of the immarcescible construction, the roses lose their petals; the house is erected, wears away and crumbles in front of the impeccable mountain wall, whose rock folds and erodes beneath an eternal sun: for every stance, there are as many gardener illusions.

The scale by which these generations live doesn't exceed the traditions of their family, but a historian would date the constructions: farm, windmill, cloister, temple, ruins, traces, marks of men who have vanished. He adds a few other levels. Each of them only preserves a human memory, one that's lacunary, sometimes written in signs, most often practical and leaving behind a few worked objects. Let's call all our history: the gardener illusion. Like the child, we foolishly believe that civilizations and their works develop in the invariant expanse of a world that welcomes them, in short, that a geography unfolding in a local or global space conditions the duration, whether short or long, of prehistory and history, like the set of a theatre in which the action would take place. But a geologist would date this set again, for it flows as much as the torrent.

The torrent and the Grand Canyon

In front of the furious flood, sweeping away with it rocks, pebbles and sand, we also foolishly say that this current tears these alluvia away from mountains that seem to us to be stable in space; we speak of erosion, as though an active flow were wearing away a passive bedrock that was always already there, like a rare channel in a massif. No, the water flows, but the cliff flows as well since it collapses into blocks and fine sands, like water and human history, in as many and even more stages or levels. Solids flow just as much as fluids do; a bit harder, more resistant, it takes them longer. If the mountain could perceive, it would see things be born and disappear downstream from it and would believe, once again, itself to be leaning back – upstream, if I may, and while it folds, rises, erodes and disappears – against a space in which the sun changes as little as the gardener before his roses: as far as any volcano can remember, no star has ever been seen to age. Behind the few hundred tiers of short-schemed history unfurl millions of levels in which the entire Universe enters into time.

At the bottom of its red gorges, the Colorado flows, but the crystals gripped in the different strata of the canyon's cliffs flow as well. From the south rim of its theatrical fault or in front of the modest farm where the child plays, you don't see two different spectacles in a similar space but a succession of a thousand springs having diverse rhythms. Of course, one spring flows at the bottom of the channel your open eyes follow without any amazement, but the others fall more and more slowly without you directly perceiving them. I invite you to see them, not motionless but slow. Imitating Galileo, I will gladly say: 'And yet all these red cliffs flow.' To the historian's and the geologist's datings are added those of the geophysicist and the chemist, who, in discovering for example how uranium turns into lead, calculate the age of the Earth: four billion years; following them is the astrophysicist, who reckons the age of the Universe, fifteen billion since the big bang, if it ever occurred, and calculates the end of the entire process in what he calls the big crunch, the terminal catastrophe in a punctual crushing. So I can no longer contemplate sun, stars and landscapes without their time carrying my eyes and body away with its tremendous flood. Yes, knowledge feeds and reverses vision.

Just as, with their mechanical science, Copernicus and Galileo reversed our old perception of the terrestrial movements around the Sun, so, filled with wonder at this new change in duration, you now contemplate a tiered series of clocks whose wheels, some of which are tremendously slow (stars and mountains), others incredibly fast (the little girl and doll), count time, each wheel with its own rhythm or rather its own tempo, swift to the pleasure of the gaze and almost motionless to its blindness.

So open your eyes newly. You see space less than time. You see objects arranged in a familiar expanse (rivers, rocks, summits or sun) less than the different rhythms of a flowing (ephemeral works, hundred-year-old houses, thousand-year-old riverbanks, million-year-old rocks, billion-year-old stars). Whereas the common representation caused time to disappear into space, dissolved it or better still concealed it like a magician hiding a flock of doves under a white veil, whereas the theatre stage of representation made the direct vision, intuition or thought of duration difficult for Saint Augustine, Bergson as well as their successors, this series – now unfurling by making millions of springs gush forth in front of me, lightning-fast or with an infinite slowness, in front of the country house or the Grand Canyon – causes the disappearance of, dissolves or conceals, in turn, the expanse behind the surgings of so many chronic rhythms.

Mosaic, marquetry

For space, then, appears as a mosaic of time, with different rhythms and tempos. The child runs and puts her doll between the walls of the house and the sedimentary rocks; let's translate: in a few seconds, three years slips between two centuries and ten million years. She is going to jump into her father's arms or cling to her mother's skirts, who examine the climate early in the morning and then, all day, work the earth, throw out the rocks and keep the soil, plough, sow and harvest with sickles, milk cows, gather eggs, hunt izard or chamois with a shotgun. Their hourly, daily, seasonal, yearly, existential … practices link together different times of the inert, age-old, of the living, domesticated or wild, and of the technological, iron and gunpowder, ancient or recent. Do they bustle about in a space? Certainly, but along the temporal ridges of their fast or slow gestures, they also link, as in a random or regular network, this composite multiplicity of rhythms that are more or less wide or fast: house, earth and rock … wheat, cows and hens … plough, pitchfork and knife … fitted together in a fractal way or mixed together and eddying, each with a different age or date. Thinking we are busying ourselves in a stable space, we mortals daily weave, weft on warp, from the ephemeral to the ancient, the slow on the lightning-fast, drawing a few fleeting lines on the billion-year-old tapestry. Space, then, appears as a marquetry of time.

Jacob's Ladder, the submerged cathedral, Heraclitus

A liquid expanse, iridescent to my eyes, widens and slows as it plunges behind the mountains and constellations; its tempo speeds up lightning-fast when it reaches us, the house, the little girl and me. This expanse bathes the endless foldings with rhythms. Time was lost in space; now in its turn, space is being submerged in time, like the legendary cathedral beneath the ocean.[3]

We find ourselves swept away by this streaming along a scale whose levels or rungs climb and descend the Universe like Jacob's Ladder. This tremendous flood sweeps away the walls of our fragile jails of space. The alpine-pastured farm on the mountain and the Grand Canyon stream with time. Liquids flow, solids collapse. All of nature, nature being born and nature dying, enters into the streaming of the torrent. The space of the old representation collapses under the irresistible impetus of these waters.

Everything flows. We had never truly believed this initiating saying from Heraclitus. We always thought that there existed, here and there, rivers in valleys, clocks between the walls of houses, a heart and a pulse beating amid the tonic muscles and a solid skeleton. In short, the space of representation was sown with several watches. We didn't recognize the universality of Heraclitus' words. We accept them today. Consequently, our perception now sees time superabound. The latter drowns our perception. Always blinded, don't believe your eyes.

This new release outside the prison of the little balcony where we and our philosophy were held stuck unexpectedly complements the Platonic exit from the old cave of space: the released prisoner formerly only added a third dimension to his perception, a dimension which would deepen the flat image he usually saw on the rear wall of the cavern. We gain, for our part, thousands, billions of levels along the universal irreversible duration. Following after the Pascalian fear before the infinite silence of cosmic expanses comes the wonder of he who floats, body and soul, on the surface in a duration with an almost infinite proliferation of rhythms and lengths that defy intuition, for the formation of things as well as in the brevity of the moment.

I imagine a living thing whose heart would beat slowly enough to perceive that mountain ridge as a giant wave whose collapsed rocks would represent the droplets of seawater streaming on its flank, and another whose rapid breath would allow it to live in a flash worlds being born and then crumbling.

Descent into the time of living things

In front of the farm and the girl, I see cows grazing, and I hear the rooster's vainglory sing out; over the Grand Canyon birds of prey fly, and among the rocks and dry grasses rattlesnakes hiss. Everything I'm describing presupposes I'm standing in front of diverse theatres, one of them rural, the others more valuable to geologists and walkers, standing, again and always in space, in front of an adjusted expanse constituted by the stage of my sight. I am again watching representations.

But who am I, me who sees? And these living things, plants or animals, mushrooms and algae, single-celled organisms that live inside me and that I don't see? Springs of time, streaming amid others. Mine, older than the little girl's, is no doubt going to dry up before hers. For my part, I only count as another step of the staircase, another rung in that universal Jacob's Ladder. Our organisms have an age, it is said; I've passed the time of roses, and the little girl has barely reached it; my life expectancy is equal to the porcelain doll's; so be it.

But my brain, to only talk about that, is composed of ancient parts in the reptilian manner, of other parts as new as those developed by chimpanzees and bonobos, lastly others still, incomparably more recent. Layer by layer, it could be dated like those cliffs whose different strata sink more and more deeply into the past. Likewise, my DNA appeared, of course, with the union of my parents, who built it the way cards are shuffled, but in its own structure it is more than three billion years old; even older still, the atoms composing it and me go back to the fabrication of hydrogen and carbon by the galactic energy of the Universe.

Who am I? Not only a step of the ladder, for the age of civil status, but also the successive rungs of a good bit of its length. I spread my time over the world's duration, or rather I plunge into the entirety of its time. Composed of varied rhythms, my body goes from the ephemeral to millions of centuries, in sum so old that my life and history itself scarcely matter.

In our behaviour and our thoughts, we could soon, we are already able to distinguish between those dating from the very formation of cells, billions of years ago, those dating from our spinal cord, hundreds of millions of years ago, those dating from others who were contemporary with hominization, and those dating from others lastly who only go back to the past century or yesterday morning. We far exceed our history. Our gestures, sensations, desires, intuitions and feelings connect, in real time, a thousand incomparable dates, the way, just now, the gestures of the tenant farmers did. As individuals as well as a community, these so vastly diverse times plunge us, up to our necks, into an oldness that's compatible with the world's oldness; sunk into this descent, our forehead reaches the threshold of history, barely, and our hair, the threshold of our existence. Thus our body understands this ladder since the ladder forms it; our body climbs or descends it almost in its totality since our body knows how to evaluate it. The history that begins with writing and the duration of my own life amount to a few steps among these countless rungs. Consequently, what weight do the sciences called social have when they only refer to these very thin layers? Milligrams in comparison with thousands of tonnes? Does our history do nothing but split hairs?

Lastly the cows, the rooster and the wolf, the firs and the ferns on the slopes also climb and descend this great staircase and just as much as we do. Old life, antiquated flesh.

Newborn old man

Meditating once more on my body and that of my granddaughter, when I consider the endless time needed for our tens of thousands of billions of cells to appear independently, to reproduce and become differentiated, to start living together by forming multicellular organisms with separate zones, original tissues, specific organs and different functions, fitted together like Russian dolls, when I count the rhythms they needed to abide by in order to reach a symbiosis, one that's viable for a certain time amid the obstacles and predators, as well as the gigantic army of their immunological defence, lastly the long chain of molecules they needed to construct in order to reproduce, without too many errors, a similar organism that would be as big, I am measuring, by the brevity of its duration, the extraordinary difficulty of this combination. Conversely, the multiplicity of the obstructions it met with causes me to be amazed at the fact that this assemblage has lasted, even for a little. Suddenly summarized for each of us in nine months of gestation, a dizzying whirlwind, this contingent masterpiece required billions of years of attempts, errors and deaths as well as this gestation, fast and successful, in order to last merely a few decades and perpetuate itself by procreating. I am measuring at the same time its long strength and its short fragility. Three years or seventy: what youth, what brevity in comparison to the enormous archaism and slowness of our composition.

New and old, we are becoming experts today in this gigantic time. By making these two operators – selection and mutation – vary, we know how to exploit it in the fields or in the laboratory. Thus we imitate the nature of life, I mean the way bodies are born, by projecting our exhilaration of speed onto this billion-year-old slowness. For biotechnologies now synchronize the times of evolution, of ontogeneses and phylogeneses. Who are we? Living things, old and new, that dare at this moment to actively tie evolutionary time to the time of history. History is changing speed, like it never accelerated before, for this decisive reason.

Our history formerly left life; life is entering into history.

De senectute: The equality of living things before time

When the Ancients wrote *De senectute* or a vain chatterer wrote doggerel about *The Art of Being a Grandfather*, they were merely lamenting or singing the short time inscribed on the village registers and cadenced by the trembling of their limbs. In addition, when assessing life expectancy, ancient and recent, their tally stopped quickly: *de brevitate vitæ*.

Rock ptarmigan and chamois, the grass of the fields and reeds, the lengths of these existences scarcely last a blink of an eye in comparison with the length of the life, counted on molecules and atoms, whose flood traverses everyone and which, in me, shines and burns. *De senectute vitæ*: here then is a true oldness, common to the dying and the newborn, to little girls and grandmothers, to animals and plants, to friends, to enemies, all of them bearers of a DNA, all of them equal in time, with the exception of two parts, the one minimal, their individual age, the other much bigger, the interval lived since their species made its appearance. I'm not taking into account thought, emotions or cultures, narrow and lightning-fast.

Thus we are all aligned together along another staircase, or we are scattered along the trunk and branches of the trees the naturalists have drawn, over and over again, for several centuries and which Darwin made dynamic. This differentiated duration of course wins out over the brevity of our ages. This common crow who traverses, from left to right, the alpine farm's platform, this alligator from the Louisianan bayou, not to mention the rare coelacanth in the oceans, precede me by a fair amount along the bifurcations of that tree in which their spring has gushed forth longer than mine. But this difference in age between the genera only ruptures this universal oldness a little, an oldness counted, I repeat, on molecules and atoms, and which makes me equally contemporary – or almost – with every living thing and, in particular, with my mammalian cousins, with Lucy and Homer, but also with my granddaughter. *De senectute omnium vivorum.* New as much as since always, this equality – at least a statistical one – of every living thing in relation to time is well worth a solemn declaration.

Next to this common oldness, my oldness, individual, and even that of history, form a slender margin. The differences by which we bake the bread of our daily hatreds, of our carnal contempts and of our little bits of knowledge thin down into an imperceptible duration; historical influences have little weight next to the immensely long causes that formed this or that neuron whose excitation contributes to this perception or that emotion. The conditions of cultural or individual diversity suddenly shrink into vanishing differentials. We are almost all as old as the Earth. Recent and rigorous, our time-counters bring back nature, in the sense where life was born billions of years ago. We are all immersed in the same alluvium. This natural equality is well worth a universal declaration.

Descent into the moment

What, conversely, should we say about the instant? And its brevity? Now, what am I holding in my hand?[4] The bursts of laughter of the cascade and the slaps of the breeze, little unanalysed perceptions but reducible into as many nanoseconds as centuries dragged by the immensity of the past. The womb of a pregnant woman experiences a million biochemical reactions per second; while I write this word, my organism is producing almost as many. As from a horn of plenty, the innumerable gushes forth from the instant. Celebrated by the ancient moralists and repeated by ten parrots, this moment in which I'm speaking and which flees far from me suffices for matter, for life, for thought to create bouquets of a thousand particles, to multiply as many cells or kill them by apoptosis, to conceive metaphysical systems. The instant depends on the scale: let Gargantua sneeze and millions of Lilliputian peripeteia unfold at length on the little theatre of his splutter.

We shall understand nothing about the sky, the Earth, life, lastly ourselves if we continue to refer our perceptions to the time of history, short, and to build our culture upon its brevity; likewise the present moment reveals itself to be interminable. Two changes of scale discover 'two infinities, of greatness and of smallness', hiding in duration.

Better, a piece of knowledge and a corresponding experience have just changed our lessons on the internal consciousness of time: our organism includes, as we now know, dozens of clocks – cardiac ones, digestive ones, neural or molecular ones – all of them disrupted by the jet lag at the end of a long flight across longitudes. How are we to think the instant and duration without referring to this internal, circulatory, existential discomfort, whose appearance indicates the organic knot where our relation to time or to the sum of durations indicated by said clocks is constructed, clocks unknown to Bergson, Husserl or Heidegger, none of whom had ever flown across the ocean? Don't these clocks play, in time, the role held, in space, by the compass and orientation? Jet lag: wild fluctuations of the chronic compasses.

Descent into the time of sensibility

The scale changes for the inert landscape and its elements, for the living body and its components; in the same way, the dating scale changes for every sensation, I mean for every relation between the body and things. Around the farm, the meadows of the alpine pastures, during this end of spring, are bursting with scarlet, orange, pale yellow and blue; martagon lilies, asters, soldanellas, columbines, anemones, gentians, rampion bellflowers, campanulas and azaleas are detailing the colours of the spectrum amid the green grass. Contemplative for a long while before this bedazzlement, my head is constellated with pixels. Better, my body feasts on them; better than nourished, filled.

The pleasure of music carries us millions of years back, to when our ancestors hailed each other with laments, and even takes us out of our species towards titmice with complex phrases and melody-inventing hummingbirds: during those times, already, these birds transmitted or received meaning before the advent of discourse. The bouquet of colours fills us in a way that's even more originary by going back towards billion-year-old eras, towards that *Univers bactériel* described so agreeably by Lynn Margulis,[5] back when the first carotenic pigments appeared, constitutive of the rhodopsin of our eyes, with the first rust- and aquamarine-coloured bacteria, violet bacteria, purple ones, yellow, orangish, drinking the light through the filter of the colours; my vision drinks its fill of these colours like they do.

And from what date do the more recent neurons come that form the processing centre for these same colours, a centre buried in a part of the brain specialists call 'the V4 complex, known as the fusiform gyrus', common to rhesus monkeys and to us humans? Luxuriously unfurling from red to violet, the multicoloured meadows give me carnal pleasures stemming from a duration whose length Darwin himself didn't suspect. Dazzled to the point of dizziness by this vertical plunge, my pleasure takes me back hundreds of millions of years in the past. In comparison, the sensations he evoked only gave Marcel Proust anamneses of a recently lost time.

The senses open the body on to the world, it is said; no, they make us descend into an immemorial duration, towards long lost environments. Empiricism holds for archaic eras and vanished universes. When we place it at the initial conditions of modern science, we unknowingly evoke a chain of millions of years.

Natural and human comedy

In front of the ancestral farm, I call my granddaughter now and see her swim towards me with big arm and leg gestures as though she were going against the current. Letting myself float towards her, I recount for her, while going downstream, the Grand Narrative, whose duration I just explored upstream, flowers, rivers and glaciers, mountains, suns and marvels. Perhaps understanding that I'm recounting quickly before dying, she abandons her doll, open-mouthed. Dante, Beatrice and their faith raised *The Divine Comedy*, eternal, to other worlds; Balzac, *Béatrix* and history situated *The Human Comedy*, short, here, there, in the provinces and in Paris. My granddaughter, today's knowledge and I recount this *Natural and Universal Comedy* via the ample contingency of the times. The landscape and us, mountain walls and chamois, we plunge into the Grand Narrative.

Here it is: ever since the big bang, if it ever occurred, began to construct the first atoms inert and living things are composed of; ever since the planets cooled and our Earth became a reservoir of the materials, heavier still, from which our tissues and bones are formed; ever since a strange acid molecule began, four billion years ago, to replicate itself as it was, then to change by mutating; ever since the first living things began to colonize the face of the Earth by continuously evolving, leaving behind them more extinct species than we will ever know of contemporary ones;

ever since a young girl, called Lucy, started to stand up in the savannah of East Africa, promising without realizing it the explosive journeys of the coming humanity into the totality of the emerged continents, into contingent and divergent cultures and languages; ever since a few tribes from South America and the Middle East invented the cultivation of corn or wheat, not to forget the worthy patriarch who planted the grapevine or the Indian hero who brewed beer, thus domesticating for the first time living things as tiny as yeast; ever since writing was in its infancy and certain tribes began to write verse in the Greek or Italic languages … then the common trunk of the grandest narrative began to grow, before our eyes, so as to give an unexpected, real and common, chronic thickness to a humanism finally worthy of the name since precisely all the languages and cultures that came from it can participate in it, a humanism that's single and universal since written in the encyclopedic language of all the sciences and since it can be translated into every vernacular, without particularism or imperialism.

The bouquet-shaped set of Grand Narratives

Yet we would have a narrow conception of it, even a false one, if we thought it to be linear and only directed towards us, as though we were playing the role of the goal and end of all things – might as well return to finality or an anthropomorphism – whereas it explodes and bifurcates in a thousand contingent ways like a tremendous flowering and ends up today at our present of course, here and now, in front of this old farm, in company with my granddaughter, but also at as many different existences as there are galaxies, black holes or bits of star dust in space, living things in the rain forests and oceans, men and women, cultures and languages on this planet, gladioluses, buzzing bees, charming young women … our contemporaries in the Universe.

Easy, descent only follows one path since each bifurcation leads back to a common branch or trunk. But, as difficult as the one Eurydice made in returning from the Underworld, the climb back up encounters millions of bifurcations, as in a maze; this ascent has endless trouble getting its bearings and choosing its way among all the routes in the expanding and multiplying explosive bouquet. This notable difference between the descent, single, and the countless possible ascents can be explained by the chaotic appearance of the process. Unpredictable when it advances, it becomes deterministic when one turns around. Like every narrative, this one, the greatest and most truthful of all, unfurls the contingent time of chaos.

Instructions for use

In the preceding text and the following ones, I make use of the word 'descent' in order to respect the double tradition of science and myth. Archaeologists, geophysicists and palaeontologists dig excavations in order to discover deep archaic strata or fossils; epic poems likewise plunge Dante, Aeneas or Ulysses underground, into the Underworld, en route to ancestral shades. All this beau monde descends to the past before climbing back up to the light, present. Natural history, biology and evolutionary theory, drawing the tree of living species, confirm this movement to the bottom of these pits: there you descend to the ancient trunk and roots or climb to the branches to come.

Alas, the image of a river and the arborescence of its tributaries, the water of which flows like time, reverses the direction of this movement: flow and alluvia descend towards the downstream, to come, and bargemen, sometimes, go back up towards the first sources. Under the Mirabeau Bridge flows the Seine from upstream towards the sea, from memory to hope. The tree of species goes towards its twigs, but, in its basin, the river comes from its tributaries, so that at the bifurcation angles of the same fanned-out form, the two diagrams reverse their course. Neither the land nor the plant run or flow in the direction of the water.

Language doesn't easily handle the difficulty of this double metaphor according to which the ascent of a river and the descents along the thickness of a cliff or the height of a tree are both directed towards the past. Yes, when I write that I am descending, I am going back up time!

Nature, the newborn

The multiple forks of this giant bouquet renew our concepts. We had abandoned the term 'nature' for good reasons. We have to, some people say, respect or not violate it, as though it were a matter of a virgin: a prosopopoeia or allegory, a statue of Flora or Pomona bedecking our gardens, how can we seriously keep this old trumpery from myths? Might as well believe that sileni and dryads teem in the thickets, might as well hear Jupiter thunder in the lightning, might as well restore a polytheism. I shall soon say how it is returning among us today.

As soon as this personified Nature disappeared, no doubt after the Renaissance, it acquired the status of an entity. Moving from deity to concept, just as easy to critique, nature began to signify the set of essential properties of a being or a thing; in defining their nature in this way, metaphysics claimed to know their reality even before analysing their properties. Worse, this nature, inflated, became the set of existents, the world or the Universe, its general equilibrium, again recognized before all examination. Laughing at these images, phantoms, abstractions or generalities, the twentieth century prudently abandoned all use of this word.

But we had forgotten what the future participle *naturus* means, *natura* in the feminine, from the Latin verb *nascor*, its root: what is going to be born, what is in the very act of or about to be born, the very process of birth, of emergence or newness. Nature: the newborn.

Let's go back over the Grand Narrative. Thousands upon thousands of bifurcations bush out, unpredictable, along its contingent course. In the vicinity of each bifurcation, an astonishing, sometimes even improbable, emergence suddenly arises: the big bang itself, if it ever existed, the baking of the material elements in the furnace of the galaxies, of the stars, of the hundred objects of the astrophysical Universe, the countless events dependent on the cooling of some planet, the bombardment of a thousand asteroids, the occurrence of water on the Earth, the ruptures of the tectonic plates, volcanism, the concatenation of an RNA, the Cambrian explosion, the five eradications of species, the disordered torrent of mutations, our ancestors of six to seven million years ago, their first bipedal walks, fire, the exit from Africa, seafaring, wheat, the ox, the donkey, the apple and wine, the invention of courtly love by the Occitan troubadours.... When I am harvesting in passing the new directions that have a bit to do with me, a thousand other gleaners would have chosen differently.

What, consequently, are we to call nature if not an integral of the bifurcations in question? A sum of births. As a result, even human nature becomes easy to define, if not to track down, as the defined integral of the crossroads that, in the Grand Narrative, brought about the formation of *sapiens sapiens*. As for nature, it would be defined as the undefined integral of all known and future bifurcations in the explosive bouquet of the Grand Narrative.[6]

Where do we come from? From this bouquet, from this Grand Narrative, from a subset of its branches, from a finite series of its contingent emergences. Who are we? The temporary result of this subset.

Why lament over the relative forgetfulness of short narratives scarcely four millennia in length when we have just gained one fifteen billion years in length? Why bemoan the loss of a local culture when the new one extends to the community of men and when we are connecting the old and singular humanities to a humanism finally close to its universal meaning?

The religious ghost: The holy and the sacred

Regarding humanism, this book on the philosophy of nature deals with it, life and man, three concepts without definitions, and talks about them without ideology, taboo or sacred since it defines them according to the lines of the Grand Narrative.

Conversely, the fears diffused today around chemistry and biotechnologies, for example, bring back the old abandoned figures of 'Nature', 'Life' and 'Man', the less defined and the more sacred the more these fears grow. Let's not tamper with 'Man', these fears say, nor violate 'Life' or 'Nature', the myths of which reappear like ghosts.[7] Yet the sciences laugh at ghosts and merrily transgress taboos and the sacred. This new distrust of the sciences comes of course from internal abuses, from economic and financial scandals concerning them from afar or even from anear, but above all from a completely different source, one difficult to discover and which I am readily calling the contemporary displacement of the religious.

Semi-mechanically, the collective fabricates gods, Bergson said. Anthropology teaches that the archaic religions, polytheistic, invented and shaped them in the past by means of violence and sacrifice, human ones in particular. The mechanism of apotheosis, for example, consists in deifying a dead emperor: the gods are born of cadavers and murders. Modern religions, monotheistic, are distinguished from the preceding ones by their commandment to stop human sacrifice.

Yet slaughters of this type today dominate our society, which shows murders and cadavers at every hour of the day before millions of television viewers. We go around saying that our media show violence; no, violence forms the substance of media images and messages. Without the flame of fear and pity, they wouldn't attract anyone. These spectacles repeat, with a stunning precision, the rites of archaic religions all the more easily because modern religions are declining and losing their audience all the more for condemning these sacrifices. Of course, these religions had promoted and generalized mediation, in particular Christianity, but when in turn our civil societies invented machines and institutions effective at this mediation, said media grabbed hold of the religious but in returning further back, to sacrificial archaism. Consequently, literally converted by this violence that produces gods, myths and taboos, our societies attack everything that destroys the statues said societies sculpt.

Are we aware that we live in a polytheistic era and that a sacred terror similar to that of archaic religions is invading our collectives, admittedly advanced as far as science, technology and reason go but thus returning to backward times? In the past and up till recently, the dominant religion, monotheistic, found itself involved in antiscience battles because it had kept a few bits of ancient trumpery from this sacrificial violence, a violence now diffused in a society in which the media, playing the mediating role that fell in the past to the churches, engender statues and civil taboos. Displaced, the religious is no longer to be found in the expected places, in the denominations and temples, rather, gushing forth from the media, it floods civil society, plagued daily by the showing of violence and murder, human ones in particular. Regressive and archaic, this particular religious, pagan and polytheistic, producing little gods and causing taboos to return, reinvents a Nature similar to the old statues of Flora or Pomona. Consequently, we adore them.

Yes, the religious changes camps: the grand priests celebrate their rites on the TV set, in front of which we bow several times a day to receive over our heads, bathed with pixels, our daily anointment of violence and the sacred. Intoxicated with cadavers, society, anxious, howls for the protection of its new gods, old concepts not defined or mastered by anyone: Nature, Life and Man, statues, refabricated ghosts – the very ones science always transgressed when it observed the stars, formerly divine, dissected bodies, once untouchable, or studied our genitalia and brains, formerly forbidden. Science and philosophy still transgress, let's hope, taboos.

The archaic religious returns into the civil. Let's learn to recognize as priests in changed garb those we revere and who are always right because they are in possession of symbols and dogmas, while alone asking questions. Conversely, the modern religious, now in the minority and persecuted, detached from society, teaches to distinguish between holiness, non-violent, and the sacred, which retains violence, freezes it and sculpts statues with it. Capable today as in the past of criticizing the society of the deadly spectacle and the taboos it engenders, this modern religious encounters, perhaps without yet knowing it, the sciences and reason.

I kneel humbly before holiness but enter the dark and archaic temples of the sacred on horseback so as to overturn the idols: on horseback, boldly, I mean with science and its Grand Narrative.

The laws of the narrative: Descent of dead leaves

Not only is it a matter of the grandest narrative ever recounted, and moreover probably true since it is continuously rectified by the reverses and advances of research, but it's also a question of a narration respecting the laws of every narration, rules I had formerly brought to light in my analysis of Jules Verne's *The Survivors of the Chancellor* (*Jouvences sur Jules Verne*, Éditions de Minuit, 1977, pp. 105–26).

This novel relates the terrible fortunes at sea of a vessel by this name, sailing from Charleston, the survivors of which, dying of thirst, ended up recognizing the mouth of the Amazon and lastly drank the river's fresh water. The narrative develops from equilibrium to equilibrium, the passage from one hardly inclined stage to the next one occurring by successive catastrophes – storm, fire, running aground – in which these stabilities totter, each of which, original, develops its own law; each rupture or disturbing circumstance allows the law to be changed.

This is how a dead leaf glides a long time in the autumn after apoptosis, first falling almost horizontally, then abruptly stalling, falling quickly so as to suddenly find itself lower, once again almost horizontal and stable, before a new stall occurs… . *The Survivors of the Chancellor's* simplicity comes from the fact that these stabilities are defined there in terms of masses, forces, movements and energies, all perfectly mastered by statics, dynamics, thermodynamics, the theory of tides, astronomy or climatology, disciplines directly interested in equilibria and movements; we don't need to have recourse to any metaphor to discover balances there: they are drawn there as on a blackboard as well as in the universal Grand Narrative, which is likewise accompanied by the sciences.

From dramatic turn of events to new development, this descent goes from suspense to suspense, in the literal sense, as though it was holding back its falling as much as possible, as though it was, counter to heavy bodies, following a kind of slighter gradient. The narrative's action obeys a 'principle' of maximal action, reversing the one discovered by Maupertuis, called the principle of 'least action'. With each interruption or stall, with each change of level, a new science is entered, which defines a different type of equilibrium, in *The Survivors of the Chancellor* as well as in the Grand Narrative. With each rupture a bifurcation emerges.

Is it a question here of the general organization of every successful narration? Tension, calm, dramatic turn of events, tension, calm, dramatic turn … reduce here to simple laws of mechanics. Few narratives deviate from this sequence of punctuated equilibria or, if they do, boredom and displeasure will arise; no one will continue to read; everyone, blind and deaf, will leave the show. All the art of recounting, all the enchantment it brings is held in the distribution and succession of the ruptures and plateaus, in the length or brevity of the latter, in the surprise provoked by the improbability, with and without miracle, of the former. A good storyteller follows a line and then abruptly bifurcates; if, after autumn, the leaf doesn't fall too quickly, it maintains the suspense, but not too slowly either, at the risk of boredom. To return to the Grand Narrative, you can see quite well that that was all I was talking about, under cover of fortunes at sea.

On the enchantment of the world

I invite into astrophysics or biochemistry anyone who proclaims that the sciences disenchant the world; the sky and the living will quickly appear to him to be filled with astonishing miracles. I chant rather the destiny that put me in the proximity of scientists, whose subtle music delights me every morning and astonishes me. Even the prime numbers, the simplest of all possible knowledge, stream with diamonds and sapphires that would be the envy of the Golconda region.

But, in addition to this minute and precious detail, such as the refined size of a simple cell or the medley of colourful stars, the flight of hummingbirds or galactic collisions, we are enchanted as well and above all by the whole of this narrative, endless and keeping us on the edge of our seats, artistically carried out through a refined composition of stallings and plateaus of equilibrium, of suspenses and ruptures, of roads and bifurcations, which leads from the big bang or its quantum equivalent to the appearance of humankind millions of years ago in the African savannah, with zero finality. Long plateaus of development broken by incomparable dramatic turns of events. Like every wonderfully well-constructed narrative, it seems coherent and directed towards some end or other when reread from downstream to upstream but goes from unpredictable circumstances to unforeseen contingencies when the direction of time is followed.

On the specialty of the possible author

The eighteenth-century Enlightenment, whose torches also threw light on the stability of the world, asked the question of what artisan had assembled such a regular machine; in those days God was regarded as the architect of the Universe; he worked with his hands on a definitive masterpiece. As order or as movements cadencing a stability, the cosmos was considered to be the model for all construction. From the author's specialty, you could infer the architectonic nature of the work and thereby that of the sciences that explained it: so the *Encyclopedia* surrounded this palace; each discipline grasped one of its profiles in order to draw a plan or an elevation. Clear and perfect, this vision excluded plunging the palace into a time that would have incessantly transformed it, into contingency and evolution, even more so into chaotic or random processes.

Supposing today we asked similar questions, we would ask instead what novelist, what writer of short stories, what dramatist wrote such a singular storyline or narrative. The God made Word develops stories so grandiose and cleverly carried out that we might call Him, should we dare, the Grand Recounter: yes, the Enchanter. In reconstructing this narrative, thread by thread, piece by piece, act by scene, the sciences keep the world and its inhabitants on tenterhooks through their suspense. *Et enarrem universa mirabilia tua*: I will recount the universality of your wonders.

The singular example of evolution

For example, the evolution of living things fascinates us and, for some, replaces religion because it follows the regime of a narrative exactly. Why didn't biologists laugh at the announcement of the theory of punctuated equilibrium, an expression that's so close to 'suspense interrupted with ruptures'? Probably because they were unaware that Gould, who probably didn't realize it either, was summarizing without changing one iota the simplest rules of narrative, which this author moreover practices marvellously; oh, paradox, he criticizes a number of his predecessors by saying that they were only engaged, along cyclic or straight times, in narratives; this argument applies to his own theory. Like *Don Quixote* or the *Odyssey*, like an infinity of short stories and novels, of plays and scripts, *The Survivors of the Chancellor*, as I just said, follows the law of punctuated equilibrium. Likewise, Lamarck, Darwin and better still Gould discover that life is recounted. And those who followed repeat this over and over again while perfecting the methods of narration. Oh, enchanting surprise, natural history makes science and literature meet. Conversely, the laws of narrative resemble the laws of life.

Better: every one of them a tributary of the Grand Narrative, the sciences, entering together into literature, find in the humanities their bed and their house. Good stories set our hearts racing as though we were watching Aphrodite herself rise, living, erect and naked, in the ruffles of the waves, of the prebiotic soup. Man and woman are born of nature.

Chronopedia

In coining the term 'encyclopedia', Rabelais drew a circle of knowledge, education and instruction. In those days, this complete and cyclic drawing of all possible points of view on the world could best express this architectural masterwork. So, complete science covered the world, the way the map drawn by Mercator during that same time did by projecting the continents and seas onto a cylinder enveloping the globe. As is evident, there are only cycles in these drawings. Therefore if the world shows a circular form so does knowledge, and the book leafed through as well. The Universe has a centre, the Earth or Sun, the way power or command has a king and creation and knowledge a God. At the beginning of the nineteenth century, Hegel still defined an encyclopedia as a circle of circles.

We now laugh at revolutions that changed centre so often and which we called decentrings. Whether it's a question of the Earth or the Sun, of the subject or the object, of the self or the non-self, these distinctions are of no matter since they all and always presupposed a centre, whatever position may be assigned to it, whatever name may be given to it and whatever movement it may command; so, the encyclopedia hardly changes since its global form is preserved and preserves its rest. The word 'revolution' itself presupposes it.

We don't live in the same spaces or the same times. At least, neither the world nor we nor any living thing are the same age any longer; we wake to find ourselves suddenly fantastically old. No space has a centre any longer, and every moment of origin or bifurcation poses formidable problems. Knowledge-wise, there is no longer any encyclopedia, but a Grand Narrative.

In what expanse does this Grand Narrative unfold? In a landscape. Today the sciences describe and attempt to patch together the pieces of these landscapes, somewhat like the way the social sciences despair of stitching cultures to each other. The most advanced theories in fact strive to stitch together: the theory of superstrings for example brings together the two pieces that are quantum physics and relativity, still scattered apart. We conceive as little order in the multicoloured unfurling of the Universe and its thousand circumstances as we see in the least cell with thousands of varied proteins or on the simple map of the Earth, sea and continents sewn together by the edges of deep plates. The order and roundness of a world seem to us today to be as simplistic as time reduced to a line. The encyclopedia's round space has had its day, like the dinosaurs.

In this landscape, we read a chronopedia.

Time and modes

Unity or universality therefore doesn't come back from the side of space, decidedly landscaped, but from the side of time, provided that it not be reduced to a line or its measurement, nor above all to what Westerners name history. Paradoxically, once again, universality comes back by what we name literature. Knowledge, as I have said, is recounted. It travels, like the Universe, life and thought. The old term 'pedagogy' told of the journey of children led by their private tutor. I hope that it henceforth expresses this travelling, fast or slow, on the part of the world, the things and the living creatures in time, yes, this new perception of the Universe, our perception and that of our children. For this rainbow-hued set of landscapes of all types, scales, forms and colours ensues from a story, the tale of this universal chronopedia. This jigsaw puzzle spurts out like a jet. Like a good theatre play or a successful novel, the Grand Narrative begins just anywhere, just anytime, strictly contingently, although it carries the succession of events in its sides, albeit chaotically. Each of its bifurcations arises like a dramatic turn of events, possible certainly, but in the very vicinity of the impossible, like a kind of miracle, like a very low probability event. The Narrative doesn't unfold but rather jumps from the unforeseeable or the impossible to predict to the necessary when it moves from the perspective of the future towards the completed past while traversing the possibilities of the present. It thus carries the contingents on its shoulders.

The metaphysics of the ancient world as well as the methods of its deconstruction follow a two-valued logic, being and nothingness, false and true, good and evil, and love contradiction. They ignore noise, multicoloured singularities, a thousand composite profiles, the landscapes to be sewn together, the unpredictability of the processual. World, life, existence, history and knowledge fluctuate among the four categories of modality: compatible with necessary laws, all things and lives run across the filter of the possible and impossibility towards contingency.

Man, the co-author of the Grand Narrative

The Narrative resumes. All the more literary because we live on tenterhooks to know what follows since it concerns our lives as well as those of others and the world. Not only on tenterhooks as spectators but active and actors.

For ever since we created world-objects, we have climbed on to the stage, participated in the work of the director and launched ourselves into the text, co-authors of the Grand Narrative. We don't merely work on the development of the story of history, an evident tautology since we go about our business, but rather exploit time, the fate of the world and that of living things; we intervene in the fundamental conditions of matter and life, the universal responsible parties for this new work. In the Grand Narrative, we henceforth take the floor conjointly with things.

Descent into forgetfulness

When, last December, in a Museum of Natural History, I asked the attendant of the skeleton hall the age of a giant saurian, he replied:

> 'One hundred twenty million years and eleven months.' 'How do you calculate such an exact date?' I asked. 'Simply,' he said. 'The museum hired me the middle of last winter; at that time, the pedestal read "one hundred twenty million". Count it up; it comes out right.'

Do we date humans to be from six to nine million years plus eleven weeks? Don't laugh, for that's how history and the social sciences talk, disciplines which obliterate with their few seconds the entire preceding year, as we are going to calculate the situation. What skeletons are caught in this dark closet? How are we to plunge human time into the time of living creatures and of things, my granddaughter and her parents' house into the torrent, the mountain and the Sun, my age into the age of my reptilian brain or of DNA? How are we to awaken these dormant memories?

A thousand disciplines, a single discovery: Chronometry

The new things the exact sciences invented along the twentieth century proliferated so much and in so many domains that we get lost in this bushiness. But one single discovery, with recent precision, unites the different efforts of all the disciplines together: for each one of them developed dating methods such that the question of the age of all the objects they deal with unifies the entire old encyclopedia into a common project. What then did the exact sciences invent during the past century? They dated the Universe and atoms, the Earth and life, all the species, humankind, microbes ... things in general. At a time when the common voice was celebrating the complexity of scientific results and approaches, a global vision come from a common computus, quite to the contrary, was arising. So the word 'chronopedia' designates, as I just said, the temporal Grand Narrative, which has been unitarily set up for several decades on the basis of these clocks, and which, with its main trunk, traverses the entire basin of the sciences, their floods, derivations and turbulences. Contemporary science restores the Chronos of antiquity to his first throne. In thus contemplating the new arborescence in a river basin resembling the Universe, who could resist the temptation to repeat the ancient gesture of classifying the disciplines, here according to the age of their objects?

To the old philosophy question, 'where do we come from?' today a single theme replies, one varied by the disciplines whose knowledge has recently been coupled with memory. How are we to define this latter? In an elementary way, as an information conservatory, a box or bank.

Triple descent

A first memory[8] recalls childhood and first loves that didn't always last; lodged in a part of the brain and body, it concerns existence, consciousness and those it lives with, what some call psychology, to which others assume an additional substratum, dark with forgetfulness. Joined to it, secondly, is group memory, scattered across objective media: ruins, skeletons, images, tools, hearsay, customs, books, archives, the internet, whose information lets me participate in social life, in human history or even in its hominization; this memory is dependent on my culture. The first treasury, personal and subjective, goes back a few decades; the second one, more collective, goes back centuries and millennia, Balzac, Gilgamesh, Lascaux, Lucy.

Third memory: the genes of my DNA bring together, in part, the genes of my two parents, of their gods and so on, until all of them, plus my own, form the treasury common to all of humanity. In it, I discover what brings me closer to the Fuegians and the Australian Aborigines as well as my proximity to the Wolofs and the Bantus; better, being common to every living thing, I measure in it my distance to marsupials, reptiles and other insects, ferns and bacteria. This genotypic memory, profound in a different way from my own or that of the collectives and their cultures, plunges into evolution and its billions of years.

Their duration

Let's count the relative times of these three conservatories taking a year as our reference: when I remember my passing romances, my first memory, which has lasted a few decades, plunges into a thin layer of a millisecond; when I learn the *Odyssey*, when I admire the cave paintings of Lascaux, the second memory, which has lasted for a few millennia, explores four seconds; when my eyes, formed by evolution, see light, when my skin regulates my autonomy, when hydrogen and carbon atoms assemble in the proteins of my cells, the third one, a billion years old, extends over the rest of the year. This last one ensures anatomy's matter and physiology's functions; the second one awakens to the world and the surrounding cultures; the first one constructs what we agree to call consciousness. In the study of the processes that animate us, do we forget this division of time and therefore the relative weights of the constraints we are subject to? Our individual existence and cultural histories weigh no more than a snowflake compared to the tons of this Grand Narrative.

In barking, grazing, spinning their webs, knotting their nests or mating, living things remember the last of these conservatories rigorously; their gestures flawlessly execute its dictates. Contrary to these genetic automatons, hominization made us into monsters of forgetfulness. Our narcissistic genius privileges, in filtering them by means of a net full of holes, the several milligrams of recent influence and plunges into the dark the quasi-totality of the year that has just gone by, before the events that only concerned me or us, the most amnesiac of living things. When we devote ourselves to history, we omit the quasi-totality of time; we remember much less than eleven months.

Not only do we forget where we just put our keys, something which sometimes allows us to invent new ones, not only do we forget the crimes of our parents and those of our neighbours, quite fortunately for morality and pardon, but we don't even remember we have a body that's as old as the rocks of the world. We pride ourselves on a few cognitive performances, attributing them to the genius of some Newton or of our cultural clan, without noticing that we often know and almost always move by means of million-year-old neurons, invariant before prehistory and my birthday. Noisy, chatty, fast, cheating, my consciousness conceals history, and this latter, more lying and raucous still, hides the honest and silent evolution whose slowness rises up over endlessly prepared inert soups. Amnesiac, all of them, consciousness, language and the pride in their performances silence the body and its age, the Universe and its ancientness. We dream of a historical or familial determinism without taking into account the vast archaism of the flesh and the Earth. We forget the body, life and the things.

Forgetting nature

Did this amnesia make us blind to the world? Hominization makes us forgetful; did this very forgetfulness hominize us? We became so historical, cultural and then personal that we obliterated with diverse codes the gigantic duration preceding these group and individual memories, which are narrow, not very reliable, thundering. We keep our nature, which obeys and remains silent, on a leash. From time to time it barks and growls, but language, technology and knowledge flog it, bring it into subjection, calm it down. Not always. Just as a written advertising poster erases the landscape's muteness, a meaningful word annihilates millions of carnal years. Just as tribes possessing writing crush tribes only knowing the oral, cultures ceaselessly blunt nature. They even lead us to disobey it. Most living things listen to the programme to the point of executing only it; some, related to us, obey it a bit less; we behave as though we had lost it. Hence the self-perpetuating cycle: the more we disobey nature, the more cultures are invented; and the more these latter develop, the more we forget nature. Does our despecialization, about which I shall soon speak, come from this fundamental forgetfulness?

A culture had to contingently invent what we call science, which, in turn, disobeys culture, forgets it, critiques it, contradicts and overthrows it, for this science to suddenly take up again with nature itself, to depart in search of its lost time-counters and end up deciphering its ancientness. As though nature played the role of a kind of unknown for cultures and as though these latter had to be quiet in order to finally let its *escient* speak, understand by this word – all the more precious because little used – the best of its knowledge.[9] Cultures plug up the natural slow duration in order to favour the emergence of other, faster, openings of time. Cultures derive from nature so as to derive nature. Even later still, conditioned by a culture to which it is in addition opposed, science thwarts this mechanism. Knowledge rediscovers billions of years behind our memories riddled with holes; knowing is *this* memory.

Oral, written

The aforementioned science dates by seeking traces in the conservatories where information is kept. At the oral stage, memory, still fairly faithful, isn't separated from the phenotypic or individual body; our brain has mnemonic zones; gestures, movements and postures are inscribed in schemas whose dynamism we retain. Verbal repetitions en famille and in public form another type of accumulation; festivals, dances, songs and stories, skirt pleats and escutcheon colour periodically revivify collective traditions; anniversaries and jubilees return so that in commemorating we remember.

It had been wanted, arbitrarily, to make history be born with writing. So the historian's work goes, next, from reading manuscripts or parchments, new conservatories, to libraries, whose collections keep written marks on books, then from there to the excavation sites where stones sometimes bear inscriptions and where other ones remain silent. Memory, already, leaves the body and becomes externalized. Forgetfulness, I repeat, puts holes in all these accumulations: amnesia lightens and rectifies our past (what would

become of us, individuals and group, if we remembered everything?);
library fires tore our antiquity to shreds; a few armed barbarians left, here or
there, ruins that have to be deciphered again after the passage of the Huns
or our scientific bombardments. History as acts – wars or fires – destroys
what history tries to reconstruct as texts; we undo with one hand what we
weave with the other.

The memory of living things, universal and long

More powerful in a different way and more durable, the third memory
therefore produced our body; this latter, more or less, unfolds its genome. In
every living thing, ourselves included, genes function as the memory of the
species and more generally as the memory of the living thing. Unlike our
memory, about which we complain, it rarely misfires; when it does make a
mistake, we call that a mutation, either lethal or favourable, and in the latter
case, sometimes selected. Like a paramecium, a bellflower, an octopus, we
bear inside ourselves, in the form of DNA, this passive accumulation of life
and of our species – for which the individual acts as intermediary – and
which itself has, in addition, enough energy to decipher its codes and invest
this treasure in a structure that's visible and moving in space.

From one memory to the other, we go from individual and singular
existence or from different local cultures and sometimes their history to the
universal, not merely of the species or the genus, but of all known, unknown
and possible kingdoms. In the first case, we have more memory or less;
in the second one, we live as memories. Discovered during the last half-
century, the universality of the genetic code unites humans to each other
and all the way down to the most elementary bacteria: every living thing
bears inside itself the trace of the birth of life more than three billion years
ago. So we remember unimaginable ages.

Memory's misfires

The meeting of two DNAs of the same species, male and female, activates
with its energy the passive accumulation of information. This is how the
memory remembers: the genome functions as the memory of every living
thing and of the particular species, which remembers in the individuals.
This remembering, likewise, rarely fails, barring sterility, miscarriages and
abortions, which must again pass into the profits and losses of natural
selection.

Thus no one has ever seen a cow in the fields get up on two legs, dance or sing in any other way than by lowing, in short, behave in any other way than as a cow: no one has a better memory than an animal, than a plant, than an alga; there is nothing more faithful than a living thing. It remembers so perfectly that we sometimes describe it as a genetic automaton. Mutation and selection, the two Darwinian operators, can be defined as exceptional misfires of this perfect memory. Our neurons have short memories; our writings have brief and lacunary ones; DNA remembers longer. The living species are memory sites; humans leave these sites.

The fourth memory: Cold strata

Yet, the discovery of inert treasuries preceded the discovery of genes, recent, by several centuries. Here, it was also necessary to find deposits or accumulations, open them and decode their secrets. Cliffs and cuttings let, beneath the face of the earth, the first mnemonic banks be seen, sometimes in the open air; naturalists discovered fossils. This descent began in the Middle Ages with Albertus Magnus and continued in the works of Agricola, Palissy and Leonardo da Vinci. In *The Mountain*, Michelet, who knew to supplement his historical work with four books of natural history, an extremely rare feat in Western culture, calls beds and strata, of different colours and formations, pages; the mountain walls forming their compilations, books; and the high sierras, libraries. With this image, he crossed the ford separating human history from the objective Earth and life sciences, but in so doing he still imported one riverbank to the other; like Newton, like the archbishop of Canterbury, who calculated the age of the Earth by the generations reckoned in the Bible, like the attendant in the Museum of Natural History, he thought the Earth lived at the rhythm of language: we read in a book that the world heaps up pages in piles, like a book.

My childhood was likewise enchanted, in Jules Verne, by Captain Nemo's dive into the classification of fish, which the author, who had never sailed beneath the sea, copied out from some ichthyology manual; in the same way a young Danish speleologist departed, with his uncle, from the bottom of an Icelandic volcano for the centre of the Earth before coming out again, like a bomb, at Stromboli; along the way, beneath the torches' trembling light, they listed off the succession of geological strata, no doubt copied out from Lyell and Boucher de Perthes.

What do these adventurers see along this anamnesis shown to them by this new *facilis descensus Averni*, this easy dive into the underworld of Avernus, underground?

Dialogue of the dead, silence of the walls

Entering into the abyss, Ulysses, Plato in the *Phaedo*, Aeneas or the chatterboxes Lucian stages in the *Dialogues of the Dead* rush down the backworlds in search of memories and vengeance; they still consider these places to be human memories. Leibniz, a manager of the Harz silver mines and the first author of a *Protogaea*, the geologists of the Enlightenment and those of the beginning of the nineteenth century open the tombs of terrestrial memory – fossils come out of graves[10] – in which lost ages are buried. An astonishing discovery awaits them: that we had a short memory, that we didn't grasp time's length because we considered the Earth to be the receptacle of recent funerals, whereas it keeps the bones of multimillion-year-old ancestors and, before them, the remains of eras without any humans and even without any living things. We thought we were the only ones to practise funeral rites, whereas the Earth itself buries its own elements.

Holding forth on swallowed-up Atlantis, the Egyptian priests who kept the temples of Sais, despite their boasting in the *Timaeus*, only went back to recent ages; neither Homer nor Virgil nor Lucian ventured deep enough or far enough. Underground, they still remain in spoken or written history, in language. Even Lidenbrock and his nephew, always preceded by Arne Saknussemm and his inscriptions, find at the bottom of the chasm, in Jules Verne who cites Virgil, a human ancestor, grazing a herd of monstrous saurians, *immanior ipse*. None of them descend more than two or three steps of a staircase with thousands of flights. The presence of men obstructs the presence of the world. As soon as these sounders of the abyss encounter familiar shades, they stop and talk. They always talk endlessly. Even at the very bottom of the backworlds discourse never ceases; books are only going to seek books; men play among themselves; words resound among themselves; history and the social sciences remain among themselves. We accused the Bible of obstructing knowledge; it would have been better to have accused the book in general, whose emblem the Bible bears, indeed, the written, language and the relations of men among themselves. Visitors of flesh and pale shades dialogue, converse about the struggles up above, watch the terrifying tortures, blind to the silent walls of the Underworld. Having a passion for vengeances and local history, nonetheless Dante alone describes, a bit, the worldly architecture of the backworlds. The other descenders continue, as above ground, to live among themselves. Perpetuating their earthly behaviour, they see rivals, never the river or its two riverbanks. Politics moves even the Underworld. Wounded by resentment, they remember the last quarter hour, never the millions of years preserved by the walls sending back to their ears the recent echoes of a history that separates them, deaf to the long silence that would unite them. These rivals from a short history have no idea that a common world, fantastically long, has formed their bones, their limbs and no doubt their speech. Behind the river Lethe, a darker forgetfulness awaits. They have no idea of it at all because neither the walls nor the earth talk, memory sites never activated into remembering. They need to be decoded; their silence needs to be translated into language.

For while living things enjoy memory and remembering at the same time, inert objects only dispose of the first – passive – one; they keep the treasure but don't talk about it; we have to furnish them with the activity of remembering. Better yet, this mute memory defines the inert. What is a thing? A memory without remembering, a mnemonic passivity. Matter means mother: behind the short generations whose chattering shades hold forth, there is the vast genealogy of our mute mother, the Earth. The sciences decipher the silence of her womb. How?

Heat counts ...

While the piled-up stratigraphy along which these descenders are walking preserves traces of time, it has the weakness of being cold, a bad clock. It indicates duration but only lets its flow be seen in the relative disposition of the strata, more or less thick, and in the slow wearing away of the rocks composing them. In cooling down, heat, a better time-counter, calculates faster. Buffon heated clay balls mixed with iron to incandescence and then let them cool down in order to calculate the age of the planet from these reduced models. Neither Newton nor his universe of forces has any memory; Buffon's burning hot balls accumulate energy in the form of heat and therefore function as bank accounts spending their money as they cool down; here is a new clock. It doesn't count the Newton-style reversible time indicated by my watch but the irreversible and entropic time of the wearing out of its parts, therefore of its ageing.

In the same way, descending deeper than Dante's or Verne's imagination, that is to say, from the visible and cold strata to the slow tectonic plates sailing on the burning hot magma, geophysicists discover that volcanic eruptions and earthquakes cadence, also like a clock, the cooling of the Earth: but its dial remains for the moment indecipherably irregular. The counting out of the bank account of the more or less burning hot celestial objects shows more regularity. We guess their heat by their colour and calculate, thanks to this mark, their age. And since we spot, on the spectrum of each one's heat, a shift to the red, we assume an expansion of the Universe and calculate its proportion or Hubble constant.

... Less well than radioactivity

Later, the heat clock handed the reins over to radioactive time-counters. The true path doesn't descend the infernal Avernus, near Naples, nor into Snæfellsjökull's vent, in Iceland, through which Verne's adventurers went, but rather descends the scale of miniaturization, going from crystal to molecules and from atoms to particles. By means of their continuous emission, radioactive elements spend these particles, very visibly. It suffices then to count the uranium and lead isotopes.

Newton's clock time didn't give things their age; Darwin's opponents therefore were first recruited from Newtonians rather than from the religious. To attain irreversible time and be able to quantify it: Buffon, Fourier, Lord Kelvin, Hubble and a thousand others had to study heat, and Becquerel had to discover radioactivity; then uranium 235 and plutonium had to appear; after the Manhattan Project, the atomic bombs had to explode; the fall of asteroids had to be taken seriously; lastly Patterson had to find the right solution by dating five of these meteorites, including the one from Canyon Diablo in Arizona. How does uranium become transmuted into a base lead? The planet's 4.55 billion years ensue from the answer to this question.

All things, in principle, act as memories. The bank-Universe contains accounts. All things are numbers; the memory-world preserves traces.

Defence and illustration of realism

Our ways of thinking are strongly sparked by the fact that this is how objects behave: subjects, we believe, human experts, date objects named by them, discovered by them, unearthed, purified, measured by them. The faculties of intelligence or memory, the acts of reading, writing, discerning, calculating, belong to them and not, obviously, to the objects they study.

The opposite idea, antiscientific, would return to animism. Yet, I have just called schists in strata, fossils, isotopes of lead or uranium memories. What could be more faithful, exact and reliable than these masses when compared to the countless tatters of human forgettings? Certain of these memories, emissive, even know how to count, particle by particle. Aren't there then, in the things of the world, functions that we believe to be exclusive to human understanding? I'm not saying a soul – a vague name – but cognitive elements?

Idealism considers things to only exist in and through our representations, either individual and subjective, or collective, corporative, scientific, political. Realism believes they exist independent of us. I use the verb 'to believe' deliberately. For while idealism can indeed be proven since reasoning itself is situated on the side of the understanding and not on the side of the deaf and mute things, realism is only defended, as weakly as can be, by a belief stemming from the senses, from raw experience and even from religion, as some people claim. For realists believe in the reality of things the way mystics believe in God, from having experienced it. Despite this weakness, I have never been able to abandon realism, hard, for idealists, soft, seem to me to have never suffered from the world as such; raised in cotton, flabby and protected, the rich, the powerful and their children believe that everything in the world obeys them like their domestics.

But, in leaving aside this controversy, in which belief gives itself away, another argument appears, inspired by the disciplines I was just inspired by, stratigraphy, thermodynamics, radioactivity, even biochemistry: in real things one finds hiding, mumbling and commencing elementary functions we utilize – better and more completely or sometimes less regularly – in our representations. Thus, to take another example, in a thousand living species, sometimes highly 'intelligent' ones, we find scattered a thousand ways of communicating which are united and combined more completely by the performances of our language. We integrate the know-how of many living things; we do the same with the inert. Something of the cognitive lurks in life and matter.

The discussions that set realism and idealism in opposition attempt to interpret the phenomenon, that is to say, the appearance, the epiphany or the hidden, the hidden God itself, if you like; they therefore presuppose a vague space inside of which the scenes of representation are played but take little account of time, which is as universal as the Universe and more durable than all the things of the world. But precisely these latter memorize and remember. And myself, I remember in part because my body and brain, equipped with matters and forms similar to the matters and forms equipping things, also know how to accumulate and then discharge time. And we remember collectively because we knew how to exploit the properties of these same things which know how to write on each other, engravings with a chisel on marble, ink marks on white paper or electronic chip circuits. Insofar as I am memory, I participate in things. Insofar as they are things, they have memory. In this respect, the things and the world therefore exist neither more nor less than I or some collective in which I am immersed do. Idealism presupposes a fight from which we would emerge the victors; I see the match as balanced or nil. Worse, I no longer see the border separating and opposing men and world.

No, I am not returning to a decried animism; I am not saying that things have a soul, or evil or beneficent intentions. But in this apparently sterile direction, which nevertheless neither the Stoics nor Leibniz nor Bergson scorned, gold veins appear. The act of knowledge doesn't link an active subject-pole to an other, a passive object, but rather both participate together in this act in which the games are shared, even if the latter of these two agencies only takes on a humble role.[11] This agency plays the first move and, with each renewal of the game, always plays the first move. If, keeping to the same methods, we had continued searching for the world's age by means of the generations, the thickness of cliffs, thermal radiation, we would never have found the solution. Another object had to appear, some element in meteorites, in which a good memory lay. Things decide at least as much as methods. The real awakens the act of knowing that awakens it. Its faculties are joined to ours in a self-perpetuating cycle.

This conclusion is only bold in appearance, so much is it universally found. No doubt, by means of this couple – active subject, passive object – we were obeying, ourselves passive as well, the *libido dominandi* and our intense passion for dominance, always the first served. We were thus continuing the line of dingoes or elk, animals that, like us, submit to victors. Idealism amounts to a form of parasitic dominance. Realism practices symbiosis, plunges into the things and collaborates with them. *Connaissance* [knowledge], whose prefix links, in its genesis, subjects with the innermost qualities of objects, takes its place among our symbiotic acts.[12] A philosophy of nature restores the dignity of these memory-things, which we always forget.

Forgetfulness sites

Homo sapiens obliviosus. Not only do you and I forget, like absent-minded individuals, not only do our cultures and their history form their past through piled-up lies, but even our species' DNA seems programmed for deprogramming. Not remembering oneself or history, losing even the species' memory all condition learning, rapid adaptation, disobedience and invention. I think like a living thing having remembrances with holes in them, having a lacunary memory. Over the course of the Grand Narrative, forgetfulness little by little became the peculiarity of thought, if not of the human race; to such an extent that for millions of years we even forgot the world, whose enormous past we have only remembered for one or two generations.

We lived, we live, we think in forgetfulness sites, as on the alpine-pastured farm or before the Grand Canyon. Let's not complain about this weakness nor about the evaporation of the past; without these faults, we would return to the hypermnesiac state of the cow or the hevea.

Let's protest against the inverse tradition claiming flowing waters have no memory, against the Greek myth of the river of forgetfulness. On the contrary, every river digs its bed to preserve a place to sleep, thus giving itself up to its lability; so if you try, by diverting it, to extract it from this enormous memory, it will return, irremediably, to the thalweg, even if it takes a long time to do so. Despite what the song says, no one has ever seen the Garonne go and warm up the pole.[13] It reposes in its long pocket like a cow in its pasture-niche, and when it overflows its little fold, it merely invades another bed, called the flood plain. Never did any river forget these two winding folds nor did its waters, whatever Heraclitus may still say about it: these waters evaporate or sometimes slip beneath the rocks and the flowers of the fields; should it rain, these same waves vaguely return, in a statistical cycle. Everyone always swims in pretty much the same river, stable course, soft banks and recurrent floods. The river displays broad and probable rhythms in the universal rhesis or fluence. It doesn't flow so much as it percolates. It remembers, like all things.

All things are memories, even flowing waters. We alone forget that we are swimming in the same river: Heraclitus' saying bears witness to our absent-mindedness. Absent-minded, we always think that a different river is making us wet. Our remembrances most often reduce to a few bits of amnesia, omission and negligence, hastily tied together. The formation of different matters as well as the evolution of living things list out memories that have an unyielding faithfulness, which is why all of them follow general and rational laws. Tattered and torn, with gaps, unfaithful, full of holes, only our life and our history know no rule, amid a world without forgetfulness. Honest, things tell true. Dishonest or distracted, we lie. And what if all our knowledge began with omissions? And what if our intelligence never stopped striving to patch up torn pieces of patching cloth?

We don't live like the inert, endowed with memory and without remembrance, therefore subjected to laws, nor do we live like the other living things, endowed with remembrances, as individuals, and with memory, as a species. Our race lost them, like so many other functions and characteristics. In order to be able to regain them, we externalize them on to living things or objects, better endowed than we are from this point of view. Conversely, we live both like the inert, without remembering, and like living things, through some memory: we differ from them but participate in them.

The question of the subject

But, once again, *who* has memory? The tradition answers: humans, their cognition, their mnemonic function, their written, engraved or drawn traces, the ones they decipher. No, for the things themselves memorize all by themselves and directly. The past is inscribed in them; it suffices to decipher it there. Dust and air particles fall every year with the snow; the ice preserves them, and cores from the glaciers of Greenland rediscover the state of the atmosphere, to the month, as it was hundreds of thousands of years ago. The thickness of the ice plays the role of a memory.

Here, again, we become decentred. What we said about ourselves – language, traces, symbols, signs and meanings, writing and memory, cognition and *cogito* – is taken on and demonstrated by all things in some way. The Grand Narrative of vast time shunts the intermediary of memory through language. Hence the status of language and of our intelligence: intermediaries between the world and the world, between things and things, a sort of brief noise interference.

In praise of Sarah

A little scene, as an aside: the experimenter asks Sarah, the famous female chimpanzee, to put the animal faces on one side and the human faces on the other. In response, the chimp places the photos of dogs, cats, even those of her brothers, mother and father on the left, and then women and children on the right; coming to her own image, she throws it in with those of humans. Let's congratulate Sarah, who, without mistake, defines them as animals that separate, choose and classify, understanding herself to be in that species because she herself indulges in classification.

But Sarah shows us another way, the way of the evolution separating us from her: even more ape, more animal and more thing than her, I descend duration to observe that dogs, with their noses, distinguish the aroma of some food or the scent of a receptive bitch; that, with their stereospecific sites or folds, proteins select certain proteins and reject others; that a given alcohol only reacts to this acid; that Maxwell's demon sorts molecules that are cold and hot, slow and fast ... Who or what then doesn't separate? Bifurcations resolve the question of classification; they date the appearance of some property or other. Producing subjects or objects, time constructs what logic deconstructs. What activity isn't shared with us by not only some animal but also by this plant, an alga, some crude body or one of its components? Rather than asking or undoing the absurd question of what is peculiar to humankind, let's let time resolve it: during which epoch does the Grand Narrative invent some activity?

Things, codes, causes:
Descent into knowledge

The stylus engraving the wax, the ink staining the papyrus or paper, the palette colouring the canvas, the chisel sculpting the marble, these objective or rather interobjective facts even condition human writing, the arts and our symbolic behaviour. With the same movement, we produce artificial memories, in libraries or server farms, and discover in crystals and molecules, pollens and stars the marks and traces of a sometimes colossal past. Commanding nature by obeying it is equally true for our cognitive performances.

The descending mass of ice forms and pushes moraines in front of it; these moraines result from this dynamic but also bear witness to it. When forces act, we call them causes, at the scale of high energy; but, at the scale of low energy, they leave marks. You see the moraine as either an effect or a fossil trace. Things don't reduce to causes but also set down codes. Things act upon each other, of course, but also make signs to each other. There isn't only physics in physics, or else we should distinguish two: mathematical physics (the mathematics of Timaeus, Galileo, Dirac) and the physics of Critias, long discredited; the physics that uses induction and the one that recounts the history of things; the one that experiments in the laboratory and the one that reconstructs the world for us. The second one returns, now exact, so that the two of them counterbalance each other: the first one seeks the effects of causes of course; the other one finds the marks of codes. The dated narrative takes place alongside refined experiments and reasoned equations. Hard things demonstrate a soft side; material [*matérielles*], of course, they too become engrammed and programmed like software. There is something of software in hardware [*le matériel*].

Not only in our brains but also in the Universe. 'Nature' is sown with programmes. Things, double, manifest causes and codes. Next to the physics of forces, we are lacking a general theory of marks, traces and signals to teach us to remember like the world and to remember the world, to write like it and on it; things are also symbols. There isn't only chemistry in chemistry: why does some element react or not react in the presence of some other? Why then does it select it? What 'faculty' in it chooses it? Large masses write, molecules read. And, even more than the inert, the living writes, reads, decides, chooses, reacts; it was even long believed to be endowed with intentions. An hour of biochemistry quickly convinces of the refined astuteness of proteins.

Does an intelligence of things exist? Of living things? Does the natural, as though in dormancy, prepare the cultural, in labour or in luminescence? The world's background noise murmurs like a *præ-cogitat*.

The gnomon and the transcendental

This discovery has ancient letters: neuter in gender, the word 'gnomon', which in the Greek language designated the sundial's axis, signified 'that which understands, decides, judges, distinguishes, interprets, yes, that which knows'; as if a thing, already, knew. Intercepting the sunlight, its shadow writes, on the dial itself, a few events of the sky and of the Earth, the solstice, the equinox and the latitude of the site. It functions automatically. 'Automatic' means: without the intervention of intention, which is subjective and cognitive. The Indo-European *men* groups together under this root – a mental one – of the word 'memory': demented, commentary, mention, mendacity, monument, demonstration, watch [*montre*], money … as though, behind the manifest meaning, the word as well was behaving like the memory of the pages I have just written.

It can be said of the gnomon that 'it knows' the way it is said that it rains. The gnomon looks like a stylus, but no one holds it in their hand. Some things of the world give themselves to be seen to an object that shows them: entirely objective, theory does without any subject. A thing, the gnomon, intervenes in the world, and the world reads on itself the writing drawn by it. This type of intrahardware software conditions our cognitive performances, like a kind of objective transcendental.

Neither knowledge nor consciousness suddenly arises to form *sapiens*. The thousand elements of their makeup appear starting from the inert – writing – or from the living – reading, choosing, deciding … Plunged into the world, we continuously forget how, over a long time, a meaning appears there. Like a temporal transcendental, certain conditions for knowing date from hundreds of millions of years ago.

Our Grand Narrative reconstructs them.

2 NATURE AND CULTURE

THE INCANDESCENT

Descent into dedifference

Our brief poverty

With the early end of a deciphering we thought ought to have lasted longer, some people were amazed at the brevity of our genome. What, so few base pairs! Around five times fewer than a small tropical freshwater fish, the dipnoi *Protopterus aethiopicus*! Since we dominate living things through research and technology, we ought to win out over all of them in richness, and here we are, reduced to poverty. Fortunately, we have known, since about 1970, that there is no correlation between the complexity of genomes and the complexity of individuals. The fact remains that we find ourselves poor here.

Specialization and despecialization

Evolution develops like a tree whose branches are divided into smaller branches that are always better adapted to the environment. Species that are more and more specialized bifurcate along this neo-Darwinian schema: some given species discovers a niche favouring, in return, the specific function housed in it and exploits this niche best. A fold in the skin, intended, it seems, for thermal equilibrium, launches reptiles into flight, and their wings become shaped according to a thousand wingspans, profiles and colours in the turbulent air; migratory birds develop a liver whose reserves allow for migration, and others develop countless beaks marvellously adapted to their diets; the melodies given out during mating season also vary in the same way. Does extreme specialization, at the maximum possible of ramification, reach a dead end?

I don't know why – perhaps someday someone will – we left this kind of duration, why we extricated ourselves from this schema. An evolution seeming to shoot out in the opposite direction, and which I have described regarding Love, despecialized us, dedifferentiated us, programmed us in deprogramming, as though we were going back to the main branches of the tree, even to the trunk. Did we forget speciation? Did this indifference, in the broadest sense, this non-differentiation, result from the forgetfulness of just now? We forget the world and time. Do we also forget our program? Can I name our species *Homo negligens*? Does it unbind itself from nature?

Does it sometimes neglect to read its own code? We doubt today whether it is even a question of a code. Other living things read it better, obeying it like genetic automatons.

Yet, along time, the organic uselessness or weakness proved to be an omnivalent technician. Thus the hand, despecialized, can be called a universal tool on the entropic scale since it hits, carves, sculpts and sorts ... but also on the informational scale since it designates and counts; likewise for the mouth since it hums, munches and chats. Likewise especially for the brain: an excellently universal tool, as soon as it takes up abstraction. Does an invention or a new gesture, whether practical or gymnastic, by the hand or the body give evidence of a forgetfulness I don't know how to name?

As it advances, evolution differentiates; should it despecialize by erasing boundaries, it seems to go backwards. In progressing, it multiplies colours and shades; in regressing, it seems to turn pale and produce a candidate for incandescence. Dedifferentiated, forgetful, we became poor; we became the most destitute of living things. Poverty again.

An incandescent indifference

Yes, we discovered – how, we will never know – that this incandescence mixes and potentially contains every colour. By losing countless specificities, valences or real powers, the zero-valent, nil-potent human became, without meaning to no doubt, virtually omnivalent, totipotent, global and infinite. These impoverishments disadapted it to every thin and precise local niche and left it with no bound or definition. Undefined in a few organs as well as in our possibilities, we became the champions of inadaptation; we don't even know how to define ourselves.

In going back up ordinary evolutionary time by dedifferentiation, we returned, if I may, backwards and went from the many species, well-named since specialized, to a kind of common genus. Non-specialized, humanity became, if I may, a counter-species: literally, it became generalized. Losing its specifying characteristics, it planed down its programme and became a generality. Humanity, that unknown: x with every value because having none.

Becoming human tends towards this white indetermination. Zero-valent, omnivalent, nil-potent, totipotent; good-for-nothing, good for everything. Every bit of progress, stroke of genius, invention or discovery originates in such a backwards movement and advances by choosing from among the range of a totality opened in this way. Consequently, human nature or, if you like, human nascence [*naître*] can be defined, without definition, as a tendency towards this forgetfulness, this deprogramming, this dedifference. Who are we? Indifferents. I exist and think in a point where nothing concerns me.

Finitude

Adapted, every species – perfect, defined; finite, filled – fits its niche to perfection. Who doesn't admire the wild corporal beauty of big cats, parrots or rattlesnakes sculpted for millions of years by natural selection? What artist has more time? So we left this perfection in definition, this exact finitude; non-finite, we became infinite. Without niche or cradle, without house or path, without borders or bounds. Poorly finite, certainly, imperfect, assuredly, but launched into an unpredictable space and time, into an open universe.

Many philosophers bemoan our finitude, a pose that provides them with beautiful moving pages. No, without bounds from our own dawn, we are unpredictable in an environment whose strangeness never becomes adapted to our opening. This infinitude frightens, with good reason. Where do we come from? From a defined integral of contingent bifurcations along the Grand Narrative. Who are we? Poorly finite. Undefined or without definition. Where are we going? An unpredictable and improbable history begins in this dedifference.

Cultural differences set sail from the natural indifferent

Starting from this generality, human time relieved, replaced, stood in for the evolution, normally and again, going towards species, but outside the body, which remains incandescent. Through the process of setting sail or exo-Darwinism I touched on in detail elsewhere, evolution promotes, via externalization, tools and cultures. Whereas with birds, evolution's duration, direct and positive, produces chickadees, bullfinches, chaffinches, hummingbirds and parrots, with diverse talons and beaks, colours, flights, wingspans and musics, with us it invents, in advancing again after the backwards movement towards dedifference, clubs and javelins, hoes and hammers ... languages, Indo-European or Dravidian ... cultures, Kwakiutl or Berrichon: tools and customs. Organic dedifference conditions technological, linguistic and cultural differences, which thus become our own external species.

Behind the relativity of cultures, the universality of corporal nature is revealed. Yes, nature: this is how we were born. For, having become this generality, humankind only produces species in language and customs when the climates, distances, the environment of flora and fauna make it Maori or Lower Breton. Whereas other living things differentiate themselves, corporally, by species, we differentiate ourselves, culturally, by language family. We differ by gods and meaning because we have the same dedifferentiated body. We have changed little since Adam and Lucy, but we become redifferentiated in myths and technologies, fashions and cosmetics, become species again by means of knowledge and occupation, peasant or sand fisher. As I've said, the human body, stable, leaks: my body and my lacrimal glands have leaked forty volumes of traces and ink. The mosaic of customs thus originates in the indifferentiation of our bodies. Why did we separate nature and culture? Because we were seeking to attach them directly, whereas they are linked by a twisted Moebius strip. When nature withdraws, culture explodes; the second one succeeds in proportion to that first poverty.

This passage must in addition be dated: our acculturation has recently taken the reins in a vastly old evolution. Objects of the social or human sciences, cultures form an ultrafine temporal film over the enormous thickness of the duration of bodies, objects of the sciences of living things, soon of the cognitive sciences. This completely naked and wrinkled newborn, scarcely out of its mother's womb, let's practise seeing it as being millions of times more ancient than the Cycladic sculptures or the drawings of Lascaux. A crowd of new cultures covers over with a few millimetres the universality of nature, anchored in a thick time. The relativity of customs and mores is also due to their newness; the stability of bodies is also rooted in this ancientness.

Let's call the evolution diverted, redressed by cultures, history. I shall speak further on about this redressing, about this re-addressing. Maybe we diverted it to protect ourselves; the more we protected ourselves from it, the more we had to throw new artificial objects into the current of time in order to protect ourselves from it even further since from the evolutionary point of view, our body, less evolutional as a result of the artificial objects, became more and more fragile. This could no doubt have been happening from our beginnings the way it continues on today. This loop maintains the flow of history, which continuously sets sail from a body that evolved so much the less, thus remaining our common ancestor who always only evolves but very little and remains contemporary and ancestral. This chapter needs to be added to the *De senectute* from just now. We all live as Eve and Adam, primitive, although recently hominescent.

The body in pieces and quasi-objects

A saying sums up and launches this history: 'This is my body.' This, this object, replaces my body, comes from it, emerges from it. This hammer, my fist; this handle, my forearm; this wheel, my ankles, hips and knees; this bow and its string, my tensor muscles and tendons … Divide up this ancestral body, present in every language, in every custom, in every culture in the world. These cultures cut it up into parts, reproduce it and devour it, feed on it in its every species.[1] Emerging from the crudest technologies, avatars of the body in scattered pieces, cultures then display the species we didn't become.

Nothing expresses this evident fact as precisely as the archaic and barbarous rite of *diasparagmos*, or the body in pieces, as the Egyptian cult of Osiris, whose sister Isis looks for the members scattered all around the Mediterranean, as totemism as well, that profound philosophy on our ways of producing. If we could unite here and now, at least in our heads, every culture, the way biologists classify species, plus every language and every vernacular usage, we would discover, as an asymptotic or virtual sum, our own body. Not an idea or a notion, but the body, of each and everyone. All this, as different as possible, bread and wine, rice and beer, stone and bronze, hoe and wheel, is summed up in my body, yours and everyone's. From it, everything arises, sets sail, separates itself, specifies itself; everything gushes forth from it like an eternally young spring. The body, our trunk barren of branches bearing cultural twigs.

Orthopaedics

It's a question of orthopaedics. For the device to slide over the organ, that organ must indeed have dwindled to the point of threatening to disappear, thereby weakening the entire organism and putting its life at risk.[2] Hence the need for substitution.

As humans, we have no definition. In that specialized philosophical language I only use when necessary, this could be stated: deprived of substance, our body produces substitutes. One of these two similar words describes the fact while plunging it into the processual; the other immobilizes an error and promotes a lie. Orthopaedic substitutions: equipped with a stump, no one can attack or defend except by equipping themselves with a hammer or a lance; nothing useful comes out of this limp hole replacing the mouth other than noise, cries, music and language, supplications and beauty.

Every living thing survives by its adapted organs. It has so much confidence in its pincer or its jet of ink, speed or venom that evolution pushes to refine or strengthen this vital and victorious solution, sharper and sharper pikes, more and more concentrated poisons, long, hard or cleverly twisted beaks. On the contrary, defeat leads to death, except in that strange case where, a good adviser, it encouraged an animal to cover itself with skins, externalized from its own skin, and whose frail back was substituted into a thatched roof. Do we know how many died before this huge detour bore fruit? At the beginning we must have died a lot; we were always on the path to extinction: children of weakness and poverty. Arrested in time, we play with death, or death makes light of us. Hence our cruelty.

Orthopaedic, behind their recommencing refinement our technologies conceal an organ which, sprawled out in this soft protective fleece, incessantly dedifferentiates itself. We will more and more resemble flabby foetuses under the lances and cuirasses invented by our lack of claws, horns and beaks.

Technology according to exo-Darwinism: Death ...

Refining their organs by mutation and selection, living things attain a new behaviour, reached in this way without finality. In this way reptiles become birds that fly; in this way former inhabitants of the sea walk; in this way parrots acquire thick, curved, highly sharp beaks. These newnesses, which then exploit new niches, require a vastly long time and as high a number of non-selected organisms or non-adapted mutants, put to death in both cases by these two fundamental operators of evolution. Hard beaks eliminate soft beaks.

When we attain technology, we invent an intention that replaces the absence of final causes. What is technology? The advent of finality in an evolution that knew nothing of it. If not the first stone, which came about God knows how, then at least the second one was carved by someone or other in order to hunt or fish, to harpoon some prey, to jab, to cut up, seeking, for an aim, new means, a newness that, for an intentionless evolution, would have taken millions of years, plus the vast crowd of the eliminated, dead by means of mutation and selection. So by carving and sharpening flint, forging bronze, making picks, lances and sabres in this way, we saved, at least virtually, the vast number of humans whose nails or fangs wouldn't have attained such effectiveness in cutting. We therefore economized first on this endless transformation of organs but also, via this short circuit, on this merciless elimination. A sublime benefit, technological invention, even the invention of weapons, saved from the work of death evolution leaves behind it. May the denigrators of technology ponder the charnel house it spares us from. Instead of killing the ill-adapted, we throw the devices that are no longer of any use into the sewage fields. What is technology? An economizing on death: saved cadavers. A thwarting of necrophagous evolution. Of course, every technological invention entails risks; but this number of dead has little weight in the face of the host of cadavers it spares us.

From having confronted death by inadaptation, we therefore invented orthopaedic cultures we could change at leisure, in the event of emergency, without waiting for a long and problematic adaptation from the genetic bank, putting the entire species at risk of extinction. The contemporary paradox immediately bursts forth: while our technological masterworks protect us from elimination, why do we, quite the contrary, think that the most contemporary ones cast us into it? We will only be able to answer this question on condition of thinking about it at this depth and in comparison with the laws of evolution.

... and acceleration

In externalizing it, we accelerate it to the point where it becomes this human history, with a changed velocity gradient. What is technology? A tremendous acceleration of the time of living things. This 'setting sail' changes our pace so much that it prevents us, once cast off, from assessing the ever so slow length of the times that preceded it. It makes us forget them. As a result, the extreme slenderness of history can in a certain way be compared to millions of years of evolution: we have changed speed. Opposition to Darwin came above all, I think, from the incapacity to conceive of such colossal durations, and I still wonder today whether we conceive of them easily. Our brief history prevents us from understanding evolution and from remembering it because the effects of the former block in part the laws of the latter.

But also because the lightning-fast acceleration of the former renders it, in a certain way, compatible with the latter. Conversely we sometimes make the mistake of saying that our human history more or less follows evolutionary laws; a correct assessment of the times, so incomparable, prevents us from falling into this trap; the several millennia that separate us from the Neolithic, during which certain of our fathers cultivated corn, have the same relation with the millions of years required by organic transformations as a book of a thousand pages does to its final letters. Such a change of scale requires different laws. Technologies, precisely, change the scale of time; their acceleration catches up, in a lightning-fast way, this vast lagging behind. Our enormous oldness outstripped us; through knowledge we assess it, through technology we imitate it. Everything is transformed by change in scale, of course, except for a knowledge that, invariant and light, flies among its rungs. Space formerly crushed us; today, time crushes us; through thought, we understand them.

What is hominization? The exit, via finality, from slowness and death. The progressive liberation from the laws of evolution. The exit from evolution? Many of religion's early books, which we hardly understand and sometimes scorn, in reality relate, although blindly, the stanzas of this liberation or this genesis. Humanity is therefore born from this acceleration and from an involuntary but real pity. Did our phylogenesis blindly practise what we call a virtue? Can we conceive that this counter-evolution engendered a morality or that this latter furthered this exit? Darwin himself did not scorn this hypothesis. This lightning-fast acceleration of time that liberates us from an interminable evolutionary pace, this change of scale, this savings of an enormous mass of cadavers prevent us from reducing technology to its practical finalities. Technology sculpted the human, which sculpted it, its time, its habitat, its customs, its morality. Technology carried history with it.

In addition, technology has cognitive virtues or at least mnemonic ones: once brought into the world, it has no need of genes to perpetuate or transform itself. Individual, collective, hardware or software, devices in turn act like memories. Organic genesis gives way here to artificial reproduction, the word 'reproduction' meaning both vital birthing and the imitation of artefacts. Transmission no longer passes through a molecular bank but rather through imitation. We learn the workmanship of the tool and the gesture it requires from the master. This is how we became, as Aristotle said, the most imitative of living beings. The most given over to learning. Knowledge begins. But sometimes we forget or disobey. We sow our memories with revolts and acts of negligence. So invention begins.

Return to poverty

Linguistic or objective memories function faster than the one lying in our genes, although less faithfully; we pay for our extreme speed with tatters of forgetfulness. We survive as cultural species, in a certain way overadapted, because we live as an organically or naturally ill-adapted genus.

As far as life is concerned as well as in other domains, poverty therefore wins out over wealth, counted in numbers, fragility over power and weakness over strength, the white and empty state over a more or less full state. Let's be delighted with our indigence and sing the praises of poverty, riskier but more adaptive than affluence. We are familiar with a thousand examples of this: immigrants courageously prepare the future of filled peoples, more attentive to their muddy dogs than to their children's education. Austere exercise is more befitting than distress or food scarcity but also than bloated satiety.

This body situation has repercussions on morality. As repetitive and idiotic as a unit added to the preceding number to get the following one, avarice heaps up figures the way gluttony does bottles and sloth or lust do beddings. These evils all proceed from envy, which compares and seeks, through pride and wrath, to win out: I put on more weight on than you; I built my house taller than yours; hence this addition whose perpetual repetition inflates the frog facing the ox but above all before his sister. These capital vices drive to violent death.

Stem cells, stem bodies and stem cultures

The whole of this reasoning has its source in the very sources of life, really in its origin. Dedifferentiated, a stem cell, in the very first state of the embryo, will give birth, during its development, to this or that other blood cell, liver cell or cell of the nervous system. It can therefore be called omnipotent since it contains in potency every specialty of cell the body will, in act, be formed from. Stem cells show the white state; every other cell shows a more or less filled state.

The prow of exo-Darwinian history, our body plays the role of cultural stem source. Omnipotent, it contains in potency every cultural variety. Each of these varieties adapts to the climate of its niche the way a species does in and through its environment. I have called my contemporaries and my successors by the name of Eve, Lucy and even Adam. See there, in the past and tomorrow, the stem body. Not really primordial in the sense of a linear time that would experience beginning, middle and end, but a kind of stem species having the potentiality of cultural actions to come by a process in which the possible comes to existence.

No doubt our body contains in potency thousands upon thousands of cultural virtualities; the fact that we are changing customs and thoughts today brings a concrete proof of this. What is to be done with a culture that only sought to preserve itself, that no longer created, even within its own framework, what is needed in order to transform? I love my culture in that it gives me the means and the freedom to reject it, to change or recreate it.

I receive from it and from other ones possibilities with whose help I try to construct a work that chance will make necessary or impossible. Contingent like a living thing, culture, a stem source in turn, opens up ranges of possibilities in which works try their luck, works mostly eliminated by the filter of impossibility, but among which extremely rare successes become necessary. Like life, culture develops in the square of modality. The stem body opens up these modes.

Descents into dormition

The spectrum of sleep

My hearing deafened by the dull and monotonous sound of the wheels on the tracks sleeps; drunk from the passing bursts of landscape, my sight becomes blurred; my skin dissolves underneath the fabric of my clothes; buried in the fold of my underwear, my genitals, folded, go absent; tucked up under the seat, my legs drown in unconsciousness; curled up inside my teeth, beneath the palate, behind my lips, my tongue is anaesthetized; my muscles are concealed, my bones are benumbed; what are we to call that which, in my breathing and my body melted into the mist, sleeps, suspended, even though I'm not asleep? Is life wrapped in kinds of sleep? The stem body inhibits its functions. In a white state, the body puts to sleep its other full states.

Roots hibernate in the ground, as do trunks beneath the bark and, without leaf or bud, twigs in the wind; the genes inhibited by interfering RNA sleep; does the inhibition vary on the sleepiness? Ecstatic animals sleep in their instinct; the soil and the inert rocks sleep, as do the mountains beneath the thunderstorm and the glaciers in their ever so slow descent, the ocean during the calm after the storm, Garonne below low-water mark and Iceland's lakes above the volcanos' fire; the nuclear lights that have been expanding in the dark Universe for billions of years sleep.

Dozing in the primordial soup, life sleeps as well; it slumbers curled up in the uterine cavity; the child coddles itself; adolescence drugs itself; what tosses old age into the rocks and the dead? Don't be afraid of dying, grandfather: an increasingly numb sleep will protect you from this fear, the way it helped, symmetrically, your childhood with the torment of growing. Institutions sleep in the dark labyrinth of the administrative moles; politics renders our obedience blasé; societies, masses, crowds are enveloped in groups in which stupidity and repetition sleep; violence and loves always sleep.

History and physics sleep in the background noise of the world. Everything sleeps: the Earth and the sky; spores and sperm, virgin ova and unsown seeds; the anchors and hawsers of a ship in route, and the same ship, conversely, at anchor or moored in port; the fixed parts of a doorframe and the standing end of a rope; our intelligence, silence, our blindnesses, the total language in our rare words, the meaning in deep things, the life and beauty beneath the cuirasses heaped up by idiocy. The dark sleeps. A few sporadic islands sometimes emerge from the sleepy blue-green sea, increasingly dark as one dives down.

Embracing the universal dormition, thought is awake. How long will I cling on to its window?

Steps of speech

In other words. I keep quiet; talk with a friend and confide some secret to her, one to one; around the table, during the meal, I speak to my family; give class to thirty pupils, or, in the lecture hall, to 600 students; in the Palais des Congrès, 3,000 experts listen to my lecture ... Here are several 'speeds' of language and wakefulness, each stage of which, of course, depends on the number but also on the quality of the interlocutors and the pertinence of the questions asked afterwards: general public, professionals, devotees, the indifferent, the hostile or critical.[3]

When I, whether a little runt or a Leviathan, adapt the volume of my voice to the audience, as well as the slowness or haste of the delivery, the rhythm of the periodic sentences, the expressive music, the vocabulary itself, the distinction and the clarity of the meaning, in short the range of techniques said to be eloquent, I feel – from the tension of the backs of my knees to the furthest point of my attention – my body climb up several different types of excitation and sometimes arouse such an overexcitement that it afterwards takes hours to get to sleep, so much does vigilant vivacity perch above the vegetative and in the end delay rejoining it. Conversely, at which stage of sleep is speech established when it whispers and lets itself go, sliding from inattention into muteness? Each level requires specific behaviours in which wakefulness and dormition are mixed, in precise proportions, all the way out to the two extreme states where the one tends to dissolve the other: white sleep and sharply discriminating and many-coloured attention.

I suspect that this staircase has flights so high at its tip and low at its depth that we ordinarily only explore a narrow part of it. Expertise, talent and virtuosity add this or that level more to this unfolding towards the top, the descent of which plunges towards as many types of stupor. Our tensor body and sharp-pointed attention can always climb up an additional step or fall lower into the delectable quietude of nothingness.

From supersharp intelligence to divine stupidity, genius comprehends the entire scale. For thought at least is not confused with the extreme apex of wakefulness. We always overestimate too much a certain light and its focus, whose point bestows clarity to explanation, and distinction and transparency to exposition, while thought, dozing and hunkering down in the numerous twisting recesses of dormition, winds about and, enveloped in sinuous inattentive virtualities, has worth: mute, deaf, blind, black, it crouches down like a wild animal ready to leap into the intuitive day. The professor expounds; the thinker listens to the background noise of the body and the world. Heavy and light, thought weighs down low, flies high and hears the entire staircase. But the word, at the peak, drugs all the rest the way it forgot time.

The descent into the body

What organ, what function, what acts are not constructed from such flights in multiple instances and unfolding landings? The entire body traverses them of itself. The bones, except when they break, and the liver, the gall bladder, the intestines or the kidneys, when they interrupt their functions, attain wakefulness less than the heart, whose rhythm is submitted to strong emotions, or than the lungs, whose tempo depends on the will or the involuntary, at will. Consult males regarding erections; this 'non-willing' that's folded or unfolded, as soft and hard, in ways so diverse that each one, it seems, is the mark of a singular partner, whether present or virtual.

We will probably never be conscious of our cells, of our DNA, of the water and carbon molecules constructing our body. These pieces of hardware, with all the software assembling them and directing their function, sleep. Almost all of the vast organic activity is buried in a happy night and only lets rare points of audible wakefulness appear. The multiple folds whose shadows and numbers are unfolded by biochemical research sleep. Sometimes pain precedes and announces the emergence of consciousness and prowls, another wild animal ready to leap, it too, from level to level. Health dozes in the organs' sleep.

Said unconsciousness, if it exists, and its irrepressible language only form some particular case, a step, in this long descent into a hundred corporal levels sometimes giving vent to the sounds of suffering issuing from their dysfunctions. Like the body, it only calls when in distress.

Descent into identity

Thus identity itself unfolds into the same ladder, as long and detailed. Who suffers, who screams, who talks and keeps quiet, who sleeps and becomes animated, brought to life, who takes pleasure, sings with joy, who vegetates and jumps with vivacity, who thinks and how? Which *I* suffers or is awake? Does it have the same 'identity' as the one who repeats or invents, who speaks and thinks at this or that level of clarity? We would be lying if we said and believed that it was, in every case, a matter of the same identity. Here rather are diverse landings or stages of equilibrium, different 'stases', several temporary invariances across variations in time and, between them, operators of transformation, emotions, feelings and thoughts: a little, a lot, passionately ... Numerous, I live ten different wakefulnesses, a thousand mixed sleeps, a hundred incomparable naps and how many deaths, ultimately? Certain great inventors confess to having received their definitive intuition in a single night, a week, a wonderful year: how did they think the rest of the time? How many differential deaths, limit ordeals, overcome pains, spurned loves has life exposed us to? After so many agonies, what eternity do I enter?

Speaking before different publics or letting myself go during this train trip, my sexuality or musculature for walking, for porterage and climbing sleep; ascending the Matterhorn's Lion Ridge, discursive thought and the speculative functions of language sleep while the sight of the slightest handhold and the tension of exquisitely differentiated muscle fibres intensify. The body is laminated; sensation and speech unfold in a spectrum; the I is stratified into stages or landings; presence and absence to oneself, attention and forgetfulness come undone into a thousand folds.

The fact remains that the one who tells of these differentials of self and their permanent swinging better than me is constantly named Michel de Montaigne. But his sharp consciousness forgot to dive, as living, wakeful presence or dormition, into colours, sounds, time and the world's sleep. Our region – Du Bartas, Palissy, Lacepède and Montesquieu – did it better than him.

The flights of memory and forgetfulness

For the body, speech, consciousness and identity, these descents and ascents with their numerous steps resemble the voyage of perception in universal time with its succession of terraces or balconies, doll, house, torrent, mountain, sky ... and even resemble the calculation of our own age: seven decades for the assemblage, several million years for the species, four billion for DNA, fifteen for atoms.

This dormition resembles, once again, the forgetting of this time and the slow ascent into wakefulness and its distinct accounting. Everything goes from a white state to another one, cluttered. Knowledge wakens perception, and, in front of the alpine-pastured farm or the Grand Canyon, around me and in me unfolds the vast scale or ladder of the universal duration of things, of the world and the living, but its astonishing forgetfulness sinks down as well: global amnesia or universal dormition.

The way we lose time, we forget the world, our bodies, our sufferings, graduated speech and our graduated identity. My body sleeps like a stem source.

Descent into incandescence

Zero and infinity, our body externalizes, into technology, its organs or functions, taken from among its infinite state; can it also externalize its zero or white state, as such?

Ploughing and grazing

Why has the peasant, for millennia, broken the ground, cleared, ploughed? To eliminate every species that could, with their wild fertility, kill the fragile domestic plant. Said weeds owe their power to natural selection, and wheat owes its weakness to that artificial selection that served as a model for Darwin and is practised by livestock farmers. Why do these latter surround the field with fences, the barn with walls or the sheep pen with planks? Why do they raise the chicken coop as well as the pigeon house? To protect the lamb and the fowl, fragile due to the same artificiality, from the wolf's and the fox's enterprises, expert and implacable because they have hunted for millions of years. Clearing, ploughing: here, let nothing remain. Livestock farming: chase out every other animal from there.

So, after the ploughing, the first *tabula rasa* and the construction of the enclosed farm, well-named, the harvest comes up thick and the fat cattle thrive.[4] In these two white, zero-valent, empty spaces, our crops [*cultures*] flourish, differentiated at leisure: wheat, corn, oats, rye, buckwheat; green grass, clover; horses, cows, pigs, turkeys and guinea fowl ... according to the environmental constraints. Every crop [*culture*] presupposes the same gesture of destruction or devastation, of nihilation: breaking the ground and ploughing. Once again, cultural diversity, in both senses, proceeds from a nature, here deliberately and actively whitened, an expression literally meaning that nothing else is going to be born or will be able to be born there. Rendered naturally virgin, axenic, that is to say, without foreign bodies, these sites produce every crop [*culture*] chosen by human free will. Just as a thousand technologies and cultures set sail from our zero-valent body, so all agriculture comes up from this white field.

The first answer to the initial question: for everything happens here as if we were externalizing the white or zero of our dedifferentiation. Objectivized, this dedifferentiation then produces the differentiated.

White house

Do you want to produce or invent? Plough, dig, exert yourself. Build a stable for a mare and its foal, a sheepfold for a ewe and its lambs, a sheep pen, a farmyard, a pigsty, a dovecote; this promises harvests and large litters. Now do your housecleaning with care: let no trace of rats or spiders, flies or vermicules remain. According to the precepts of this method, your niche becomes smooth. Field or room, let the white body export, here again, a white site. It will live there; it will make it its abode.

If it left the least stain there, it would appropriate it, the way an animal marks its niche with its excrement. On the contrary, in whitening this site to make it clean, aseptic or axenic, it makes it into a hotel that can receive everyone and anyone comfortably. This cleanness, this white, this zero, this nothingness become a universal hospitable space. Like the cereals in the breeze or the fowl in the farmyard, all humankind will feel at home in this new site. What should we call it: drawn out of everything, extract … abstract? Do you want to produce or invent? Is abstraction born from our bodies, in the fields and at the hotel?

General equivalent

From the *pagus*, where the peasant exerts himself and where he is going to bury his old father, his wealth rises up. Which wealth? The wealth counted in heads of cattle [*têtes de bétail*] – *pecus* in Latin and *cattle* in English – and this is where the words 'capital' and 'pecuniary' come from. Long ago certainly but now no longer, for these cattle, heavy and slow, are not easily exchanged. The wealth counted in Florentine florins, Byzantine bezants or ducats struck with the doge's effigy? Formerly certainly but not today, for these coins can be stolen, again too heavy and precious. Why does money, now, have changing and abstract appearances?

Because, in divesting itself of all of its concrete attributes, this token is worth everything because it isn't worth anything in itself. If value consists in what fulfils needs and desires, we can't drink or eat this symbol, nor can we take shelter under a roof it doesn't offer, for value resides in us, in our desire and not in it, therefore become, by our own decisions, a general equivalent, a kind of stem thing. So, from these white dedifferentiated coins proceed, once again, barley and bulls, movable goods, the immovable house and farm, the social bond, all the rest of the differentiated values, even the ploughed land, the clean house, even – alas! – the body of the other. Equivalent to everything in the world, this treasure replaces field, niche and flesh.

White money, without odour or taste, virgin and fecund, growing beyond the limits of need or desire, contractual and fought over, diabolical and divine. It has every attribute, even the most contradictory ones, for not having any: a rich fool is rich; a poor fool is a fool. White, transparent, without responsibility, administration takes every power, for those who manage know everything, are in charge of everything, build bridges and roads, know better than scientists, invade political and cultural posts, direct everything, always and everywhere present because they aren't worth anything. White money is worth everything, can do everything, rules over everyone, omnipotent; the administrator who manages money in our societies obtains a hyperpower there because he parasitizes it. Money and administration devour the entire social bond.

A little interlude for days of worry: Auguste Comte invented sociology, the word and the thing, against the economics of Jean-Baptiste Say. The positivist was the first to understand that money dissolves the social bond and that this latter must be reinvented. Today we are witnessing the end of the era inaugurated by his philosophy. In the West, money has invaded everything, destroyed everything, by taking everything up into its measure. Traditional societies, consequently, try to defend the ties they fear to see destroyed or undone; they try to bind themselves again. But do we know what bond gathers us together? Neither the politicians, in practice, nor, in theory, the social sciences know or teach this invisible adhesive.

Poorly named because new, contemporary war sets two twins in opposition: terrorism's invisible hand versus capitalism's invisible hand. For how can we effectively attack white capital, whose global enterprises employ individuals who are not responsible, without having recourse to local individuals who are just as ghostly and unlocatable? But, even more profoundly, the social bond as such, still present although translucent, collides there with abstract, white and transparent money, which tries to replace it by dissolving it. Of course, the terrorist with the invisible hand fights Adam Smith's invisible hand, mano a mano, but again Comte is still waging war against Say, sociology trying to hold up against economics. Who will win? And what should we call a fight that only sets invisible beings in opposition? End of the interlude. We shall return to this.

Balance sheet: by externalizing a white land, a white house, by externalizing relations whitened like this, the body enters into abstraction or into a symbolic world. Better than to a species, it belongs then to a genus, a generality.

Symbol and tessera: *Tabulae rasae*

Our behaviours called symbolic thus proceed from such a whiteness. Beyond its market value, the token from just now attains precisely the greatest generality. Assigning a meaning to a sound or a sign presupposes white signals and free relations. Broadcast, transit and reception presuppose that the multiple spines of the chaotic primordial commotion have first been carefully razed away with a plane. Filled with the stones of language, Demosthenes' eloquence rises over the sea's fracas; it first confronts the chaos of waves and the background noise of the world. Between the howling of the wind, the thunder of the earthquakes, our squawkings, moans and sobs on the one hand and music on the other, a certain acoustics smooths out the waves. And the sound whitens the noise. Just as no one can speak without this prior planing down, no one can write except on virgin wax, a smooth parchment or white paper, on the page that derives from *pagus*. He who wants peace – also derived from the same word, *pagus*, the field – raises a flag, white as a page, so that no one can mistake the message. Cultures, languages, styles and later words redifferentiate these previously whitened signals. And the relations between signs and meanings also become planed down. We wouldn't understand one another without these three sandings: of *tabulae*, of signals and of the links putting them together. And, once again, the white body externalizes itself as these *tabulae rasae*.

The word 'symbol' describes this process. When they parted, the host and guest would divide a tessera, a token that was witness to the hospitality received and given; the random fracture of this terracotta piece, broken to be shared, follows a fine jagged outline, one that's haphazard, complicated, inimitable, specific. Upon meeting again, recognition would take place when the two broken edges were reunited, adapted like a key to its lock: συν-βολον [*sým-bolon*] expresses this con-vention. No more spines, ridges or teeth on the piece reconstituted in its totality, the joint playing the role of the plane. The smooth piece thwarts noise's treacheries. The piece has become white again. This is my body; do this in memory of me.

Specialized, equipped with sharp teeth, spines, ridges and claws, species adapt to precise niches, fractally scattered on the planet. They enter into the background noise of the inert and of life. Despecialized, our body produces white pages or completed tessera thanks to the bonds we maintain. Who are we? Living things that are close to symbols and coming all the more closer the more we multiply our relations. From this whitened body, our white behaviours proceed, of course, but whitening, in their turn, our acts and our bodies, as in a cycle feeding into itself. Who are we? A *tabula rasa* species, a symbolic genus. Generality has visited us twice.

The occupations of the whore body

So we return to the body. No longer genetic, but individual, it practises gymnastics: even though the old Greek word means naked, I see this nudity whiten. Stretches, jumps, limberings and rolls open up a thousand possible positions and movements to the practicer; they again transform his body, thus ground up into virtuality, into generality. The physical education teacher carries out on it a work similar to the work the farmer does in his field or the scribe on his *tabula rasa*: they all produce a white page on which a differentiated bouquet of specialties will appear. Well-versed in all gestures and expressions, gymnasts and their brother dancers therefore make symbols of their bodies, better yet, semaphores. Objective or collective, all the preceding practices, stemming from the body, return to its singularity in order to dedifferentiate this singularity again.

Consequently, it can practise every occupation in the world because it excels at the oldest one: whore, as they say with good reason. 'Pro-stitute' signifies: situated in front, the way 'preposition' signifies: anterior position, the latter denoting an elementary relation and the former a first site. A corporeity that's courtesan and, as they say, professional: plastic and suited to every occupation; a white land that receives every domestic species in its furrows; a white house that lays every guest in its bed; a general equivalent body, the husband of every woman and wife of every husband, giving itself in return for money. Our practices proceed from there? A gymnastic body, a dancer, prostitutable, therefore an actor, changing masks with each performance; an interpreter, going from languages to cultures and a traveller, running from mores to customs; a shopkeeper, exchanging wheat in return for beef and anything in return for money; a clever handyman, making use of every means at his disposal and making of necessity a virtue;

a thief making off with whatever presents itself; a politician, representing each individual of his group … a philosopher, running along the flow of the chronopedia … losing all substance in favour of substitution.

More authentic, since ingenuous, than Plato's Socrates, the Socrates of Xenophon's *Symposium* defines philosophy as μαστροπεια [*mastropeia*] or pimping. A procurer, open to every stranger because axenic, purified, cleaned of all excrement, a universal host or exchanger, the philosopher places his body, a white gymnast, under the angelic sign of Hermes, the father of skillfulness.

Agora, templum, tribunal

Through conflicts and disputes, hatreds and rivalries, we never, of our own free will, stop paving hell on earth. We can only with difficulty conceive of a paradise where all these energies would be pacified. Leibniz described it, quite rightly, as the omnitude of new things; again a totality that's contradictory – how can we conceive something new when the whole presents itself? – and white. Yet, we construct, here and there, sites where we carry a little bit of this hope, just as ineradicable as war. The *agora* or marketplace couldn't exist without a tacit contract allowing the general equivalent to circulate in a site without any conflict other than debates over price. There is no fighting in the souks. This zero of violence allows everything to be bought and sold there.

Likewise, the temple draws the cut out of an enclosed space inside of which holiness imposes behaviour opposed to that of the outside: don't kill your son but only the ram whose horns are caught in the branches of the neighbouring bush; reconcile with your brother before bringing your offering here. Not only does war die down here but what is called lawlessness rules here: the police don't enter this place. The sacred and the taboo cut out a white space whose definition boils down to the literal meaning of 'definition': a site surrounded by a boundary, *finis*. In ancient Rome, in the round temple of the vestals, whose white chastity watched over a pure fire, the filth they swept up had to leave by a door said to be stercoraceous: a clean expanse, even whiter than the agricultural *pagus* or the smooth page, even more than a cleaned house, as virginal as each of these young priestesses. What religion doesn't purify ritual sites as well as the bodies of its officiants or of the pious flock seeking an impeccable soul? *Lavabo inter innocentes manus meas.*

Lastly, in the tribunal everyone brings their cases and accusations; opposing forces balance each other there; the word replaces wounds, lumps and blood; actions are debated there, as with the general equivalent in the market. A symbol of the contracts entered into there, here is the flat and level equity of a balance in equilibrium.

The above are white spaces and a white object, and without them no social practice could appear.

The *apeiron* as origin of knowledge

This generality of our condition doesn't only unfold within the horizon of practices, whether work practices or social ones, but within the horizon of our knowledge as well, which for its part is also infinitely open. Just as the common zero-valence of our nature conditions the multicoloured omnivalence of cultures, just as the common nil-potency of our bodies conditions the virtual omnipotency of their acts, just as the field's white space opens up to every crop, just as white places and white objects condition all life in society, just as money tends to replace all things and every social bond ..., so our various pieces of knowledge come into being in this incandescent emptiness. Before receiving our language and its singular syntax from the tribe and our mothers, we bear a totipotent capacity to speak. Likewise, do white cognitive objects exist?

The origin of geometry, no doubt of philosophy, maybe of all knowledge, is revealed in a fragment from Anaximander, which calls this origin *apeiron*, an indefinite stripped of bounds. Rigorous and abstract knowledge becomes differentiated into principles, proofs and theorems starting from that very thing to which neither definition nor programme can be given. For the sciences to be born, whether formal ones like mathematics or applied ones like mechanics, it was necessary to regress to this totality in potency having no determination. *Geometry* (pp. 3–36) already called this formal space – in which, since the Greeks, we have lived body and soul – white, a space later defined and mastered. This space received, fairly quickly, the name Earth, which is measured and mastered by Geo-metry. This space, which was invented and described over and over again by Plato, Theodorus, Euclid or Eudoxus extends the ploughed square, the house of men, the temple of the gods, the agora, the tribunal to the Universe, to the world and to the backworlds. The global meaning of *geo* in the word 'geometry' is akin to the global meaning of the *apeiron*, our indefinite habitat, open and white, the definitionless world of our being-in-the-world. An indefinite living thing wandering in this white space and haunting it – this is the process of knowledge.

At the origin of algebra, a thing (the *cosa*, as the first Italian algebraists said) called x takes on every value because it doesn't have any value of its own. Again a symbol, again a white token or a general equivalent. We already carry in our incandescence the potential origin of our knowledge; we have already said of the human: this unknown = x.

In the same way, when he tried to draw the first horizon of our research, Auguste Comte assessed the driving couple formed by the generality of the problems we had posed from the origin and, secondly, our incapacity to resolve them then: minimal poverty equipped with a maximal potential. Like Pascal, he touched on the two extremities of our condition, nothing and everything, zero and infinity, minimax and maximin, but better than him, he joined them and drew the power of a dynamic from this. For our totipotency can be described as a universality that is at first without any specific or singular expertise but already at work unfolding such details. Anaximander describes an indefinite expanse, whereas Comte shows the positive dynamic from which our indefinite time shoots up.

De arte inveniendi

Do we thus attain an art of inventing? Does every advance, here biological, human and cultural, there cognitive and technological, elsewhere artistic or religious, require everywhere, at its beginning and in quest of its driving force, this regression to a kind of totality equipped with a radical erasure?

The flat balance of suspended judgement in Montaigne, hyperbolic doubt in Descartes, different ploughings, new purifications leaving nothing behind their annihilations; the 'sentiment' Jean-Jacques Rousseau seeks in the *Reveries* and which he seems to discover during the ecstasy that comes over him lying in his boat in the middle of the lake; indifference or idleness, absolute standing-aparts sometimes professed by the eighteenth century; the transcendental named by Immanuel Kant; the epoché or putting of everything and myself between brackets among the phenomenologists ... these are so many varieties of white erasure. In his *Timaeus*, Plato calls a virgin expanse χωρα [*khôra*], imprint-bearing wax, a space onto which we can put any topology, the primary uterus in potency of all things, that feminine womb about which we shall soon say that contemporary biological research rightly said that it is an exception to all the organs since the immune system doesn't always defend it from the outside, hence a fecundity issuing from the open welcome that results from this non-aggression; a *pagus* womb and page, a white house, a universal hostess, our bodies all began in this very space. And in his *Symposium*, the same Plato celebrates *Poros*, Expedient, and *Penia*, Poverty, whose union produced Love, therefore every human. We are born from a defenceless womb and from an extreme destitution that calls for, promotes and exalts resources.

The more we whiten, the more we invent; the more we set sail, the more we externalize, the more we whiten. The more we produce, the more we become innocent: by this holiness, you will recognize a discoverer. Invention extracts from the dedifferentiated body a flow of differences, technological, cultural, cognitive, and as this exo-Darwinism functions, we become dedifferentiated, even more disposed to make it function. Innovation gushes forth, exponential, never ceasing to feed on itself; this dynamic explains its multiple and vertical spouting up.

Not only do these specific functions set sail from the body but this latter also externalizes its global dedifferentiated status from itself. We surround ourselves with spaces and objects that are as white and immaculate as it is. And thanks to this corporal indefinite, successively subjective, objective, collective and cognitive, we invent.

By means of these whitenesses, which philosophy discovers and describes via that generality it makes its specialty, philosophy invents nothing singular, neither tool nor theorem, rather it anticipates a global world we will live in tomorrow, equipped, before this horizon, with these instruments of action and thought. It is therefore concerned about and gives itself the mission of inventing the dedifferentiated habitat of differentiated inventions.

The white relation

We don't maintain any definite relation with the *apeiron* or with these sites or 'objects', except that, through a kind of symmetry or face-to-face, they require us in our entirety, without any bound of any kind, without any work programme or specialty programme, without any specially cut out organ or 'faculty'. We think about them with all our floating and indefinite attention; we remember them with all our vague memory; we imagine them without any image; we attach our reason to them without any reason; we apprehend them with our seven senses; our entire body bathes in them, bones, muscles, genitals and skin; we desire them, love them with all our heart, await them with all our soul … A flame suddenly burns in us, melting our focalizations into a single one, indefinite in turn. We go back up to our own incandescence. Like the 'subject', the object becomes *apeiron*; like its 'object', the 'subject' itself becomes *apeiron*. Translucency upon translucency, nothing separates them. What living thing constructs this white relation like this?

But above all, we invent our encounters starting from this wide land. For a half a century, I have been seeking to construct a philosophy, one that has been lacking, of relation, moving from saturated models – Hermes, Angels, the Parasite or the Hermaphrodite – to the generalities this philosophy requires – translation, communication, a bouquet of prepositions. In any case, human freedom produces, in each of us, the capacity to construct with others links that are even more singular than the individuals linked by them. Slavery makes them fall back on prior models.

The class of white concepts: Freedom

If then there exists a class of white concepts, whose indefiniteness distinguishes them from the concepts defined and refined by the sciences so as to make them falsifiable and operational, Freedom belongs to it. How many women and men live free? Slaves of a party, of an ideology, if it's a question of politics, of societal conventions, of cosmetic or intellectual fashions, of any pressure group in which clones surround a perverse leader, of voracious appetites disgusting to others, of an organized network in which the paths always lead somewhere, would they agree to pay the price of a free life with open relations? Who doesn't instead rush towards a directed existence and directed relations, as though having a passion to carry an emblem, the trace of a classification, a brand of party, car or clothing, all relations of belonging? In its school, each fish orients itself parallel to the others, directed by some social magnetic field. It doesn't invent its relations.

Yet, indefinite, the human bifurcates from animals precisely through the minimalization of a pre-established programme, of a required speciation or specialization, of fixed direction, of ready-made relations. Thus its natural birth takes place in freedom: the human is born so transparent, so incandescent that freedom enters into the white class. Not only does freedom concern us, it identifies us. When the Declaration of Rights announced that man was born free, did it know that it was touching on the biologically, on the genetically correct? Freedom takes on the colour of the evolutionary cradle of men and women, becoming attached to their bones, their flesh, their hands, mouth, skin, brain and blood, to the billion-year-old whole of their cells, in brief, to their incarnation; to the tongue that speaks and shouts to others, to the genitals-hyphen, to the entire expressive and receiving body.[5] Universal twice over, in its comprehension and its extension, therefore in its content or its signification, both indefinite, and its transcultural application, freedom therefore can, it even must be said to be natural: in the literal sense of birth, in the genetic sense of deprogramming. We are born despecialized, therefore free. This indeed merits a solemn declaration.

Whoever renounces freedom loses his stem body and drifts towards another living kingdom: leaves this minimalization, loses this poverty, grows richer, becomes specialized in a relation, like a parasite, in a pressure group like a cow in its pasture, in a party, in the bestial passion for power, the vice of avarice or envy, an opinion, becoming shark, crow, asp, ivy or mycobacterium because of it; a predator rarely, a host frequently. We live surrounded by companions undergoing animalization, in the course of metamorphosis, the way Ulysses' sailors became swine under Circe the enchantress. Our fetishist ancestors sculpted it; Aesop and Kafka recounted it; Ovid and La Fontaine bemoaned it. The daily effort towards freedom is measured by exo-Darwinism's divergence; we must continuously leave life as such, the powerful impetus of its flow, not lose the temporal distances separating us from the bifurcations taken by the other living things. Plants, animals, mushrooms, single-celled organisms obey their programmes or the environment or both at the same time. We abandoned this automatism; we entered into forgetfulness. This transparent becoming of incandescence made us free.

Incandescent man and woman

As early as terrestrial paradise, Adam and Eve disobey. They choose freedom over their Creator even though He gave them a delightful place to enjoy everything in abundance; they prefer freedom to happiness; less due to passion than to nature; better yet, they define it then and only then. The departure from paradise gives birth to humans, who no longer remain among the plants and animals they enjoy and have just named. They choose poverty over this obese wealth. It would therefore be better to suffer and labour, but live free. Freedom is paid for with the pain of work.

Knowledge, the serpent says, who knows a thing or two about programmes, will make you like God, as invisible as He is, as transparent. In storybook images and religious paintings, I see them incandescent, at least as much the gleaming angel with the flaming sword chasing them out. Incandescent with pain, poverty, guilty disquietude; incandescent with anger and disobedience; incandescent with expectation and improbable future; incandescent with solitude and sin, with misfortune, with possible knowledge and holiness; incandescent with hominescence.

Ecce mulier et homo. Naked.

METAPHYSICS

The group and not the class of white concepts

A white concept, freedom is born from the other white concepts: from our totipotency, certainly, from God, assuredly, who infinitely allows us to disobey his weakness. Faced with any power of this world, no thought opens more to freedom than the one that whispers: if God exists, He surely doesn't sit on this throne, on these cushions and in the light of these gildings; beneath this canopy rules a living thing that's other than human, tiger or shark, oak or reed, a vegetable, some animal. Better yet, this thought, like this behaviour, opens to invention. Do you want to invent? See to it that you remain free. White concepts form a group rather than a simple class: they proceed from each other. Seek freedom, and you will know; seek knowledge, and you will invent; seek knowledge and invention at the same time, and you will not be able not to love.

Let's call metaphysics the discipline that deals with the group of white concepts. Universals. From the deprogrammed body set sail *pagus* and house – objective; next, from the relational set sail money and signs, to return in a loop to the subjective; then, individual and swept along, the body leaves again, in turn, for other externalizations, to the temple, the marketplace, the tribunal – collective – to all professions or kinds of work – objective – to the cognitive: symbol, *apeiron* …, lastly to the freedom that sums up and starts the loop again. Thus this class is structured as a group.

Work and metaphysics

All work, all practice, all invention depart from these dedifferences, imitators of the body, and from these relations, indifferent, so as to differentiate or redifferentiate. At work: when the mother matter, hyle without specification, from which everything in the world is made, becomes wood, stone or metal, crystal, molecule, atom, particle, quark, then we toss the idea of matter, become useless, into the trash. When space, the translucent and basic content of everything in the world, becomes Euclidian, relativistic, projective, topological and multiplies its dimensions, we no longer say anything about it, and it disappears from our concerns. When biologists claim life is no longer being interrogated in laboratories but rather proteins, their foldings or kinesin, they are saying that life, dedifferentiated, has reached the extreme of its differentiations. Vitalism vanishes like some kind of ghost.

Metaphysics has the worst of reputations at the end of its practice but the best at the start. For without its ideas, which end up no longer saying anything at all, we would never have been able to begin; we erase conditions and premises; we always kill our parents; we forget our beginnings. The cognitive sciences speak little nowadays about our understanding, a *tabula rasa*; does theology still discourse on God's understanding, the sum of eternal truths? And yet, how can we do without an invariant of truths before constants arise without which no science can progress? How can we do without a universal cognitive function, undefinable God, about which we can only say what He is not? Would we merely speak about, would we conceive what we know without these white premises? Can we begin to think without these universals? What can we do with them except for falsifying or redifferentiating them? Do we dispose of an axiom of closure to limit the list of these white concepts having, I repeat, the worst possible of reputations? Can we, for the sake of our future, do without metaphysics? When it reaches, like evolution, the limits of dead-end specialties, can science itself, entirely human, in order to revitalize itself, not reinvent new global concepts, even if difficult to use?

What is metaphysics?

After having asked for an axiom of closure, I will now ask the decisive question: is there a bound, a lower limit for dedifferentiation? Can we determine a lethal threshold of minimal despecialization below which a body can't survive; where a field becomes sterile when stripped of even its bacteria; where a page loses its inscriptibility and the general equivalent its value; where a language, stammering, loses its syntax, its meaning and falls back into a noise bushy with spines; where a society, with attenuated bonds, no longer holds together and gives itself over to wars in which it risks eradication; where none of our knowledge has any dynamism or content anymore …? Yes, there is such a limit; the whole of Metaphysics itself draws it, provided that it be given the general extension of all the whitenesses whose sequence we have just listed off. The prefix *meta* designates this threshold. It doesn't signify beyond, as has always been said, but below.[6] Below metaphysics, wheat doesn't grow, for lack of elementary life; cattle and horses die without reproducing; all exchange freezes up; language no longer has any framework or meaning; knowledge and freedom vanish; the collective comes undone; the body itself no longer lives.

What is metaphysics? It describes the minimal thresholds of our despecializations, whether corporal or externalized. The thresholds of whiteness, abstraction, symbol, the low limits below which we cannot plunge without dying. What purpose does it serve? To watch over these dangerous critical points. It watches over our mouths and our hands, over our white organs, over the species with the symbolic body, over gymnasts and dancers, over ploughed fields, dovecotes, the marketplace, bankers' accounts, temples, churches, the balanced scales of courts, the diverse bed of whores and derived occupations, the boards for actors, political meetings; it watches over the minimization of the social bond, over the cleanliness of our houses; it watches over the *tabula rasa*, Anaximander's indefinite, geometry's earth, algebra's unknowns, matter, space and life; it watches over the Universe so that the whole of living things and their places won't regress – below its minimal and precious whiteness – into the abyss of nothingness and nonsense, where neither plant nor animal are found, not even a bacterium. It erects a guardrail: above, our hominization; below, the chasm and its commotion. It watches over the human source.

Programme, syntax, white and black tablet

When I use a computer, I change software depending on whether I'm word-processing a text, setting out a household budget or having to find my way on a trip; my language on the contrary has a single syntax, a minimal one, which serves in every possible case, whether I'm writing, calculating or planning a trip. Dedifferentiated to the maximum, metaphysics likewise supplies a minimal tablet, one as razed as language's syntax, ploughing's *pagus* or the house's cleanliness. It proposes the idea, even before Plato distinguished 'the idea of bed' or of tablet;[7] it imagines, in sum, the other world of ideas. It tells of matter without specification, well before crystal and molecules; the individual, before Pierre or Paula; consciousness before it becomes 'the consciousness of something'. It imagines backworlds from which the justice that rewards life's acts is equalized; in brief, it constructs zero-valent *tabulae rasae* of being and knowing, of fate and meaning, of acts and relations, in imitation of our white body, always present beneath these enterprises. And this zero-valence, once more, opens up to the omnivalence of all the differences unfolded by our actions and knowledge. It thus conditions knowledge, founded the ancient world and will found the next one, reinvents my body and that of my female neighbour.

Below metaphysics, the states of things vanish, the social bond dissolves, societies kill each other; death is always present beneath these enterprises. The simplest tablet, the universal tool, such that none simpler could be built. Is the success of theology in the style of Saint Augustine or ontology in the style of Heidegger due to the fact that they attempted, particularly when the sciences had tossed the ancient universals into the trash, to move back again into dedifferentiation, to construct tablets that were even more razed, where the name of God or the verb being and its present participle were repeated in every mode?

Would the virtuoso pianists of the baroque or the accompanists of songs, through exclusive love of Couperin or of Brassens, scorn the piano itself, built as a universal tablet suitable for playing any music and to compose even more of it, new and unexpected? What could be simpler than such tablets since time hardly changes them, unlike so many techniques? Of course, this common succession of white and black strips, this tablet without prior music is no good for anything without scales or arpeggios, without practice or finger exercises, without tonal or atonal decision, without harmonies bounded by wrong notes, without virtuosos or composers. But what would all these talents do without this tablet? Here is a white syntax that's as visible as the ploughed field, the smooth page, the clean house, the virginal womb, the temple of Vesta, the wedding of *Penia*. Metaphysics abstractly, that is to say, in a white way, expresses all these *tabulae rasae*; it constructs the most razed tablet below which there aren't even any more tablets.

Who and what purpose does metaphysics serve? Its incarnation

Nothing could be more 'useful' consequently than despecialized metaphysics, despite the mockery of the specialists who seem to be unaware of how destitute of future its absence would make them. Metaphysics serves to remain human and not die from it. It allows the subjective, the collective, the objective, the cognitive to survive. It ought to serve to build a new peace during these times of new war in which invisible beings put invisible beings to death. Who does it serve? At least it doesn't serve anyone, whether tyrant or guru.

What purpose does it serve? There could be nothing more useful, even indispensable, in the visible and concrete than metaphysics because it imitates our body, comes out of it, returns to it, both of them dedifferentiated, both of them properly human; it is born of the body and stops at death. A triumphant result whose newness is enchanting: nothing could be more carnal than this apparent abstraction of quintessence, nothing could be more incarnated, closer to the hand, to the mouth, to the womb, to the naked body, to the very gymnastics whose movements practise for everything, to the nervous system, to the repertory of gestures that give signs, free, to music, to dance, to the voice that sings or speaks, to the labour of the earth and to the relation to living things. Corporal, peasant, gymnastic, vital, metaphysics marks the threshold below which our body can no longer be dedifferentiated without mortal danger. Highly physical, metaphysics positions itself at the boundary (*meta*). Below it, the gravestone, the statue of the Commander, better, the totality of *Statues*.

Return to incandescence

Our nature blows, flows and burns, incandescent. Our totipotency makes the class of all these white concepts possible: the beyond of all knowledge and all experience, in which the heart of my silence prays to the silence at the heart of all things; eternity in time; our bonds in fusion, the serene peace beyond battles and all resentment, all of them concepts that have been banished ever since knowledge no longer trusted in anything but defined and falsifiable formats, ever since we no longer heard that call in music and without voice, audible nevertheless ever since we received the chirping of birds and the cries of ancestors buried in the Africa Rift, ever since we suffered from thirst, hunger, cold, poverty, solitude or being crammed together, ever since, children of poverty, we gaped from lack, ever since prophets psalmodied absence, ever since scientists gropingly began to know and rejected lovers to weep, that call we no longer hear and which nevertheless murmurs like the air and the sea and the fire that surround or beat the earth and can destroy it, the earth defined, delimited, rigorous and exact like the scientific disciplines, conditional and founding like a cognitive science, solid like experience, the earth, habitation and niche, support of the species, of their wanderings, of their wars and their labours, but always surrounded by the rumbling of the immortal sea, enveloped by furious and turbulent or calm and transparent air, an earth devastated, nourished, dug up, annihilated, reborn through fire, serious exactitude edged with the trinity of incandescent elements.

We have quit earth for air, water and fire. Humble humans with the name of the earth, we live on it, depend on it, on its multicoloured immanence, rendered so by grid-patterns, mosaics, landscapes, networks of a thousand forms and varied circumstances; we carefully and without dreaming keep our two feet on it, our hands on things and eyes lowered; we cut out a white *pagus* on it, which reminds us, in us and around us, of that large encircling on the part of the blue-green sea, the translucent air and the pure white fire.

Elementary immanence and elementary transcendence

Of course, no one can work or write except on the crystalline solidity of the earth, well differentiated, never on the blurry water, in the capricious air or on the untouchable fire no one traverses without dying. But the earth, full and black, awaits the white in order for writing to be read or transparent fluids in order to bear fruit. We don't merely dig into the writing media, we must still shed light on our scarifications for reading and comprehension to occur; we don't merely plough furrows, we must water the plants and the aerobic seeds for fruits and harvests to occur. The earth therefore needs the water and tears stemming from the seas, the wind and its ceaseless sobs, flashing fire and burns, so much does brilliance and fruitfulness come from passionate joy and pain.

The form and bounds of work and meaning, of course, come from the earth and its immanent hardness, which is dry, rigorous, exactly precise, but no form, no bound could be read there without formless and boundless incandescent transcendence. We wouldn't understand the first word of any knowledge or the first benefits of any work should this beginning of light, heat, movement and flux be absent. Just as the earth shows its borders in its ocean robe, beneath the atmospheric scarf and in the aura come from the Sun and the constellations, so the plane of immanence plunges into a volume without which this plane could neither exist nor be thought. There can be no earth without the other elements; without the Universe, there can be no world; no chromatic state without white state. Work, language and meaning would remain black without this first and indispensable light. Useful immanence, cold and black; burning and shining transcendence, conditional. Recent, complicated, cooled off, the Earth descends from hot fluids and primitive simple bodies, from elementary incandescences; and meaning descends from the divine *apeiron*; and the range of colours from whiteness. Just as every culture proceeds from the stem body, so all our thoughts, all our feelings descend from the white.

Who should we love?

The same goes for desire. Certainly, we fall in love with him or her, but the infinite, before all and after all, tempts the totipotency of our condition of being a stem species. Our deprogramming erases every orientation and places us before the possible totality. After the list of the thousand and three women he loved and abandoned, Don Juan ended up praying in a monastery, his face lifted up to the infinitely populated empty heavens. Except in known pathologies, mysticism doesn't reduce to a sexual frustration. Or rather, our white, infinite and symbolic species cannot avoid frustration, its daily bread. Who or what can fill our desires? Who, even filled with riches, hasn't at some time experienced in his flesh that humans are more often fed by privation than by satisfaction? That they drew what they did best from this inexhaustible spring? That hundreds of thousands of years have trained their metabolism for lack, hunger, shortage, dearth, scarcity? That obesity overburdens and kills us? We quit specialization even in desire. Destitution, our condition.

If, positively, love sometimes experiences the excellent seraphic union in pure and naked eroticism, this satisfaction alone however, even if perfect, whether punctual or of long duration, never fills the ineradicable – because infinite – lack of an inaccessible totality tied to our infinitude. Widowers of God, we love all women and the world, our neighbour and those who are far away, plants and animals, landscapes and life, the world in its *tabulae rasae*, deserts, high seas, white mountains, existence and death, good and evil, being and non-being, the Universe and women again; there is no love but universal love, directed towards that inaccessible integral of our acts of love called God Itself by wiser people than I.

And if I love you, I know that this totality visits you, becomes concentrated in you and inhabits you, singular. We live in nothingness or infinity, sometimes plunging into this finite milieu in which other species have their niche. To zero or to all, many does not matter. Loving him or her, named, occurs when the All becomes condensed in him or her. A lightning-fast experience that creates a short circuit between emptiness, named frustration by our incomprehension, and the filled infinity of the pleroma. Mysticism prowls around all of our loves, which are always universal.

Saintliness, poverty

So the Greek innovators of the abstract set out an *apeiron*, humanized here under the idea of a totipotent stem species that was born of a reflux in the reverse direction from evolution and starting from which all cultures are born. Mystics experience it as the sum of desire and knowledge, as the God they can only speak of apophantically, that is to say, negatively and regressively, only saying what one cannot say about it. It remains indefinite. Paschal fire.

Who bears witness to it? Since, put into networks and professionalized, our sciences function on collective intelligence, we have less need of genius; since wars have become impossible under the threat of atomic eradication or reciprocal invisibilities, we are wary of heroes; we feel today an enormous lack of saints, who return to the same deprogramming, to transparent indifference. This latter whitens them so that they become invisible, in the image of God. Discreet, secret, without any halo of glory. Witnesses.

Poor in language: silent, transparent, almost absent from the world, who could locate them? Poor in intentions: virgin, naive; saying yes infinitely, without any no. Poor through gift, pardon and abandonment. Poor, period, without any determination by luxury or superfluous needs. Poor in mind, learnedly ignorant, limited to carnal metaphysics. Poor, seeking total – and without any condition – humility before the Earth, life, thought, the different cultures, the others. Destitute: without self, without I, without subject. They have wandered so much, without any roof over their heads, that the differences met with have noiselessly planed down any differential spines in them. Forms, lights, shadows and colours have been mixed in them by the meeting of humans, the Grand Narrative of time and the trip around the world.

If we don't all decide, individual and collective, to become these poor people, as we genetically are, we will die. Poverty: the hope of humankind and the future of the world.

Identity, belongingnesses

We, I

Since, irrespective of porous cultures, absurdities still exist as outmoded as borders between nations, you have to show your passport or identity card to one of the functionaries who keep watch at those walls. He first makes sure the photograph of an inimitable face matches the singular one, passing before him, between your shoulders. Then, if he is in doubt, he reads your last name, first name, age and sex, written on one or the other of the documents. He verifies your identity. But is it really a question of identity?

No. For depending on whether you are called this or that, your name, carried as well by ten or a hundred thousand people in the world, doesn't designate you in any way: you merely belong to the subset of those men and women who answer to the call of Martin, Chang or Gonzalez. You likewise belong to the subset of those men or women called Sarah or Bruno. You sometimes meet, on your journeys, pretentious people who bear your first and last name. At least for this homonymous reason, the one, even associated with the other, doesn't make your identity precise in any way but merely an intersection of two of your belongingnesses. And depending on your sex, you again belong to one of two subsets, male or female, lastly to the subset that saw so many births in such-and-such a place and at such-and-such a time. Who can boast of having alone been born there and at such-and-such an hour, such-and-such a week? Your supposed I plunges into diverse *we*'s.

Confusion between belonging and identity

Thus we always confuse belonging and identity. Who are you? On hearing this question, you state your last and first name, and you sometimes add your place and date of birth. Better yet, you claim to be French, Spanish, Japanese; no, you aren't, identically, such-and-such, but, once again, you belong to one or the other of these groups, of these nations, of these languages, of these cultures. Likewise, you say you are Shintoist, Catholic, Democrat or Republican; no and no, once again, you merely belong to this religion, to some political party, to some sect full of obstinate people.

But who are you then? This verb opens up to meanings that are so vague it would be better to put it on hold; we shall return to it. So say your identity. The only truthful answer: yourself and only yourself. And this is so especially as the principle of identity is stated as follows: p is identical to p, logicians and mathematicians being in the habit of writing it down with three little horizontal bars in order to distinguish it from the 'equals' sign, which only gathers together two of them. As for belongingness, they designate it with a little sign shaped like a barred semicircle, literally resembling the Greek letter epsilon or a kind of euro, and whose presence shows that such-and-such an element is part of such-and-such a set, the way you are a member of the Portuguese, the Muslims or such-and-such a football team. The confusion between belonging and identity then begins with a grave error in reasoning that a teacher of an elementary class would punish.

Customs and excise, police, FBI, taxes …

Of course, most often, your last and first name are sufficient for the police to locate you. We, alas, no longer remember the indignant protests against the institution of identity papers uttered by those who refused, only a few decades ago, to be issued a card by the government like a whore. The Nazi state humiliated the Jews in this way by obligating them to carry such a document on their person and to show it upon command; the men and women said to be free found themselves exempted from this, whereas the women and girls who were victims of this measure were all equally to be called Sarah. This decision, as can be seen, eliminated identity so as to only keep belonging. The method of location used by the police shows that belongingness functions as a kind of address; if the police want to apprehend you, it is enough for them to ring at your place of residence, whose department, city, street and number is known to them. While you are asking the question: 'Who am I?' the FBI is resolving a completely different one: How can we find you? The mistake in reasoning concerns two distinct disciplines: you are confusing ontology and anthropometry. Maybe you are even forgetting the freedom allowed by a certain anonymity. Conversely, carrying this card protects from murder; I have heard ten African friends envy it, saying that at least their state counted toubabs; if one goes missing, they search for him; it becomes difficult to eliminate him.

Life and death

But the list carried on the passport, the identity card, plus all the administrative, bank and medical papers, not counting telephone, gas and electricity papers, does not exhaust, and far from it, the belongingnesses of a woman or a man. Should they learn a language said to be foreign, they will be plunged into a new community, inaudible to the neighbouring one and often to their own; should they practise a profession, they will be in a company, a department, a division, even launched into competition; a sport, they will be on a team that, next Saturday, is going to oppose some other team; should they become specialists in a discipline, they will be participants in a knowledge, in a department, in a corporatism; should they take delight in opera, dance, the piano, they will start an appreciation club. This series of belongingnesses grows all the longer the more you possess a concern for living. It allows you to share your experience with others, and its openness increases your accomplishment. So don't hesitate; multiply your belongingnesses; your bonds will become proportionately richer. This series doesn't close; you will only finish weaving this network the day you die.

Once again, say your identity: supposing it is decided to be the union of the intersection of all these subsets or the sum of the series of all your belongingnesses, you will not know your identity; no one will know it, except at the ordinary moment, solemn for you, of your death. If and when it exists, it may reduce to the sum of belongingnesses, but never to one or the other of them. Does there exist, at the limits of this series or of this sum, an accumulation point outside their unfolding? Either your identity integrates the niches you passed through in your existence, the doors you forced open, or it (another identity?) always resides in some site irreducibly exterior to this sum. Only the tautology 'self is identical to self' rigorously closes this bushy immanence or this inaccessible transcendence. But the white transparency, the incandescence of this repetition doesn't teach anything.

Drawn in this way, two cards tend towards each other: the belongingness card runs towards a complication increasing in number and intersecting overlappings; the white identity card, silent and smooth, shines.

Racism and its two reductions

Now, for quite some time scientists, politicians, journalists, regionalists, lastly everyone, have used the word 'identity' ad nauseam without first seeing in it that pure logical error that slides into a worse mistake. For let's examine what is covered over by the expressions: cultural identity, national identity, religious identity, masculine or feminine identity, African, European or Islamic identity.

Shocking injustices and an unbearable poverty can arise from these ways of speaking and thinking. What does the racist say? He treats you as if your identity were exhausted by one of your belongingnesses: for him, you are black or male or catholic or red-headed. He loves the verb 'to be', as vague as it is reductive. Racism draws its power from an ontology whose first act of speech here reduces the person to a category or the individual to a collective. It nails you into a compartment the way an entomologist sticks some insect into his collection with a needle; hunted, killed, pierced with steel, it incarnates its species. No, you are not Muslim, a young woman, Protestant or blond, you are merely part of some country and its spring fashions, of this religion and its rites or of a sex and its changing roles. As much as logical identity determines a rigour, so much do belongingnesses fall and float like time, chance and necessity. So much misfortune sweeps down on to the world from this that it would be better to correct this error that quickly turns into crime.

Racism can be defined by the reduction it carries out between the relation of belonging and the principle of identity. Don't use this word anymore, so widespread when it's a question of culture, language or sex, since the logical error becomes a social and political crime there. The racist reduces the I to an us. Who hasn't experienced that this simple mistake in language conceals an attempted killing? So consider the following expressions, so common today, to be definitively racist: cultural identity, sexual identity, religious identity, national identity.

Ethics: Inclusion and exclusion

Corresponding to these elements of logical and sociopolitical order are now things that are as highly simple in ethics. For belongingness, as is little said, implies a singular libido and drives more burning than the drives said to be of the body and the mind, attachments that flame in contemptuous attitudes, during heated discussions, and in war, during which everyone defends less his identity, or even his ideas, than the glue [colle] of his collective, sect or corporation. These pathological delights sometimes find their treatment (the learned say 'catharsis') in the rows of the stadiums where soccer is played; better of course to watch while shouting the victory of the Blues against the Greens in the number of shots at goal, which never kill anyone, while waiting for another competition for a tin-plated cup in which the results will be reversed than to bury a hundred thousand useless dead the evening after a battle of my country against yours. Belongingness's terrifying lust, from which perhaps comes all the evil in the world, is expressed in a universal, although unspoken, rule of conduct – 'love one another only inside one's group', – exclusive on the inside, excluding towards the outside.[8] So belongingness again repeats the verb 'to be': this one is one of us. I spoke of a subset, and here we find it closed.

If some individual belongs to this subset, this presupposes that there is at least one other individual who doesn't belong to it; in fact or by force, we will expel this person outside our walls if perchance he crosses their enclosure. Outside this boundary drawn by belongingness, this other cannot benefit from the same benefits: inclusion implies and explains the exclusion. Thus certain animals practise extraspecific murder. The question revolves around the Other. Since identity merely applies the self on to the self, identity rigorously expressed remains innocent of this exclusion; but the belongingness or gluing of the self into the us rejects the others from this inclusion.

The libido of belongingness: Exercises

With, as driving force, this unleashed libido of ours. Does every evil in the world come from belongingness? I'm inclined to think so. Evil prowls in these boundaries, closure and definition, ensuing from comparisons and the rivalries they incite, it being roused by this libido's heat.

May you, once a day, in order to cool it down, forget your culture, your language, your nation, your dwelling place, your village's soccer team, even your sex and your religion, in short, the thickness of your enclosures. Women do change names after marriage; travellers change address, and emigrants passports. Translate [*traduisez*] some foreign word; betray the easy dialect in your mouth; imagine that the person being accused of betrayal is traversing, in the literal sense (*traducit*), a border, is quite simply travelling and that, whether an importer or exporter, he is giving across this barrier (*trans-dare*). Call this traitor an exchanger instead. Bless the translator [*traducteur*]. Women, marry your brother's enemy. If you live in the shadow of a modest church tower or cathedral, look upon it once a day, at noon for example, as a ziggurat, a pyramid, a mosque or as a shadowless pagoda. Happy religions whose founding narrative doesn't deify their own land but on the contrary blesses an entirely different one, distant, said to be holy and so inaccessible that the land upon which real life unfolds becomes a valley of tears and place of exile. Where are we from? From nowhere, from elsewhere, from transcendence. Let's lastly practise, during this hour of light, dressing our friend up as a Persian and seeing our dragonesque beasts as beloved princesses calling for help. May we, from time to time, forget our belongingnesses. Our identity will gain from it. With peace, on top of that.

An admission by identity: Entirely innate, entirely acquired

I love the fact that the principle of identity reduces to an empty tautology, the ontology supporting identity becoming, by this stroke, nullified. My face takes on the form of a white circle, my body that of a candid coat. A portrait without lines or traits, a piece of wax that's as malleable as you please. So the populated card[9] is projected onto the white card, every different thing being imprinted on such an incandescence: the beauty of some female friend, the ugliness of American cities, the sparkling Sahara, the transcendent Andes, the currents of the Baffin Strait with its successive icebergs, Japan's triangular volcanos, bandits and saints, the humble and kings, crane operators, labourers, hookers, ministers, killers in power and love's secret lovers, knowledge and music. The noisy echo of a thousand voices, the white light with ten colours.

I love the fact that the sensualist philosophers, during the century of white enlightenment, plunged the self into this virgin wax. The world is figured and disfigured there as much as you please; the others hold an infinite conversation there. In my body, my soul and my palimpsest-understanding, a thousand texts and drawings arrange to meet each other, heavily overburdened, speedily forgotten, memorized, overlapping, ceaselessly erased and nonetheless always repainted and rewritten in reshaped furrows. Everything written on this absence; or: no one plus the others; that's the self. *Ego nemo et alii.*

Identity, vacuity, virginity. From this emptiness, every possible thing that can fill it jumps forth. The pleroma or plenitude needs a vacation. A virgin becomes a mother who becomes virgin again after her pregnancy. Almost all living things, plants, animals, mushrooms, are born endowed, only know what they have been given, marked, equipped with stiff limits resistant to learning, in sum, programmed, innate. For us humans, everything is acquired, as I just said, like traces on wax or colours in the colourless. But our native identity precisely includes this possibility of acquiring everything; given at the start, this is an omnipotency, a totipotency, in the sense that everything sleeps in potential. We find ourselves universally endowed by this whiteness itself, innate. There is no discussion or contradiction or even proportion between the acquired and the innate, between the two cards I'm talking about: entirely innate, entirely acquired, humanity is formed by this strange addition.

The compound body

Objection: an extreme difference on the contrary separates the self from the non-self since the immune system defends the organism from the outside by recognizing the others with enough precision to better attack them if they invade the place. This then is a counterexample in which identity becomes confused with belongingness, closes off its borders and wages an implacable battle against intruders. Everything happens as though an entire defensive army was keeping watch from the battlements of the numerous walls included in the organism, skin, pia mater, dura mater, pleura, peritoneum, tunica externa, cellular membranes.

But sometimes one organ is an exception to this rule: the uterus, in which, if I may say so, a partial lifting of immunity rules. For the womb mustn't defend itself against the intruder the male puts into it; femininity must actively welcome alterity since, in the contrary case, it would kill or expel the spermatozoids, single-celled organisms that are always foreign. It accepts them without fighting them. As far as immunity is concerned, every mother remains virgin in some way. She can receive the semen of an infinity of males, which she doesn't protect herself against. Otherwise we would never have children. The uterus resembles the self, not defined by some belongingness but by the transparent principle of identity. I love the fact that this incandescent identity descends into the belly of women; love this welcoming organ.

What then should we say about identity in addition to the tautology of its principle? Either it follows the ordinary rule, arming itself and multiplying cuirasses and walls, engaging in a battle against any alterity in order to end up expelling it; or it prefers the womb, sometimes outside immunity; so, immersed in the uterus' possible, identity disarms any defence, whether collective or particular. Our body puts together both solutions, combats and doesn't combat, closes and opens, forbids and allows passage. If you choose the solution of the intestines, the liver or the skeleton, you opt for individual life, the life that lasts for the time of mayflies and passes like the grass in the fields: a blink of an eye, fighting, death rattle; you will have lived for the useless flash of wounds and bumps. Should you prefer love, unfurl the white flag. The time of a new narrative occurs then.

Three bodies, three lives and three times?

The individuated body, the phenotype and ontogenesis fight but, buried at least inside the uterus, phylogenesis invents a peace in order to last in a different way. Does a secret lie in this origin place? A war always costs more than the conditions of a prior armistice that would allow it to be avoided. Always ultimately beaten, does the individual organism pay the price for its defensive system with death? An enormous cost, in truth. It only survives, partially, in and through the organ that's sometimes without defence. Everything happens as though we were living two lives, one of the individual and one of the species, as well as two times, short and long, because we have two bodies, with open doors and crenellated walls, the one in white identity, the other in belongingness.

Hidden in the depths of the vagina, the peaceful solution causes another life than our own to be born, another time, the time of a narrative that surpasses the duration of roses. Does the identity of humankind lie in women's wombs? Does human culture lie in feminine nature? I love this metaphor.

Third body, third life, third time: four centuries ago, Montaigne met a 'savage' from the New World who dazzled and disquieted him with his strangeness. Under the various pretexts of these differences, we normally kill each other. But we have just learnt that our common forebears, coming out of Africa, separated several millennia ago; with our cells bearing a code akin to the one carried by that Indian dating from the Renaissance, we meet again as close cousins. The Age of Discovery opened culture and the social sciences up to the alterities scattered in space; the time of the Grand Narrative brings them back to the family; predominantly natural, it relativizes the former cultural differences.

Life and the self as works

So we take up again, over a longer duration, the slow patience of our contingencies. Thus the self is founded in the work of time and assembled like a work that grows, in turn, like the destiny of a life. All of them together begin with blessed encounters, at random, and develop by epigeneses. Like the self and time, the work advances, falls back, never linearly, bifurcates, returns back along itself, sleeps, dreams, rests, explodes for a long while, suddenly empties, often becomes muddled, and also fills with hopes that die and unpredictabilities that shoot up like jets of water, abundant for a long time or gone dry the following day, parching or flooding the rare lands that are erased, revised, transcribed, the mixed places, the whole coded on an initial whiteness. Contingent, time and the self expand or collapse like the work.

When Flaubert says: 'Madame Bovary is me', he only reveals a small part of the truth. Precise and exact, this identification only goes in one direction, from him to a character. He could have, at leisure, identified just as much with Bouvard, Salammbô or others. In reversing the direction of the famous sentence, in therefore seeking the author's identity as such, we would discover to what extent his self is swarming, overloaded with princesses and Roman soldiers, with Saint Anthony and erudite theologians, with simple hearts and complicated bourgeois, with Norman landscapes where cows splash in the mud and dry African shores, with Telliameds and Pécuchets. This identification in the forward and not reverse direction, an identification unfolded then like a fan and not reduced to a single one of its branches returning towards the pivot, says as much about an author as about the self in general.

Certainly Balzac and Zola identified, in their works, with ministers and murderers, washerwomen, miners, duchesses, bishops, women peasants or men of law just as much as George Sand, Cervantes or the Countess of Ségur did, but the former objectivize on paper, the way others paint on canvas or sculpt marble, the thousand and one figures of a self that's common to everyone and thus always constituted as a coalescent and slow work. Just as 'author' means augmenter, these great proper names enlarge a process that everyone experiences, even if minusculely. The former make this process set sail from their body, and the others keep it, hide it, sometimes even forget it, as though it had shrunk; but it's always a question of the same process of mimetism and assimilation. Alterity penetrates in droves into incandescence, as does the chaotic card into the white card. But how could these identifications reach such a number, such qualities, this leafy, sonorous and hued landscape complexity if the self eliminated, if it expelled, if it didn't function like a uterus, welcoming and sometimes without defence, or like the trunk of a wide family? Dense with legions, each of us assembles his whore-identity from this crowd that's encountered, accepted, not merely tolerated but actively invited. Thus each life, each self, each person's time is constructed like works. A single precept for behaviour holds: build yourself, life, body and duration, in the patience and the suffering of a work of art.

Pedagogy imitates the organism

Why wouldn't the pedagogy of human children follow the evolution of this organic map, composed of territories of belongingness and terrains of reception? This pedagogy consists first in coding them; I was going to say whatever form the code might have. Its work, later, will plan to be decoded, to return – why not? – to the incandescence of virgin wax or learned ignorance, to be recoded, to change languages, sounds and images, but it won't be able to do so unless it knows how to code. Why not consequently accept necessity? The first code, inevitable, consists in receiving one's own culture, the subset of one's earliest belongingnesses, even if it means refusing them later. Transmit your language, your customs, your religious rites, in short, your ethnology; don't scorn them. For how can we avoid these necessities of enrootedness? How can we, impregnated, not love them? Up until my death, I will retain my accent, tails of inveterate habits following my ethnology, certain bad table manners, a streak of Gasconitude, the practice of Christian and courtly love. The generation that didn't transmit the codes it had received is learning, too late, that it was unduly arrogant, believing it understood what it hadn't mastered and criticizing to the point of abandonment what it hadn't understood. So don't let the wax stay virgin, don't let the child choose always and too much, for learning, always difficult, consists in letting oneself be scarified. A harsh ordeal. In order not to remain naive and foolish, plasticity has to learn the act, less passive than is believed, of receiving. The verb 'to capture' designates this mixture of capturing action and captive passion that's at the common root of the learning words: perception, concept, interception, reception. The predator hunts and kills; the charmer attracts to her. On the one side, the capturing immunized organs, on the other, the receptor. On the one hand, one's own ethnology, which tends to defend itself, on the other, the journey of life, which laughs at these fortifications and which fortifies itself by not defending itself. Yes, I live with demolished defences.

Look at the tapestry, put together during the day and undone at night, on which Penelope draws and erases the map of her sailor husband's wanderings. The cartoon develops with time, depending on the storms and calm seas, on the position at noon and at twilight, on the bearing and explorations, on the monsters and enchantresses; the self resembles the changing couple of the weaver and the seafarer, resembles the single body formed by the organs that remain in Ithaca so as to defend themselves every day against the odious suitors, who, invading the palace, seek to devour the heritage, and by the other who becomes transformed on Circe's island, hides beneath the ewes' wool to escape the cyclopean prison and sometimes also makes himself deaf with balls of wax in order to pass through the sirens' strait safe and sound. This one and double self, named Nobody and who at leisure captures the monsters met with in the inhabited lands, is constructed, by time, like the *Odyssey*, a masterpiece of art. Travelling and stay-at-home, its narrative is striped with an inextricable network of warps and weft, of verses sung and then written, nothing but crisscrossed scars or traces of wounds. Learning requires actively enduring this passivity, formerly called feminine, of receiving. I live scarified. Wounded, almost destroyed. A hundred times shipwrecked, therefore wonderfully living.

Temporal invariance

For the past few pages, time has occurred. It forces us to go back over the name, the one the identity card bears. Apart from the belongingness to the subset of those who are called in the same way, the name at least ensures that the person who was born there and at that hour, but who subsequently became an adolescent, an adult and, sooner than can be believed, an old man, remains the same: the naming guarantees a constancy across time. The principle of identity – P repeats P – remains outside of every framework, of every order, of every place, of every time. Yet, its opposite, the principle of non-contradiction states: P cannot at the same time be non-P. For example, I can't simultaneously be someone else, nor can I at the same time remain a newborn, a young man, an adult and dying. Yet time makes us go through all these stages; they therefore do not contradict each other if and when duration occurs. This is why my identity can be defined as this constancy in becoming.

A good definition of time therefore eliminates these contradictions so well that many recent philosophers, taking everything in the opposite direction, made the mistake of engendering time through contradictories. On the contrary, it recovers them through identity, in such a way that it transcends and combines these two first principles of logic: time makes identity stable across contradictory states. Far from any place, duration creates me. It stabilizes my contradictions. Terrified by wandering and time, those who seek places flee, if I may, into the space of belongingness and think that only statues ensure perenniality, as in the niches of Paris's Hôtel de Ville. A bad sign, only these people are seen. The self stays as invisible as the principle of identity. White, transparent, the colour of constancy. So finally say your identity: incandescent, I remain; contradictory, multiple and mixed, I plunge into time. These are my two cards. Does their confluence ensure that I live, a little, in eternity?

The end of two-valued logic?

All belongingness presupposes a subset; every subset is defined by one or more properties. With the libido's help, we have a tendency to consider ourselves as being part of a community endowed with a human property, the others – women, children, strangers or animals – being excluded from it and gathered into a complementary subset inhabited by those who are not human. Consequently, there are two subsets and two only: ours and this opposing one. The verb 'to be' and ontology conjugate this logic wonderfully; we will say being and nothingness, the human and the non-human, true and false, good and evil. The deconstruction of this operation carries out the same gesture as the metaphysics it wants to bring down since it adopts the same two-valued logic in triumphing by positioning itself outside Western metaphysics: here we see the return of the same division.

Yet it suffices to understand, as I just said, that I grew for thirty years in order to think that I am big and small at the same time, modulo time, without my collapsing for all that; it suffices for me to learn a language or music in order to think I am capable and incapable, modulo these recently acquired specialties. Two-valued logic is used wonderfully for certain demonstrative systems, but only there. Life is hardly acquainted with it, nor time, nor learning, nor projects, nor construction in general, nor the Grand Narrative.

Which fluctuate instead in a four-valued modal logic: possible, impossible, necessary, contingent. This possible, plastic and in a certain way totipotent, plunges into an environment in which it encounters the impossible and the necessary so as to blossom into the contingent. When the impossible sorts among the bouquet of possibilities, we never emerge except as a contingency sculpted by necessity. Time and life flow from and to the possible, passing through channels percolating with impossibilities; the past immediately becomes necessary there, the future remaining possible and the present contingent. Even the physical theory of chaos is better understood within this framework, a fortiori vital and historical phenomena. Philosophy thus frees itself from two-valued logic.

Intersections

Outmoded, your identity card only included two or three of your belongingnesses among those that stay fixed for your entire life, for you remain woman or male and your mother's child; you can no longer change your date or place of birth. Such logical poverty confines you to destitution because in fact your authentic identity is more greatly detailed and even seems to dissolve into a thousand categories that change with time. For your travels, jobs and the things you've been trained in, your professional, sports and political experiences quickly make the number of groups into which you are integrated grow: tomorrow you are going to be part of those who speak Vietnamese, play rugby, know how to fix a moped; nothing augments the number of collectives of your peers at the same time as your personal characteristics as much as pedagogy or the acquisition of new competences.

So how can your identity be described? As an intersection, fluctuating across duration, of this variety of belongingnesses. You never stop sewing and weaving your own harlequin's coat, as many-shaded and multicoloured, but freer and more flexible, as the map of your genes. So don't defend one of your belongingnesses; on the contrary multiply them so as to enrich what we call, by common accord, your self, all the happier and stronger precisely because it gradually frees itself from the places you wanted to defend. In doing so, you even honour your earliest culture better. Never do I feel more Gascon, more French, than at the other end of the other hemisphere.

Towards a first limit, the multicoloured multiplicity arouses singularity, strengthens it, as though this singularity gave its main colour to the whole of the painting. At the other limit, it rejoins universality. You as well as me, her as well as him, African or Eskimo, let's present such a many-shaded palette to everyone. Humanity arrays itself with bright colours. You will recognize it by this harlequinade. The distinctive feature of humankind? This sort of mixture. Incandescent like Pierrot; many-shaded, mixed like Harlequin. The more you imprint others onto the self, the more it becomes established as singular – for no one else presents this remarkable colour – but also the more it runs towards a sum as white as the wax we began with. This whiteness can be regarded either as a colour or as the integration of every colour. Pierrot tends towards Harlequin; Harlequin tends towards Pierrot; this double incandescence forms human time.

So universal humanity becomes that virginity that was received at birth, achieved at death and whose plastic becoming we recognize in ourselves. We will therefore give it two identity cards, the one white, the other multicoloured.

A new identity card?

Imagine going back over a border in front of the border guards, equipped with a variable passport resembling the instantaneous cartography of your changing aptitudes. New technologies allow the chip you show to the customs official to be instituted. The official will pinpoint each person and yourself among everyone since this chip describes the changing profile of singular identity, but above all we see mixing in it a thousand collectives corresponding to your experiences and the things you've been trained in. Each person can even show it to potential employers who have less of a need for specialists than for fluid aptitudes or intersections of various expertises. A diploma, for example, only tells one of your belongingnesses, first of all old, often forgotten, always stiff due to its unicity. In fact, your aptitudes must be said to be, in the closest sense of the word, polytechnic, I mean at the intersection of a thousand expertises, understanding by this repairing mopeds as well as translating Sanskrit, running computers as well as an infinite sympathy towards those who are poorer than you. Fingerprints formerly came close to such a drawing, but it would in addition be necessary to suppose them changing in real time. The self becomes identical to an inconstant finger. As wrinkled as the skin and as mobile as the face, smiles, winks, tears and old traces of crying, this Harlequin coat therefore varies, whereas the thumbprint, given at the start, never changes. Easy to create, such a chip, as universal as the virginity from just now but in addition eminently singular, paints your portrait in real time. Might such a chip contribute to putting right the aforementioned logical error and injustice and, all in all, a great deal of human misfortune? Or should it be kept in secrecy inside each of us?

Balance sheet

In total, this description of identity traverses the following domains: logical, through the principle and its tautology, temporal invariance across contradictions; sociopolitical, in the critique of racism and the process of exclusion; biological, through the immune system and its fluctuating uterine exception; psychosociological, since this description defines a libido of belongingness; it ponders space and time and identifies, to finish, the self with three states: a virgin plasticity, a complicated landscape and transformations vibrating from one phase to the other.

ITS CULTURE

From identity to belongingnesses, we slide from the I to the we. For I at least belong to a culture. How should we define it?

The culture of the 'Honnête Homme' or 'Gentleman'

The French language primarily detects two meanings of this word. Cicero long ago called philosophy the cultivation [*culture*] of the soul. The humanist sixteenth century repeated this signification with the 'development of intellectual faculties by means of appropriate exercises'.[10] Our Italian colleagues use the expression *uomo di coltura* to designate the signification French classicism recognized in *l'honnête homme*, common throughout France for so long and become now rare. For, inherited from the Latin language, from a Christianity equipped with its Greco-Roman and Middle-Eastern roots, in sum from what two or three centuries later will be called Renaissance humanism, this ideal that's corporal, intellectual, scientific, moral, aesthetic and also sometimes religious remains in a few consciousnesses and still irrigates certain lives with health, sensitivity, and gentle [*honnête*] behaviour. Our German friends call this education made of knowledge and courtesy *Bildung*. But social and political correctness considers this education to be academic and elitist, sins that are now deadly.

Born with the translation of Greek philosophy into Ciceronian language and ancient languages into European languages, based then on the 'humanities' today in danger of going extinct if not vilified, it started dying at least a half-century before the new technologies; so the latter did not kill it. Reading a thousand books taking Piraeus[11] to be a man and reheated banalities to be postmodern discoveries allows us to observe the ravages produced in the head by the absence of perspective brought on by the ignorance of antiquity, of the Middle Ages and the seventeenth and eighteenth centuries; a few university specialists frequent these dying humanities, specialists themselves suffering the symmetrical ravages of the ignorance, just as serious, of the exact and social sciences, which this cultivation entails. The university only had to separate, on the whole recently, men of letters from scientists for two families of imbeciles, crammed full with repetitive formats, to be born. Where can we find a lantern whose light, strong enough to shine during the day, would discern the 'cultivated' person? This latter would strive to reconstitute a humanism based on truly contemporary requisites.

The cultures distinguished by anthropology

A second meaning, rather Germanic in origin, prevailed during the nineteenth century in the wake of Kant and established itself in anthropology. For the *Aufklärung* and then the social sciences added to 'civilization', a term of a more Latin origin and judged to be more normative by said sciences, that culture which today signifies 'the set of acquired forms of behavior in a singular human society'. The adjective 'acquired' highlights here the opposition between the cultural and the natural, the latter gradually losing lots of ground to the point where human nature became negated, as in Sartre for example, at the very moment when the discovery of DNA was giving us the hope of redefining it with exactitude and generality. So the ethnologist describes the Aboriginal, Berber and Gascon cultures; the sociologist analyses their shock; politicians and ministers defend their exception during international negotiations since, it seems, cultures are bound to territories, to places, to climates as Montesquieu said and as is also said for the wines of Burgundy; do cultures thus find the agricultural meaning of the word again? Since economic globalization vaporizes the identifiable differences between the zones in which cultures are born and live, they must then be defended in the same way as the living species, which themselves owe their survival to local conditions and constraints. Since the parallel with biodiversity is imposing itself, we shall speak of a fragile culture or a language having few speakers as endangered species or of already dead civilizations as eradicated phyla.

Going-returning

I like to say that culture, in the third place, ceaselessly transits, in returnings and goings, between the second of these meanings and the first one. Those who, distinguished, only know the aforementioned humanities, the Salle Pleyel, the Paris Opera and the entrechats of ballet are to my eyes lacking in culture if ignorant of the cuisine of pig slop and the rites of greasy grub they sometimes scorn; I see them at times being more horrified at the knife stuck into the pig's throat by the slaughterer than by human murders represented in images, especially if these distinguished people have any power. Conversely, the pork butcher cleans up the mess smeared all over him to enter the Louvre.

The cultivated man departs from his roots – dialect, customs and mores, ceremonial clothes and rustic expressions – so as to steer his way towards the distinguished convention of his group or at least tend towards it, without forgetting to return to the servant's hall where the kitchen boys live. Such a coming and going never ceases with great artists: from his tower at the edge of the Mediterranean, Gascon-accented Montaigne frequents Plutarch, Virgil and American Indians; laughing at the learned, Molière caresses maidservants; conversely, washerwomen sang refrains from Couperin and Rameau while the Court, in ribbons and lace, danced their minuets; Shakespeare, in the forests, Giono, a peasant, Céline, a suburban doctor, never fail to get us lost on this always intersected path where Don Quixote, a man of the book astride his charger, can't do without the proverbs strung together by Sancho Panza on his donkey; Cervantes makes the mounts of his two twin heroes run *ex æquo*. Without dung or grease, there can be no dignified academy; archangels visit humility. Great art builds this entirely human-arched bridge where a crowd, whose members converse with and teach one another, bumps into each other. Masterpieces have long embodied what we proudly call multiculturism.

Local and global

A redefinition has recently imposed a fourth meaning. In parlour games or television quiz shows, the questions said to be about culture mix the first two meanings – 'What did Cervantes write?', 'What was the Australian Aborigines' favourite weapon?' – with this other one, where I always stumble: 'What nickname were the half-naked girls who wiggled their hips around some singer in vogue several decades ago known by?' Mass culture thus designates the whole of what the glossy magazines, radio, cinema, television channels or websites broadcast or make accessible between their advertising pages. It has come to this.

If culture has this fourth meaning, then yes, it is becoming globalized and brings in cliffs of dollars for those who control access to the media. To defend against an invasion that seems to some people to be as dangerous as the Flood, which we know covered over the terraqueous globe, some people advocate a quick return to the second definition, the anthropological one. So a war begins, which Rabelais would have called Picrocholine, invaded with acid bile, between the local and the global: McDonald's from everywhere crushes the blue cheese from Roquefort; Hollywood erases Pagnol from Provence and Guignol from Lyon; let's wield Astérix against Disneyland. Museums where the elite line up and concerts with hoary heads are opposed to the crowds got moving by the decibels in which young people romp about. Cultures in the second and maybe even in the first meaning then would amount to particularisms, to conservatisms, alas, to folkloric old-fashioned things. Consequently, a thousand risks spring up; fundamentalists and fundamentalisms are in return fed by this war. We find ourselves condemned to choose between multinationals and Taliban. Our current terrors come in cultural forms.

The question of space

For this stupid and monotonous dialectic to have any meaning, culture would have to be born, live, be spread and rule for only one type of communication space, whether divided or not: homogeneous, isotropic and transparent, it allows everything to be done and everything to pass; so a powerful financial group can control access to public noticeboards, newspaper advertisements and rumours in order to monopolize all definition of culture and, by repeating this definition in all places and at all times, transform it into dollars.

The word 'universal' always seems to conceal an imperialism. Often true, this accusation, a falsifiable one, ignores several non-violent global expansions, to which I shall return, like the expansion of fruits and vegetables, a quite old expansion, one which saved many scattered families from starvation, or the expansion of mathematics, whose theorems were not imposed in time and on the five continents by force. Whatever people may say about it, the universal exists – we'll speak more about it later; agriculture, the linguistic and practical root of culture, has shown it for several thousand years; the exact sciences have followed agriculture for more than two millennia and have thus contributed to a few curings and to making our labours easier. These sciences in principle succeed without imperialism and utilize this space that has no obstacles to their spread. Should merchandise and money transit there, this favoured exchanges in the Mediterranean as soon as coins sprang forth from Lydia and the river Pactolus. Did this invention create the space I am talking about? We indeed find ourselves in the domain of 'laissez-faire, laissez-passer'; does this space adapt to cultural circulation? The question of knowing whether a cultural 'product' reduces to a merchandise comes down to the constitution of this space. Did it exist beforehand?

No, because a thousand mountain chains raise as many obstructions. 'Truth on this side of the Pyrenees, error on the other side.' 'How can someone be Persian?' There are only exoticisms and exceptions. Let's accept universal laws for the rectangle and gravity, the stock market fluctuations for the value of aluminium or coffee, never for works. The set of boundaries inscribed in this communication space – become then, conversely, opaque, heterogeneous and obstructed – draws cultural world maps in which archipelagos of islets and islands, of departments, are defended by inaccessible shores and walls; to each his truth, his tastes and his beauty, defined then as local specificities; forbidden to talk, think or taste outside differences, a motto repeated ad nauseam.

Although opposed in appearance, this global and this local agree about the space in which they confront each other. For at first sight, only it exists, considered in its expansive totality or thousand differentiated parts, a space bare or entrenched, traversed with various networks in which armies can circulate freely or blocked with customs gates to stop them. Chicanes to slow traffic only exist due to this homogeneity; barriers only exist because of this free flow of traffic; we will block passage because everyone can pass. Conversely, we will seek to overturn borders that are absurd because conventional. The Alps never did stop smugglers or their donkeys; not only did the armies of Hannibal or Bonaparte cross these natural borders, porous, but so did languages and religions. There are different truths on this side and the other of the mountains because you built shacks there where a duty must be payed. Since no one likes taxes, let's all stay home, where we eventually cultivate distinctions that will someday seem natural. Local because of the global; global owing to the local; global and local, the same battle. This simple, stupid, repetitive and dangerous evident fact of space organizes everyone, violence first and foremost. What luck, we would indeed have to tear each other's guts out.

In truth, on both sides of the Alps, the Piedmontese speak a language that mixes Italian and French; Basques and Catalans, sometimes the Aragonese, live on horseback on both sides of the Pyrenees; Blaise Pascal, a native of Auvergne, was clearly unaware of this. This is how Alsacians and the people of Karlsruhe speak and act on both sides of the Rhine. Is there really only one space, I mean the space of roads and fortifications? No, for there are infinitely more types of expanse than it appears; we have long known a thousand other topologies and in particular those of the human habitat.

Confession

Forgive me, please, for continuing in the first person an argument that up to now has only concerned groups. Not out of narcissism but for better precision. Like many people my age, such as a Guarani or a Scottish

Highlander, I have a culture in the second meaning of the word, yes, an ethnology. Proof: people more learned than me, without any lived experience with the place, already hold colloquia about it. Some family of farmers and bargemen installed there, on some quay, waiting for the barge, instilled in me the trades of my forefathers, land and water, along with the customs and appropriate languages, expressed in Occitan. One day, I shall try to write with that portion of language that, still sonorous in my breast, becomes caught in my throat, silent, in public. None of this happened without our rural customs, some hard labour, tools that have vanished with time, an oblique vision of the world, typical human relations, a disquietude regarding the social inherited in an obscure way from the Cathars, a joy in the body and a cult of laziness, dark beliefs, light doubts … Local culture?

We shall see, for already my father, born in Gascony on the river Garonne not far from the confluence with the Gers, between two catastrophic floods, was often opposed to my mother, stemming from Quercy, by the dry and pebbly hills of vineyards, like a foreigner to an exotic woman, distant from one another by thirty kilometres, which in the past was equivalent to an astronomical distance. Since they loved each other, they adapted to each other; since they adapted to each other, they loved each other. But when they argued for a little bit, each reverted to their own dialect, for they didn't quite have the same words said with the same accent to designate bread and salt. Although nurtured on a tiny particularism, I nevertheless experienced what the latest racists today call the clash of civilizations. The smallest municipality is granitized with sub-localities the way an atom is composed of dozens of particles. There is no Occitan or Gascon language, strictly speaking, but a multiplicity of subdialects, the dentals of the one sometimes being opaque to the ears of the other; so there is no local culture in the above sense but rather a spectrum of nanocultures scattered from Bas-Quercy to north of Moyenne Garonne, and this is still too big.

Consequently, culture, even in the second meaning, doesn't stop at the borders of Quercy, of Berber country or the Zulu mountains because it has its source there, as though tied to a place, already composite, where it would quickly suffocate with lethargy by becoming atomized into tiny hamlets, but throws out around it random roads geometers call analytic continuations and, happily, crosses the thirty kilometres separating Quercy from Gascony so as to end up at the wedding from which my body came. Culture leaves a local that I can no longer define so much does its size diminish, from the region to the village and from the *lieu-dit* to the farm, all the way down to families whose generations invent words only belonging to them, leaves, yes, a place so exiguous it is sometimes reduced to a point; culture therefore leaves this tiny roundabout point, not always to invade the world, by imperialism, but first and foremost to be amazed at the vicinity, like the rat of the fable, my father temporarily angry at his wife or the shepherd practising transhumance. It therefore walks step by step, hesitates, visits in small stages and, shy, educates itself; marries from outside its locality, the way my mother, Quercynoise and a winegrower, married my father, Gascon and a bargeman, water and wine, like Sabine in Rome and Camille with an Alban. Often exogamic for, endogamic, it would perish from incestuous rapes and mortal jealousies.

I therefore didn't become *uomo di coltura* by remaining Provençal, a naming that's already global and not local, as is believed when one isn't acquainted with this vanishing local, but because, travelling when young in Guyenne and in Armagnac, 'I had passed the mountains that bound this state',[12] then, older, in Spain towards Andalusia, in Germany, Hanover and Leibniz, in Ireland next, lastly in Japan, where the spring bedecks the almost Aquitanian valleys with flowers, towards Alice Springs, where the flora and fauna amaze, and to Pretoria, where during autumn blue leaves fall in the streets, but transiting as well in the lightning-fast times of histories and the longer time of evolution, I took, little by little, at each stopover, what I found to be better than back home. I make my bed in the German way, wash my face in the fashion of the Quebecers; my religion is rooted in the writing prophets of Israel, who are so far removed from my ancestors the Celts; I know of nothing more delightful than Brazilian handicraft nor more intelligent than Bulgarian and Malian popular musics, nor better engraved than certain cave paintings of the Aborigines of the Outback. I have merely continued the footsteps left by my Odyssean father when he departed to become betrothed into unknown lands where the peasants had no experience of rivers.

The crude opposition of the local and the global shows that those who find their delight in this single space have neglected to launch their lives into the cultural adventure in order to, on the contrary and like everyone, devote them to war. For this latter takes place on the imperialist world map of barriers that are put up or taken down. So the real world is reduced to the space of its map, the one being as homogeneous as the other. In wandering on the contrary from proximity to vicinity and from foreignness to remoteness, they would have quickly noticed that while national, political, military or economic borders, in short the whole infernal kit and caboodle of power and of public convention, open or close, culture's borders, porous, permeable, evanescent as well as individual or innermost, filter and percolate so much that I would readily define culture itself as this process of filtering and percolation, therefore as a process of acquisition, of digestion, in short, of acculturation. How can one become a philosopher without speaking Greek, Latin, German and Sanskrit, at least? I think, in the French language, like a half-breed pieced together with Anaximander, Lucretius, Leibniz and the Vedas.

Am I defining culture by acculturation? It's less a question of a tautology than of a succession of foreignnesses. Never did art sound more French than in the seventeenth century and yet Molière, impregnated with Italian, Corneille with Spanish, Bossuet with Latin, La Bruyère and Fénelon with Greek at first seem to come from somewhere else than Lutèce or the banks of the Loire. This mixture occurs when, in space as well as in time, a Castilian discourse opens up a singular road to Rouen before spreading to the city and the court via a theatre expressed in an uneven and alexandrine French, when the *commedia dell'arte*, the botanist Theophrastus' *Characters* and the Latin novel clear the paths by which they will spread into France and when the latter welcomes them in an incomplete fashion. For how on the contrary did it happen that, having set sail from London to the mouth of the Seine, a hundred English sailing ships rushed into the port, a few cables' lengths away from the house where Corneille wrote, and Shakespeare's plays, already old by several decades, never embarked under those sails? One long road runs from El Cid Campeador to Normandy; another one, short, running through the English Channel, gets blocked. This defines an original expanse, neither global nor local, neither homogeneous nor sporadic. We have to change spaces in order to understand the 'cultural'.

Cartography

Don't try to draw the cultural as a frame or an isolate, nor as an imperial invasion, as an isotropic block, nor as an unconnected archipelago but strictly speaking as a marquetry or a mosaic where the local sometimes resists and sometimes yields to the global, where the global sometimes goes everywhere but sometimes retreats from the local and where also long-distance attractions operate even though neighbours don't know each other. World and place mix their scopes, cross their paths, combine their colours. We must even leave the mosaic, already too divided into units and pieces, so as to appeal rather to paintings in which colours mix and whose drawings often lose their clear edges, as with Turner or the Impressionists. There can be no culture without this mixture, intimate here and lacking elsewhere. In an expanse as intertwined, as crumpled, as mixed as the universe of the things themselves or the universe of time, we travel with as much ease and as much difficulty in the vicinity as very far away, and rarely uniformly. I have lived longer in San Francisco than in Limoges and longer in Kyoto than in Narbonne, although I understand the inhabitants here better than those over there; I read Borges, not Mistral, Steinbeck more often than Jasmin, who was nevertheless born in the same city as me; I deciphered Russian music earlier than that of the troubadours, my direct ancestors. I regret it, but there's nothing to be done about it. Conversely, I delight daily in prunes from Agen, white wines from Sauternes or Graves and reds from Médoc, hardly tasting guava, kiwis or wines from California, nevertheless quite close to my residence at Stanford. Our cultures draw our matters of chance at least as much as our belongingnesses. They retain traces of our random journeys, of the lessons received from people chanced upon, of tastes contracted any old how, by the side of the road. They resemble stars with multiple and unequal branches, or better yet, those neuron tissues certain axons of which endlessly lengthen and traverse the brain whereas other ones stop short, Darwin or God knows why. Such chance tastes made me prefer, when quite young, downtown Hanover over the village of La Haye-Descartes. When a certain distant becomes my near at the same time that a close relation, unknown, therefore very far removed, neighbours another close relation who is intimate, the drawing is no longer engraved on a space divided into local gridding and unitary global but guides towards a singular topology where unexpected distances must be incessantly defined and measured. When Isidore Ducasse, a Uruguayan, signed Lautréamont, was he saying that two people were coexisting in him, one of which resided in Tarbes while *l'autre-est-à-Mont-evidéo* [the-other-is-in-Mont-evideo]?

Thus everyone carries with him his singular cultural chip, variable with the time of his trainings, as different from his neighbour's as the design of his fingerprint or the count of his DNA, natural chips, and travels over a multicoloured cartography in which, a half-breed, he celebrates weddings at unexpected crossroads. Culture invents many-coloured topologies, spaces that are entirely different from the space of battles, history, politics and the economy; the space of these latter, always geometric, metricizes the earth in order to master it.

The universal and the singular

Thus conceived, singularity can attain the universal as much as it requires exception. Thus some visual neuron, unique, traverses cervical space and connects to all its functions. Likewise, original and highly rare, masterpieces can reach men and women of all ethnicities. If we limited ourselves to our cultures said to be local, the Irish Celts of the first century shouldn't have converted to a religion of Semitic origin any more than Westerners should have gaped at Chinese opera. And yet who among us doesn't fall over with admiration before certain African masks or Aboriginal divinities as much as in listening to Bulgarian music or Renaissance harmonies? Better, in this strange space where distances and durations are abolished, the more home life attains the authentic, the more chance it has to open up to the Universe.

Banal and profound, this assessment defines what was formerly called substructure. As long as we stay in the same space, we remain in the superficial framework; armies, parties, businesses, currencies or fashions confront each other there, striving to conquer fortified towns or parts of the market, at the distance of regions cut out from this same homogeneous expanse; nothing new under the sun nor across monotonous history. But we enter the foundation when, changing spaces, we reach a terrain without points of reference for distance. Just as topology founds metric spaces, so the substructure of human constructions lies in culture.

In biological descents, the distribution of genes, shuffled like playing cards, sometimes produces similarities on the other side of the ocean and strong differences in the same lineage. What traveller hasn't encountered his twin in exotic places, while his own brother, a homebody, never left the house? Hardly several decades ago, who would have guessed this paradox which establishes a connection between work and existence, culture and nature? What's surprising about it, since both of them augment us and contribute to life?

This is the fifth meaning, first topological, then substructural, lastly vital and temporal, of the word 'culture', even more singular than the second one, but, profoundly, even more universal than the first one, humanist, and than the fourth one, commercial and financial, in that everyone's aleatory bouquet of paths, multiplying at leisure the comings-and-goings of the third sense, runs towards the vision of an asymptotically common space-time. No doubt there is culture only in growth towards the human universal.

Joy

So if globalization merchandises culture, I don't see culture as being in danger since it's not a question of culture. Whatever maritime experience *Titanic* may claim to stage, the film remains a gigantic turkey, as comical for someone who sails as *Vertical Limit* is for the alpinist. If ridicule killed, Disneyland's pasteboard would collapse into pulp, without any harm to civilization and with benefit to the rearing of the children of men. It takes a lot of courage or deafness to call music what one sometimes hears by this name. Don't confuse philosophy and *Sophie's World*. These are merchandise. They are consumed and consume their consumers, who come out of it diminished, sickly, discouraged. *Post Disneyland omne animal triste*. The *Iliad* and *Le tombeau de Couperin* aren't consumed nor are they consumptive; they augment with age and augment their readers or listeners.

The burial, the strangulation of culture in a place embitters it, suffocates and kills it just as surely as mercantile globalization. I don't know of a single one that, having closed its doors to the others, didn't die from it; nor any that, crossing borders to conquer customers, didn't collapse into monotonous tokens. The true one lives on acculturation, where broadening contributes – oh paradox – to home life. You recognize it by the joy.

The crumpled network

Precisely the internet takes shape today in the same way, topological or in networks of diverse neurons. We formerly imagined it to be a homogeneous space of transparency and freedom allowing access everywhere and always. It has evolved, like every place where interests, desires, base acts and power, generosity, humanitarianism and longings for knowledge confront each other, with as many obstructions as passages. Mixture took place, increases and gets denser every day. Just as several maps of a given territory exist, so the internet presents, under a thousand cartographies, a topology that's crumpled, granulous, as mixed with local and global as cultures themselves. Little culture takes us away from the internet and a lot of it brings us back to it.

Spaces and times

Topological and projective spaces

A new identity card would mix the thousand and one different belongingnesses life meets with, undergoes and invents; in a completely different space from the one whose uniformity permits the war of cultures, an individual or group mixes influences at unexpected distances and times. These two varied representations accentuate, and ultimately define, everyone's singularity, whether individual or collectivity. How are we to describe, positively, this card and this space? Can their particularities converge towards a common humanism?

That such a thing can happen has been known for millennia since an adventure told starting from an island as narrow as Ithaca turned the inhabited Mediterranean upside down before entering further afield into the world and since another adventure, come from a distant Roman province, Judea, gave more than a billion and a half humans in every part of the world their faith. Particularism sometimes leads all the better towards the universal for seeming to abandon any such pretension: leaving from a hamlet in La Mancha, Sancho Panza travels in the world on the back of a donkey and, closer to us, Cyrano delights audiences everywhere when only the inhabitants of Bergerac ought to understand it.

A hundred scenographies for one geometral

Having had the experience of its possibility, how should we conceive this passage now? By changing spaces, once again.

Look at that terracotta vase in the middle of the room; you who have just entered perceive it from behind and don't see its handle or what decorates it; you on the contrary can, from the middle of the room, view it from the front; while ascending the staircase towards the landing opening onto the room, I perceive, from below, its base instead; perched on a chair, my grandson sees its upper opening and its curved edges … In short, everyone only perceives a profile of this jar or a projection of it as geometers would say, or in architectural terms, according to the plan or the elevation. Nothing could be more characteristic of a singular point of view than this scenography of an object or a landscape.

Ten lines of reasoning about relativity draw their arguments from this: for the thing as such, if it exists, hides from every eye beneath these different and sometimes contradictory profiles; for a given section on the cone of vision that leaves our eyes towards its contours, you see a circle with a centre, I see an ellipse with two foci, and he sees a parabola with asymptotic curves. Conversely, what a delight it is to see turn at leisure, on a computer screen, exquisitely folded molecules whose various sites would be poorly seen from a fixed point of view!

Perfectly conversant with these respective particularities tied to irreducible views, marks, they said, of our limitation as finite creatures, seventeenth-century philosophers, Leibniz for example, wondered if they could conceive and if there existed a privileged point of view, a kind of site adding up all possible sites, from which the one who found himself there would see the object as such or in itself. We never see it; we nevertheless believe it exists since we say the vase in the perception example or the building for the architect's drawings, like we say language or music in spite of or owing to the variations of style, accent, instrument or musical score.

Leibniz conceived there the integral of the points of view or of the endlessly unfolding human scenographies. He pushed this site back to infinity, as if the cone of vision specific to everyone became at the limit a cylinder. Situated thus outside the finite, God sees the integral of the profiles, revealing the object in its reality. Leibniz called this integral the geometral of the object or its ichnography.

When we talk about language, even though we only read styles and only hear specialist words in oblique accents, when we cite some piece of music, even though we only hear interpretations of it, when we say the vase, even though we only see its sides, when we designate the flower, even though we only smell the rose or reseda, we silently or blindly designate this geometral. We think the universal daily without knowing it. Leibniz even readily added that we know how to read the geometral behind every profile. Why wouldn't the same line of reasoning be renewed for what concerns people and human cultures?

New space

At the end of 'The Unknown Masterpiece', Balzac describes the portrait of a woman nicknamed '*la belle noiseuse*',[13] a canvas taken by the painter, its author, to be the ultimate accomplishment of his genius. Long kept in secret and then suddenly unveiled, it appears to the young Poussin, a student of this master, as well as to every visitor who looks at it and can't believe their eyes, as an inextricable chaos of colours, blurred boundaries and vague tones, in an indecipherable disorder. The work of a madman, the decline of an old man, a brilliant presentiment? The identity card [*carte*] I just spoke about as well as the multicoloured map [*carte*] of a culture both resemble the painting by Frenhofer, the hero of this short story. The canvas is also named *The Noisy Beauty*. The noise or sound doubled with fury conceals the beautiful woman in it, veiling her and making the visitors blind to the perception they could have of her body.

Poussin and the others stoop and bend down in order to see better but don't succeed in comprehending. And no one can because the painting, more anticipatory than crazy, changes spaces. It's no longer a question of representation, equipped with relief, distance, forms and the colours that highlight them, nor of perspective, projection, point of view or a scenography cut into the expanse common to seers, but of an entirely different space, precisely of a topology, which Leibniz had intuited and Balzac conceived and painted before Riemann and Poincaré invented it.

Remember: before the alpine-pastured farm, you also changed spaces and representations so as to see an overlapping mixture of time.

The trace of the step[14]

But, Balzac recounts, in the margin of this jumble without any apparent order or reason, the figure of an admirable sole of a foot appears, as though saved from a mad accumulation of ruins, a foot whose delightful tonality seems to emerge from the catastrophe. But again, the form of a foot left on a medium – a dirt path or deserted beach – is said in Greek as ιχνοσ, *ichnos*, the mark of a step, or more generally the trace of someone absent or the one left by a murderer who can be discovered by means of this vestige; this is how detectives, historians and commentators proceed. Ichnography therefore signifies the writing of the trace. But if noise means rumbling sounds and violence, here the distinctive mark amounts to a stigmata or a signal that can be distinguished from the white noise.[15] However indecipherable and mixed a singularity plunged in this commotion may appear, this indication signs an absence or, better, makes this absence present. *The Noisy Beauty* remains noisy, singularly, through this chaos or through this individual background noise but appears itself in its beauty through the emergence of this mark. It, beautiful, through the *ichnos* or the trace, noisy through its individual scenes. It, singular like you or me through this mêlée or mixture, but bearing in a corner, like each of us, the signature of the Universal. In each of us, amid the noise of our multicoloured card or culture, there exists somewhere an indication of the Universal or of beauty, a trace that's faint here, illegible there, elsewhere warm and sonorous, and sometimes, in a rare place, dazzling.

You will recognize a work of art by this mark, whose sign never deceives. Don't give an inordinate amount of attention to the singular signature of this man or that woman, a signature scattered in the noise of the work itself, so particular it nears the closest vicinity of noise, but rather give your attention to its indication of absence, to a form, a sound, a word, emanating from a hole of universality, to the trace of a step marked on its blurred wax. The scar left on the envelope of a seed by the filament or nutritive cord breaking off is called the hilum. Nihilism rejects the very existence of this hilum, this filum, this hardly visible scar, this often broken thread attaching us to the species, the genus, living things and the world.

The Universal hides or shines in the singular the way the world does in Ithaca, Bergerac or the village of La Mancha, the way the ichnography is concealed or appears in the scenographies, language under the styles, a palace on its plans and the beautiful woman in the noise. Equipped with its elements at infinity, projective space aids in representing such a lost secret. Let's seek the Universal less by making our way towards this infinity – our limitation would wear itself out doing so till the end of our lives – than its trace in the singular. It is hidden under a stone, in the straw of the stable, on the sparkle of your smile. Eternity itself sometimes seems to mix with passing time like the gold lost in the ducat or this perfume filling a moment with an herbal fragrance. We can never find or give anything of it except a fragment of thread and then pull this thin end up until it breaks – I would like to invent a hilism – but, like a straw of hay, it glimmers on the ordinary tablet of the work and of singular existences. The intensity of its light flickers.

The trace of the step towards the universal

Follow this thread, difficult to read but visible, like the foot of the noisy woman in the middle of the painting: amid the ruins of Greek culture, some Cycladic sculpture; amid the Latin rubble, some lamentation by Lucretius; in the Etruscan silence, two people betrothed united over their tomb, resurrected from the night; amid the Khmer jumble invaded by the jungle, some Angkor bas-relief; in the middle of the dances of the Australian Aborigines, some dazzling painting Westerners call abstract; and amid the oblivions into which the classics of the West are falling today, the Knight of the Sorrowful Face and the melancholy of Couperin. Beauty leaves, left and will leave its trace amid the incoherences of every cultural singularity so that everyone, near or far, in space or time, stranger or intimate, may one day recognize the trace of its step.

Differently: of languages, we only hear the singular noises, sound and fury; but, in the course of a sentence, Virgil or Cervantes lets language be heard such that everyone can hear it; they find the shadowy hole through which it gives out signs in the middle of the squawking; of an object, we only see the noise, sound with a thousand profiles, fury of opinions; but with a lightning-fast stroke, storytellers, prophets, painters or musicians indicate it, and we suddenly find ourselves in its presence; at a blow, they pierce the thickness of the scenes and unveil its nudity. Of beauty, we only perceive the noise, sound and fury; but in a corner of a painting, in a fragment of marble, in a yellow high note, Bonnard, Houdon or Chopin bores the tunnel through which it flows; of the true, we only know its noise, sound and fury; but in the intuitive course of a theorem or a poem, Galois or Apollinaire scarifies its mark. The foot or the trace of the step of *The Noisy Beauty* opens a gorge in the painting, from noise to the beauty, through which we pass, one by one with all of humanity, from the other side of the mirror of profiles, from time to eternity.

The time stemming from projective space

If we want to achieve a common humanism, we therefore have to change our vision of the world, therefore have to first conceive new spaces, topological or projective, abundantly supplied by the mathematical sciences, themselves common. Next we have to try to decipher the rare signs amid the noise. We must also change times. This effort, more considerable, especially concerns what we have learnt under the name of philosophy of history.

Ezekiel, Jeremiah, Amos, the writing prophets of Israel conceived history. Before them, time didn't exist. They invented history, in the singular sense we give this word in the West, and have handed it down to us. Before them, it didn't exist. They were the first to know how to read a notable mark, unique and divine, amid the sound and the fury of battles, successions, inheritances. A God that's difficult to decipher, as though behind the cloud that guided the Hebrew people through the desert, but always present and absent, always in the state of being a trace, lost, found again. Hoped for among some, later already having come among others, the Messiah-Individual, contingent and necessary, first figuratively represented and then incarnated this trace of the universal in the noise of chaotic time. The realization of the transcendent God across the immanent, haphazard and contingent history of the people of Israel, the fulfilment of the promise or the achievement of the figuration which are described in Pascal's *Pensées* show that here history unfurls this mark-bearing confused space by repeating more and more clearly this signal, this call, this *logos* that emerges from the noise, this breeze that blows on the originary commotion and even on the psalms or the Song of Songs. Time unfolds the ichnography across the infinite series of scenographies. The project unfurls projective space.

Chronocentrism: The battle against the first windmill

Readers of the prophets, Bossuet and Pascal inaugurated the philosophy of history, followed by Condorcet – who put science in religion's place in order to battle against this latter, while repeating its schemas – Hegel or Auguste Comte. An evolutionary flow, continuous and linear, sometimes broken by obstacles in the dialectic fashion, advances in such a way that individuals stemming from certain nations or these collectivities themselves seem to progress or fall behind in relation to other ones, like species that are more or less developed. As long as the only and universal God realized itself as a trace in the history of a single people, the comparative question was not often asked. As soon as history, globalized, invites every nation on Earth, how can we differentiate their respective states of being? By considering, in a truly racist manner, that the spirit descended upon these nations, one after the other, the last to thus receive this unction being – oh, manifest surprise – the philosopher himself's nation.

These judgements, still very widespread, surreptitiously transport into time the various 'centrisms' erased with great difficulty from space. Some such centrism, triumphant, finds itself less in the Sun's place, the middle of the world, than at the extreme point of a temporal process conceived as a progress, while its rivals remain upstream, in the primitive, the archaic, the unfinished. Without it always being precisely seen, this point replaces every centre of space. These abuses could be called chronocentrisms. Instead of taking the place of the Universal in space or giving this place to his own collectivity, the historian-philosopher seizes it in time. The spatial centre becomes the most advanced point. The others have long since disembarked from the forward-moving boat and are drying out on the bank on which time has left them. Imperialism passes from space to history.

A thousand travellers have thus thought that the men and women of their age that they encountered elsewhere, of course, but even in the now, *illic sed nunc*, were nonetheless living in times anterior to their own under the pretext that they wore strange clothes, inhabited different latitudes and were subject to different legislations. Did they perceive phantoms or ghosts? How did it happen that we were able to believe these absurd datings? Yet even today, when we allude to the different degrees of development of the nations on the planet, we make the same logical and experimental mistake, the same moral and political error. Conversely, in the *Supplément au voyage de Bougainville* or in the *Supplément au voyage de Cook*, Diderot and Giraudoux attempted to date our customs and mores back to a time that's archaic in comparison with the positive evolution of these good savages.[16] Not to the left, not to the right, we are all contemporaries.

The second one: Narrowness and breadth

The battle against the first windmill is easily won. The second one is outlined against another hill, one better defended. When Pascal and Condorcet invented the idea of progress, when Hegel predicted the coming of the reign of Mind and Marx the reign of the classless society, the duration of time they were examining always seemed to us to be so long that almost anything at all could be said about such vast intervals. Like Haeckel and certain naturalists of his time, Auguste Comte compared the march of humanity to the successive ages of individual development; positivism sounds the hour of adulthood for the one and the other: from the fetishism said to be primitive to the dominant sciences, this scale still appeared to be interminable to us. Here the optimism of the seventeenth century stops. Husserl lamented the crisis of European sciences, Heidegger the forgetting of Being. A despair follows the triumph, a despair that tinges the colour of the flow without changing its nature.

These evolutionary schemas that sought universal laws from now on err less through too much breadth than through narrowness. For the adventure of humanity unfolds first in this living world, and this latter, in turn, unfolds in the inert Universe. We had no idea of our common oldness, nor of the oldness of our life, nor of the oldness of our common earth, nor of the oldness of our universe. In our recent individual noises, the innumerable traces of the Universal date back to periods that are unintuitable due to their billion year age. So I love to recount again, but differently, Balzac and his *Noisy Beauty*: not far from the craters formed by falling meteorites, tiny fragments of radioactive material had to be unearthed in order for the exact age of the Earth to be reckoned on them. Amid the enormous disorder of the things scattered on the planet, a minuscule trace – a thread, a hilum – suddenly says its global time. In the middle of the East African Rift, a few bones reveal our antiquity. Admire how much art and the aforementioned humanities have preceded, and by far, the methods and visions of the world that the sciences only discovered long after: universal time is read today on atoms and particles, as improbable and difficult to translate as the trace of the step in the painting's chaos, as beauty in the noise. And by the new scale, our philosophies of history amount to a few seconds.

Four extensions

Seemingly long, the tradition drawn by the narrow thinkers in fact broadens today at least four times. We are taking the Grand Narrative up again by starting, at leisure, at the big bang, if it ever existed, at the cooling of our planet, at the appearance of RNA, around the Kenyan Rift, according to whether you are dealing with the Universe, the Earth, life or *Homo sapiens*, at the four respective times of their emergence.

In these four cases, the entirely subjective belief in a globally positive or, on the contrary, globally negative gradient of a simple and linear curve seems naive today; global progress or general regression, this depends on your digestion, whether clear or grouchy, from the night before. Lastly, while we may have spent the century laughing at these prophetic judges in assessing their overly extensive aims, therefore open to criticism because indeterminate, these aims seem to us today to lack broadness of outlook; by excluding non-Europeans, other humans, all the living species, the inert planet and the world as a whole, these corporatist intellectuals, believing themselves to be alone in the world, practised a universal racism.

Hence the new access to the Universe. For the Grand Narrative truly invents globalization by virtue of the fact that it attaches itself, for the first time, to the fate of the entire Universe, of the entire Earth, of all living things, of all humanity while only attaining politics and cultures at the end of the account and contingently, both of them minuscule in such a picture. Certainly not a *Légende des siècles*, but by contingent backwards steps and advances, a probable truth over billions of years. When philosophy doesn't open up to these extensions, it dies from smallness and repetition. By virtue of the fact that it pours onto all things, this Grand Narrative imprints onto them a trace of the time that passes like a step, a rare indication, not very visible, difficult to decipher, but an indisputable trace of universal time in different and wildly mixed physical, living or cultural spaces.

That a flash of thought of mine, with a life as ephemeral as the life of that insect that dies the very evening of its birth, attains this almost unintuitable universal duration is a miracle that charms the moments that remain for me to live.

Prescription

Short time, long time

Already Sunday, already the return of winter, already my old age. We all experience how fast time passes whether mature in years or juvenile, at work or on vacation. Production rates, financial due dates, circulation of goods and information even speed up; the media glue us to a so-called piece of news, without distance or space.[17] We sometimes envy our predecessors who, deprived of fresh news, without planes or electricity, enjoyed slow trips and dawns with hues in endless gradation. This comparison bears a strange contradiction inside itself.

For the old and everyday perception of this dragging duration was accompanied by a short estimation of history: during the era of the pedestrian and the horse-drawn cart, the world was four or five thousand years old. Conversely, today when we are living at the speed of light, it tallies fifteen billion. We used to move step by step in a recent Universe; we now manipulate real time and simultaneity within a horizon of an astounding ancientness. Save for a few generations, we don't experience the same space or the same time. What's more, during the same interval, the life expectancy of these generations went from thirty to eighty years. The adverbial phrase 'a long time' no longer has the same meaning. But only today do our lives become brief.

Analyses of our hastes abound; thanks to the mobile phone, we no longer need to plan a schedule; a person can live at the other end of the Earth while continuing to be, thanks to the internet, our neighbour. But these true remarks lack a symmetry and a balance. Reversing our ancestors' experience, long time reached us at the same time or just about as short time. At the moment when our technologies were plunging us alive into the lightning-fast, our sciences were immersing us into an inconceivable slowness. We easily adapted to the lightning-fast without seeing that we needed to, as a counterbalance, bring our knowledge, consciousness and perception into line with this slowness.

Our old age

Tremendously old, our organs and our bones; old, life and old, the Universe. Woven with entirely different durations, our existence changes natures. Sometimes fixist, our predecessors dated their ancestors back several thousand years. Inasmuch as the human species emerged six to seven million years ago, as life appeared three and a half billion years ago and the Universe fifteen, we laugh at the old precept, both poetic and moral: 'what is a hundred years, what is a thousand, since they can be erased by a single moment?'[18] But we laugh without understanding, for the intuition itself of this new duration escapes us.

Today we have to carry out a theoretical effort as well as an existential one: trying to live and understand the content and stake of this new ancientness. Let's first look at our hands, our skin and those of our neighbours, whose texture dates back incredible epochs; we have murmured music, no doubt, for hundreds of thousands of years; let's next contemplate hens, sparrows, oaks and reeds, companions that are sometimes even older than us by millions of years; let's lastly consider the mountains, wind, sea and stars, by means of new clocks, to be a billion-year-old environment. Undergoing these sudden ageings being-in-the-world changes both being and worlds.

When changing scales, a thing often changes natures. We can conceive a span of several centuries; learning history trained us, from a young age, in this exercise. If need be, we can imagine, without too much trouble, several millennia through a simple extension of this training; we have seen the caves of Lascaux, the cave paintings of the Australian Aborigines, Lucy's skeletal remains. Modernity now requires of us an entirely different extension of this temporal intuition. Conceiving the durations demanded by life or the formation of the Earth and the world, this seems difficult to us. I will try, at the end of this book, to outline this other time.

War and peace

This theoretical and existential stake goes hand in hand with another one, a political one. As long as we were only imaging centenary durations, even millenary ones, we could still think we were all different and hate each other intensely. For, at these small scales, languages and customs had already bifurcated; borders were bristling up on the face of the Earth. By the action of the sun and the climate, our initial black skin had long turned whitish, yellow or more scarlet, and the degrees of latitude had long shaped, according to the cultures, customs and laws, the truth sometimes. Recent, these variants had caused the exotic, the barbarous, and tribal wars to be born. Longitudes, languages and cultures had already created such differences that we could already no longer understand one another. As soon as memory scarcely surpasses written texts or even traces visibly left, the vendetta is nonstop.

As soon as, on the contrary, we estimate real time in its breadth, we yield to the evident fact that we separated not long ago: around one hundred millennia. If we don't succeed in conceiving this duration, in filling it with a living chronic intuition, we will never be able to think humanity in its genuinely lived adventure, that is, as a species stemming from the east of the African continent, which a handful of a few families left, and we will never understand how cultures and languages descend from adventurers who were so few in number.

The small global family and the enormous African diversity

In comparison to Lucy's three million years or the six to seven of other Chadian ancestors, this separation took place at a recent date. Direct heirs of these scattered travellers, all the peoples of the world who see themselves to be so different differ less genetically from each other than the populations of Africa today. The colour of the skin and other visible traits count less than these several scattered emigrations that invaded the planet. Conversely, calculating genetic distances permits us to know or confirm these early diasporas. From a never-ending flat curve, a lightning-fast vertical one suddenly shoots up; our adventure bifurcates at a few recent and rare points.

As long as history starts with rare writings, our truths set us into opposition; if it follows our common duration, in which these decisive dates appear, two genealogical trees, the Africans' bushy tree and the narrow branch of the other peoples of the world, bring us together. World wars set brothers into opposition, and the conflicts shaking the African continent cause cousins to fight each other. Having history start with writing is something I willingly accept but on the single condition of extending our own selective, manual, engraved or printed writing to the natural one coded with four letters in the intimacy of our bodies, in our germ cells, by long combinations of our DNA. Our history starts with this writing.

The aforementioned old culture ...

A theoretical effort, a simple intuition regarding numbers, can therefore have consequences for social ideologies and peace. As soon as, in a calculation by thousands of years, we replace four or five with a hundred, from being strangers we become friends. Changing numbers, the family is brought together again. For this reason at least, we have to reform the teaching of history and, to do so, think time and space as quickly as possible on a scale compatible with the human adventure, the many species, life, the world and the Universe.

Our new old age teaches a wisdom. The old man of antiquity, whose wrinkles and hair are preserved in sculptures of white marble, the old man the Christians named and still call priest, an origin word designating he who reaches a great age, that old-timer lastly revered by every culture, these figures of wisdom remained individual. Their testimony was limited to memories acquired over several years, and their tranquillity calmed us in the face of short lives and mortal imminence. Scientists sometimes, they found in books the broader memory of history, I mean the old one, the one that starts with written texts.

From now on let's all become immense old men according to the writing given, imprinted and decipherable in the secrecy of our bodies and before whose beauty unimaginable ancestors have buried their dead, have drawn, painted, sang and trembled with emotion for hundreds of thousands of years. Humanity as such, in its entirety, you, me, those near and those far, surpasses the patriarchs. Humanity attains the age of wisdom. Not in rare individuals venerated for this, but in community, as a species, within the secrecy of each and everyone's bodies. You old philosophers, bearded prophets, Greek sages, Hindu ascetics, Tibetan monks, Brahminical gurus, sachems of the prairies, Christian priests, you all become children.

... Becomes childish

At the end of *Hominescence*, I asked why our cultures weren't sufficient to contain our violence. They even seem to fan it by displaying our differences. Discover why: because they never got beyond the possible experience of an individual and the collective age of a merciless childhood. Civilizations that are too young, never calmed, always showing their excrement in the potty like little children or the superiority of their biceps like teenagers in the schoolyard. Oh paradox: these ever so juvenile judges laid claim to the wisdom of those who had amassed lots of time! In front of the young folks arguing philosophy, Plato staged, at the beginning of his *Republic* and the *Timaeus*, an old man, Greek in the first one and Egyptian in the second, as though he wanted to double green reason with a mature wisdom and recent philosophy with a kind of outdated or at least archaic sacred. Like the patriarchs of the Bible, these ancestors seem today to be young greenhorns, victims of short memories, despite all their boasting. Of course, they do say they remember a few diluvian floods, volcanic eruptions and earthquakes: from a past without thickness. Think four thousand years in the best case! They only see the surface, not the deep tectonic plates.

Our wisdom now places Lucy before Pliny the Elder, the scattered bones in the valleys of Chad before Homer the Blind and Noah the Winegrower, and our African father and mother before Eden's Adam and Eve, before every ancestor venerated by every culture; this wisdom reads the genetic code before the Code of Hammurabi. There, it's a question of humankind and not a chatty and malicious whitish man contemptuous of the scarlet barbarian. Next and again deeper, it's a matter of life itself; we arrogant Westerners have only recently caught up with cultures that claim with good reason that an animal or flower species preceded their ancestors: did they have better clocks than ours? I sometimes read Darwin in certain traditions said to be fetishistic and on the steps of Aztec pyramids.

Return to space and time

That was for four, five or a hundred thousand, three or seven million, various quantities or numbers; that was for the results of a change of scale and of a conversion of our intuitions, cognitive consequences that allow us to hope for the construction of a new common culture.

Of course, regarding space and time, we have long been in the habit of making major efforts, theoretical and existential. Ever since Plato freed us from his cave, we had learnt to change dimensions, as many times as necessary, in order to account for things that are more real than perceptual appearances. Better, we were no longer contented with a single space, that of Euclid, or a single time, that of Newton. For we conceived spaces without measure, or other ones, projective, abstract no doubt, but that also allowed us to understand certain perceptible circumstances, of sight, touch, facility, tension and bodily movements. We sewed and knitted in a topological space; our sharp eyesight was practised in another, more projective, space, while our masons and architects still built at old Euclid's place. We therefore imagined a thousand spaces. Likewise, we had learnt the multiplicity of times: the reversible or circular one, the irreversible ones of entropy or of evolution, the time of contingency and of chaos, unpredictable, and that of percolation, which varies according to thresholds. A thousand efforts that allow us to better grasp the flesh and mind, things and life, our destiny sometimes and history.

Reunion, accord[19]

But here, the effort seems to me to be at once simpler and more difficult, more decisive as well for humanity. Simpler, for it doesn't have to do with the nature of time or space, highly delicate problems, but with their measurement and their scope, a quite easy thing. Simple certainly but difficult in fact because, as I'll repeat once again, a change of scale often results in subtle transformations in the very nature of things when they are put at various levels. Constructing a reduced model only requires paper or cardboard; building full-size needs steel. So going from local and singular cultures fragmented across the continents to the progressive scattering of a small human group into global space transforms our vision of the world and of duration. The mosaic of space gives way to a temporal crossfade. Are we starting to believe again, without any myths or mystifications, in the primitive unicity of languages? Globalization began about a hundred thousand years ago. At the middle scales of the usual history, there are only differences; at the scale of the real human adventure, the universal is the rule.

Hence the decisive character of the new Grand Narrative for the future history of humanity at the very moment when humanity is renewing contact, still lacunary of course, under the impact of the new technologies.

We separated at the stated dates, and here we are today finding one another again. Who could be surprised that at the moment of this reunion the memory, in sum fairly recent, of our separation comes back to us? At the beginning, I told of our paradox of playing at the speed of light and at ubiquity when we learnt the extreme old age and tremendous slowness of our destiny. Retracing the links that united the meagre family of adventurers who ventured outside our African cradle, our networks thus aid in the establishment of this new culture that's, yes, universal, as ancient in millions of years as it is recent and lightning-fast in electronic speed and next to which the Renaissance merely stammered out its Greco-Latino-European incapacity to define humanism, a culture henceforth common to our species. And now that you conceive this finally completed, general and on the whole true history, think of the smallness of the numbers the old one wanted to be imagined!

There is always already prescription

Of course, perpetual peace doesn't immediately ensue from the fact that we descended from common parents since twins, even more than strangers, find reasons to strangle one another. We are not ignorant of the mimetic origin of human violence. But we can as little ignore the pretexts it seeks in difference. The learned discover these pretexts in texts, I mean in memories, traces left by history, history taken in the sense of yesterday. As we go back up the stream of this time, these marks become scarce, to the point that we have to dig deep into the earth and have to have an ultrasharp expertise with these excavations to recognize them. They precede, they exceed the written texts and visible traces, as pre-texts, in the literal sense.

So I invite the reader to meditate on the legal term 'prescription', whose obvious meaning expresses the exhaustion or extinguishment, after some given period of time, of all legal proceedings concerning a crime or offence. This use of prescription requires us to decide which is stronger, time or law: does time extinguish law, or does the latter withstand the wearing away of the former? Using prescription seems to violate law if and only if law prevails over time. Conversely, if time prevails, prescription becomes the foundation of law, for without it violence, always resumed, would enter into the eternal return of the vendetta. If you don't, at some point, extinguish the proceedings concerning the crime, the victim's heirs, to the umpteenth generation, will kill the heirs of the murderer as well so that no one will any longer be able to tell the dead and the murderers apart or even the reason for this interminable and insane dialectic. This discussion, revived on the occasion of imprescriptible crimes against humanity, but nevertheless a traditional one, doesn't take into account what this term itself literally signifies.

Prescription means: writing at the head, or as a title, or as what always precedes what the text written after is about. Regarding the English and Latin 'addiction', a legal and drug term, I had, in *The Five Senses*, already encountered this precedence of certain unsaid gestures over written or even spoken language. Here, when we are discussing which prevails, time or law, we forget that the time we are talking about remains in history, therefore in the written, as subordinated to the written. In this case, prescription presupposes that some written law encounters something written before it, literally pre-written or prescribed. This limits time to highly narrow limits.

And since we are practising thinking time beyond the borders drawn by ancient cultures, for example the very laws that are the most ancient, we find ourselves forced to transgress their edges by asking ourselves the question: what testimony do we have from before the written? Answer: rare remainders that testify to a time such that written law appears to be strangely recent. So I am seeking less something written that would precede every possible piece of writing than what radically precedes the written. What then is there before it? A colossally long prescription. In other words, prescription precedes law; it even precedes all writing: the word itself says so. Whatever pretext you may give for your war, there is always an immensely longer prescription before this war and before every text. This prescription signifies that from the point of view of time our differences vanish, for we all descend from the same lineages.

But, once again, the written returns, for the preceding sentence itself is read in a real text that's prior to every text inscribed by any law, pre-written therefore in comparison to everything we have written from the dawn of history, therefore well and truly prescribed, but in the DNA of our brothers and cousins. The genetic code, to which scientists of every language have given a name similar to that of the written code or law, precedes our real and possible writings so that time prevails, and by far, over law, and this given, lasting and transmissible code prevails over those we compose by hand in clumsy letters subject to wearing away; always anterior, this prescription founds law and founds it in nature; if peace prevails over war, it owes it to this natural code.

3 ACCESS TO THE UNIVERSAL

ITS NAMES

Attempts[1]

Hesitating over my identity, what am I called then? Near the Pont de Recouvrance, between two corvettes, someone who resembled me, they say, frequented a house in Brest, then lived in another one in Toulon, not far from the old Sentier des Douaniers; he built three of them, one in a small valley where a stream runs to the Garonne, two others on the flanks of Gergovie, in Aubière and in Romagnat, then renovated what appeared to him to be a hookers' hotel not far from the Château and the Bois de Vincennes ... here a Breton sailor, there from Auvergne, never truly Parisian. As his second homeland, he loved Quebec with its winter shores. Curled up for a long time by the Chesapeake Bay, in Baltimore, then in the humidity of São Paolo, after that in Buffalo, near the Niagara and its falls, did he live anywhere longer than in Palo Alto, between the Pacific and the Sierra Nevada?

When Finistère's breeze wraps him in its powerful gentleness, when he hears the Saint Lawrence moan like a lover during the debacle with its squeaking ice, when he recognizes, beneath the green grass of the Dômes, the red-black mouths of Iceland, the Andes or Mt. Etna, when he gets back to California's climatic equilibrium between the desert's dryness and the ocean's cold, he feels at home, as though in his own house. Where then is his niche situated? In the middle of Japan, whose fragile power he loves, in the Alps, in a climbing team between crevasses and bergschrunds, in ecstasy on the summit of the Matterhorn or Cotopaxi, in Nepal with the Sherpas almost naked in the snow, on foot in the Saharan dunes, across the Australian Outback, under the Alice Springs sun, in Montevideo, along La Plata River, or towards Paraguay, at the top of Irazú Volcano, of Piton de la Fournaise or the cliffs of Cape Town? Everywhere.

Yet I have never stopped living in Poulère, farm and barnyard, never stopped diving under the arches of the Pont de Pierre or the embankments of the weir at Beauregard, never stopped walking along the *Chemin des Cressonnières*, so much does one inhabit childhood, starting from which vague camps temporarily advance elsewhere. Garonne still flows in my arteries. I only left the local house with a regret close to being torn up. I have suffered a hundred deaths from pitching my flying tent like a nomad, here and there. Thus I've left a bit of blood on the road, lots of sweat and, like snails, a great deal of saliva. But today, land and sea, mountain and volcano, savannah and forest, river and lake, I sing my global house.

I am beginning to inhabit the map of space.

* * *

Another clone built, beyond Occitania, a castle founded on Greek tragedies and the Psalms translated into Latin, the French of the *Essays* or the *Imprécations de Camille*;[2] he founded it, even lower, on the dark masses kneaded by certain of Chopin's *Nocturnes*; Couperin's motets and the *Tombeau* Ravel erected for him traverse it in its heights; Carpaccio's Venetian landscapes and Poussin's enchanted Roman countrysides surround it, nonetheless immersed, sometimes, in Turner's mists and the rural peace of the Flemish masters. The background noise of its world bustles in Goya so as to rise up to Cervantes and Saint John of the Cross. Its flesh of language, its walls and floor vibrate with Celtiberian waves.

But he lived for a long time in the wings of the Platonic palace, where mathematical analysis organizes its galleries of light, where algebraic structures unfurl their counterpoint and where new algorithms explode, combined, not counting the patio where fluid mechanics shoots up in its fountain basin, the hearth where thermodynamics blazes or even the architect's plan of the several-dimension future city projected by superstring theory ... he lastly found the inhabitants of the world in molecules and codes; bacteria, algae and mushrooms enter one after the other, before Flora and the fauna, to inhabit his ark, whose beauty was lacking billions of signals throwing out their vivacity.

Yet I only confess my love in the Latin, Spanish or Gascon languages, as though the emotion amounted, body to body, to ancestral music. But whatever language I may hear, I resonate to the reason of the encyclopedia.

I am beginning to inhabit the map of knowledge.

* * *

He built his house, you can really say that again, with rocks, cement and sand, in the company of masons and bargemen, his true people, with whom the early hours of the dawn were shared, when the shovel doesn't yet make you sweat so much; he built roads with asphalt in the burning of tar, drove heavy trucks, bulldozers and sand transports, worked on the wharfs of Bordeaux, between dockers and crane operators, sailed on big and little ships, between fishermen and quartermasters – these are the early professions of his proximity. Even though on balance he spent more time on books, he keeps in his possession the impression of having only practised these public or maritime jobs and that he would return to them tomorrow with an entirely natural pleasure. Despite a thousand moltings, he never gave up his peasant's back, his worker's arms, plus two sailor's legs in shifting equilibrium during bad weather.

But he has worked since in ten places of science, solitary ones but cluttered with permanent staff and visitors, whether current or vanished, in crowds, Archimedes and Lucretius, Darwin and Monod, Hermes and the angels, no one and lots of people, met ambassadors and Prime Ministers, little-recognized geniuses and more or less stupid crowned heads, stars and the homeless, glories that will stay or fleeting fames, humble people and arrogant ones, the poor and millionaires, cardinals and country priests, Nobel Prize winners and ignoramuses, sages and swindlers, female saints and murderers, quickly convinced that no category wins out over any other and that, far from engaging him in dated street demonstrations, the world in labour demanded that politics be reinvented as quickly as possible.

But under every gilded ceiling, above every red carpet, in the shantytowns, the luxury hotels and the favelas, my soles bring the land and rocks of my working-class origin.

At home in everyone's home, I am starting to inhabit the human world map.

Viator

Here and now applies to plants and certain animals. A slave to its stake, the goat lets itself be eaten by the wolf, wandering therefore intelligent. Who will tell of the advances achieved with the first evolutionary steps of fauna, freed from floral immobility? Who will sing of the freedom of the one who escaped from his mother's womb, left his soft cradle, quit his home, walked, set sail, set off out of Africa millennia ago, populated the planisphere and occupied the lands attained by lands and seas?

Can this itinerant be named? Ephemeral and local, this human who is attached to the humus, the humble product of humility, tied to hunger and desire, finite, as they repeat, I call him viable, that is to say, fit to survive, because viable, that is to say, suited to launching himself onto roads, that is to say, even composed of roads. *Via vita.* There can be no human life without journeys, at least of initiation or learning, at most of prehistory and anthropology. But even beyond our fate: there can be no life without roads. The word 'viability' is said for the one and the other.[3] Everything moves, even trees, in which sap circulates and whose foliage whirls in the north wind. Everything moves, even the molecules in the minutest cell. Everything lives from communicating. Everything exists from exchange. Relation conditions life and precedes existence. The lack of a general theory of signals and their roads in our biological sciences therefore conceals the secrets of life. For, from lemurs and hummingbirds to single-celled organisms, from whales, which call from a distance, to jellyfish, whose tunics pierce the darkness of the sea depths with their flashes, from synapses to kinases, life unceasingly exchanges sounds, lights, molecules, in short, a thousand signals. In order to survive, it launches itself on to as many roads. *Sine via non vita*. There can be no life without roads.

One, human, transcendental quasi-subject[4]

Yet, to the eyes of the homebody, nothing could be more dangerous than travelling on these roads or off them. One risks one's life there, of course, owing to the precipices and the highwaymen, but above all one wears out one's identity, one's belongingnesses, customs, beliefs, attachments and passions, in all, the very essence of the subject. He who doesn't leave his niche retains his childhood; the blessed person who roams the streets loses it. There the infantile I plunges into the other, who plunges into the others, who plunge into the adult. The ages of life make themselves independent. For time, nothing is preserved like the sugar in jam; it makes the child change. How? By losing the narcissist I in the hazards of alterity. At the extreme limit, the subject transforms into '*one*'. I become other, then the others, everybody, lastly 'one'. Undifferentiated, white, 'one' – a magnificent pronoun, a true transcendental subject – is modelled identically on the noun *homme* [human].[5] A few philosophers were ashamed to become 'one'. From fear of the common run of human, they sought to become extraordinary; perhaps they had even got into the habit of philosophizing in order to become this out-of-species rarity, without realizing that everybody tends towards this banal anomaly; nothing could be more commonplace than wanting to tear oneself away from such commonplaceness.

Luckily and fortunately, I have become 'one'. The thinking and speaking subject slides into the identity of everyone. 'One' adds up the I, the you, the we and the they. This sum forms humans. 'One' or token for pronouns. Far from scorning this general equivalent, this ferret that runs in the woods, my ladies, it would be better to define it as a quasi-subject.[6] Just as chemists don't think a hydrogen or carbon atom without the number of its bonds, the subject of thought remains unthinkable without the relations that precede it. This quasi-subject therefore adds up the 'atomic' subject and its communication routes. It envelops or integrates the set of these relations in an indefinite way. Stripped of these 'valences', how could it add I with you and we and she? The 'value' of the human is assessed by this sum. A transcendental quasi-subject and condition for global space and its practices, one achieves the accretion or the coalescence of humanity in me and in us. One approaches the Universal.

The roads leading to the various habitats on the map of space allow us to attain this quasi-subject unifying knowledge, space and time, allow us to attain this general equivalent of people and groups. The Incandescent is named one.

New virtual attempts

To what slim chance do I owe not having become a peasant, following my ancestors, a contractor of dredging and of public works, like my father, a grocer or an equine fly protector seller, following my mother's family, a sailor, without leaving the Naval Academy, a member of the National Assembly, as my department asked me to be towards the end of my studies, a pianist and composer, the melancholy regret of my existence, addicted to music as others are to alcohol, above all a monk, my second deep vocation, one dug into my gorge like a vertiginous cone whose spiral screws its descent all the way down to the soul's nothingness? By what last-minute hesitation did I not flee abroad to Brazil, the United States, China or Japan?

I picture myself a weary minister or a failure of a village mayor, in any case having nicer things to say than those who read their grey literature in the assemblies, a pacifist admiral or an officer demoted for having flooded the ammunition store, in love with every ocean, a concert performer or a piano bar employee, incapable of writing or saying essential things in words, sure of being able to express them in motets, a wise abbey or a monastery gardener, intoxicated with God, an engineer signing contracts to dig channels in ports and build bridges or a clumsy warehouse worker beneath his hard hat, wandering above all, always alone, going from here to there, like Cain, Lapérouse or the Jew of the legend.

A contingent chain of infinitesimal decisions, life only goes towards its truth if it adds up, more than the facts that have become obvious, the non-lived that has remained possible, the non-lived that is regretted and sometimes rediscovered thanks to the slap of a breeze bringing back a seed full of promises, as before. Life lies to make one believe one could start again. Wherever another direction might have led me, tears would have accompanied me by every path, as on this path, finite. I would have wept over you on the sea and the rivers, by sonatas or quintets, in Asia, in Chile, monk, hoodlum, poor, sedentary or traveller, in the slender branches, virtual and flourishing, as on the boughs, real and old, that are surprised by the first signs of spring.

So I would prefer *My Virtual Clones* to be the title of a hetero-biography whose hypertext takes into account possible and untaken bifurcations, abandoned adjacent branches, sometimes more important than the boughs that develop as the main ones. These stumps leave recognizable knots on the trunk, like wounds whose scars identify the tree. Do these virtual clones, which I recognize with delight inside me and outside me, reconcile the inexorable necessity of ancient metaphysics with the contingency understood by contemporary chaos theory? Don't these gigantic and unexpected bifurcations which, one after the other, shape a life result from the branches this life has removed and as though cut from the real tree, branches therefore remaining virtual? Does the branching that alone remains seem to come out of just anywhere, like an unexpected event, because the gusty breeze tore out all the others, one by one, from the densely foliated bouquet that included, in particular, its unpredictable twig? Necessity advances, of course, but it also weeds and thus produces what is taken to be contingency. We can as little predict the bud that will survive as those which, around it, die every day.

Who am I then? What remains of the dark cuts that killed, as soon as they were born, all these virtual clones? My reality survives these dead we toss into oblivion due to their disappearance. Does this survival retain the fittest, as is said for natural history? Who could guarantee that I developed the best one of my possibilities? It suffices to evaluate this question by the weight of my regrets or by the flight of a few hopes: if God exists and so wills it, I think I'd spend – I know in whose company it would be – my first million years of eternity composing music in order to rid myself of the pressure of meaning on the sustained flow of the pathos of writing. During the following million years, I would dance more than I have ever danced before – I know in whose arms it would be. In addition, I'd see to it that I'd sail, straight ahead, without taking position or seamarks into account since the oceanic expanse, out there, becomes lost, I suppose, under the striking absence of time. Through the heavenly or hellish virtual, I will gather my clones together. I will reunite myself. I will regraft the entire tree; I will reconstruct the bouquet. In adding up these contingencies, I will hope to become necessary. What use is eternity, I ask you, if it doesn't repair the leaks in time, if it doesn't make good the losses of history, that castrator who threw my scattered members to the four winds? I will rebuild the lost time not by means of vague, lying, narcissistic memories but through addition or grafting of the men and women I have been lacking because the path has cut them from my body. For life leaves behind it the cadavers of those I haven't been along with those men and women who have abandoned me. Eternal life will resurrect them. My God, what a crowd around each of us! Restored, 'decastrated' of all its cut-off clones, re-membered in this way, this is how I believe the glorious body celebrated by Saint Augustine will be reconstructed.[7] The 'Platonic' reality of this eternity will add all these resurrected virtuals to the poverties of the individual who is so divided.

I speak about all these virtual clones in the past tense, as vanished friends, in the future or the hypothetical tense, hoping for reunions, but also feel them in my present flesh as a rending lack, scattered or phantom limbs. Sharp-edged, duration makes us into skeletal trunks starting from a blossoming of virtuals recommencing at every moment. We cannot not choose, sort, cut, as though linear time compelled us to cross one abreast over its rope bridge, thus forcing us to throw a thousand suckers into the torrent roaring in disorder at the bottom of the gorge. Could we not prune, preserving the entire bouquet in its natural state? Can we reinvent time so that it advances en masse, the way a glacier descends its slope while pushing its terminal moraine? The razor of the excluded middle was used on my clones: the one or the other on the bridge's thread. No, I want both the one and the other and this last one, too. I want to grow richer, to become moraine, river, legion, 'one'; and the entire human species to become more virtual.

You knew it well, my Malian friend, who refused to give me the status of being a toubab; you also recognized me, my Chinese friend, who asked me what minority I belonged to, east of Beijing; you cannot not have a Jewish parent, they told me in Israel; in the Atlas mountains, I found my old brother and in India my younger sister. Distributed across every part of the world, the human race is reduced to a family that's narrower than one might think.

The white 'one' sees, if not his clones, at least his cousins everywhere. What should we call him? I name him *Pantope, Panchrone, Panurge, Pangloss, Pangnose, Panthrope*, a man or women who's integral six times over. Far from escaping from the common run by means of exceptional qualities, she or he, hidden in the incandescence, melts into knowledge, humans and horizons. The return of the Great Pan unites them. *Nemo* becomes 'one', that is to say, everybody. How?

Pantope, Panchrone

Since our astrophysics unfurls, in millions of light-years, a Universe, with the solar system only opening a derisory nook of it during the seventeenth century, we now measure the narrowness of the 'infinite' spaces Pascal was frightened of. The fact that the expanse grows around us however only gives us a bit of acro- or agoraphobia. Those who fear mountains and their walls already experience this slight dizziness. The old reed becomes thinner, that is all.[8]

But the fact that world time, estimated by Newton himself during Pascal's era to be four thousand years, suddenly extends to fifteen billion or to four billion since the beginning of life on Earth, this becomes difficult to conceive. Duration doesn't expand like space. But, like space, it changes things. The Emperor of the Moon returns from his journeys claiming that everything resembled the things here, but what would he have said if he had travelled to the Cambrian, when the first hard organisms exploded, or if he had descended to the ever so hot first second following the initial explosion? The Euclidean expanse transforms neither profiles nor sizes and so leaves the comic reasoning of the *commedia dell'arte* intact; we therefore imagine travelling to nearby planets, but who would survive in the archaic eras before the reed even appeared? Travelling in time stifles our breath, breaks our bodies down into elements, wipes out thought, denies our existence. Therefore as much as I might easily merit the name Pantope by going, a pilot, from Lapland to New Zealand, or by jumping, an astronaut, from the Moon to Mars, the name Panchrone doesn't seem easily accessible. Travelling in pure space would leave the subject invariant; travelling in time does away with it. Panchrone has trouble being born, for he immediately vanishes; ten million years from here, he is already a quadruped; a little more and he crawls like a reptile or flies like a bird; lastly he is reduced to a single cell.

Nevertheless this Panchrone comes even closer to us than Pantope, a contemporary of Gilgamesh, Ulysses or Pantagruel, simple walkers, plus a few obstacles, shipwrecks, enchantresses and sirens. For here the subject, the observer or me, we have to quit precisely our subject status or observing position, our pride in thinking or our site as the final work of evolution so as to dive, like Empedocles, headlong body and soul into the river of burning lava where time, turbulent and chaotic, percolates, destroys everything upstream and gathers the disparate downstream. This new journey would sooner resemble the journeys by Ulysses, Aeneas or Dante into the Underworld, where they descend to the pale and translucent souls. Consequently, Panchrone metamorphoses, becomes every species, by going back up evolution, fauna, flora, algae, single-celled organisms, and still farther upstream, chemical elements, primeval hydrogen, particles, energy and light. Who is he, this Panchrone, who am I then, if not this provenance in return, this traceability, this river of unpredictable fire, this interminable descent where this contingency that thinks today is constituted from almost nothing? Pascal said of space: through thought I comprehend it; for thought could occupy it because the space-object leaves the subject-reed of thought invariant; did Pascal suspect that he was thus praising space rather than thought?[9] For what could thought do if space made it vary? Panchrone says of time, which precisely does make thought vary: through time I change, disappearing in going back up it but constructing myself in following it. I carry in my body the constituent elements of the Universe and, although differently, the constituent elements of myself; my organs are composed of thousands of billions of cells; there isn't a single part of my flesh that isn't left from a bifurcating event of this time – I am, live and think from these traces and marks; even the composition of my interior milieu resembles the composition of the oceans from which we came. Thus, starting off from particles, I became a mirror of the Universe, not a spatial or optical representation mirror where rays walk in space like you or me, but a temporal one, by strata and traces that were contingent in the past, necessary today, constructive in any case.

Consequently, Panchrone wins out in universality over Pantope who, compared to him, amounts to a simple phantom, unstable and restless, who, from his wanderings, only retains images, fragments of stories, in total not much and sometimes retains lies. Who has never suspected Ulysses and Dante of boasting in the manner of Pytheas the Massaliot or Marco Polo? At each stage, on the contrary, Panchrone, menaced with death, is constructed. There is not an atom of his body that doesn't testify to his duration as honestly as the beauty's foot in the noise painting. Body and understanding, he is made of time. Better, in him as in a tree, the Universe folds or unties its flows. From the air he breathes to the water drunk, nails, faeces or noble neurons, Panchrone is several billion years old. Who, just a half-century ago, would have believed this great antiquity of our flesh? Thus I, Panchrone, conspire to the totality of things, to what lives and does not live, to the species and to the elements. I comprehend time and the world, what they make of me and what I know about them. Panchrone percolates like Pangea. How can we not declare this me to be universal and 'natural'?

Pangloss

Even though its flesh incarnates all times, the Incandescent will never speak every language of men and angels. This sum surpasses an individual's effort. But each of us can – and must – remember. During the days our ancestors left the African cradle, even before they diverged, before their separation was dug deeper, next, by the mosaic of dialects, how did they communicate with one another? Did they use an archaic Nostratic from which that explosive sum of languages descends? How can we rediscover this first language of ours? We retain no trace of it.

But what do we still have in common now? Music. We don't know of any culture that doesn't have dancing or singing, that doesn't have ululation or threnody. *Homo musicus.* Every instrument is different of course and every composition, but I seem to hear the cry, the tone, the low vocalize that joins them together and from which they will emerge. Blocked, buried, hidden between the hubbub of the world, of our own body and of the crowd, on the one side, and, on the other, the compact multiplicity of heard languages moans what cultures have since played by the name of music: the source of languages, emanating from the world's background noise and supplications, sliding between Genesis' commotion and the prophets' chanting, occurring before the Word was born in John, well before every language received this Word at the same time on the morning of Pentecost, humanity's *ur-musik* or primeval tonality howls in the double well of my throat and my ears, in the double fold of storms and my desire. We have never had anything but such music to say time: the allegro, vivace or lagging tempo, the melody so that time runs or is interrupted with silences, measures to give it rhythm, rhythm to give it measure, double bars and da capo so that it turns back ... in his first two études, allegro and presto, of Opus 25, Frédéric Chopin even lets us hear its whirlwinds ... . From Panchrone, Pangloss is born.

But also Pantope, in return. Space comes back on the wings of time and musicians. For we aren't merely related to titmice and hummingbirds through the invention of songs in the springtimes of our loves, the storms of anguish and the distress of solitude but also in the subtle relations of nest and niche. The woodcock, the greylag goose, the wood pigeon and the stork raise their broods in the cold of high latitudes and bring them back in the summer to temperate climates or go from these latter to the tropics, showing thus, by migrating thousands of kilometres and sometimes at high altitudes over the Alps and the Himalayas, that their global niche includes, here or there, a local nest. The entire mystery of their behaviour is held in this double inhabitation, non-contradictory for them as well as for me, inside a narrow place, their family shed, and across the wide Universe, their elective biotope; a portolan before their eyes, in their heads and beneath their skins, full of sextants their glands guide them, lead them and bring them back to positions whose fixity marks out a niche compatible with the planisphere. As old as life and its journeys, this globalization characterizes a thousand species. This is how spiny lobsters in columns behave, as well as bison in herds and gnus in hordes, schools of herrings and eels, flocks of cranes and locusts; this is how cells and organs in the course of their development behave; this is how parasites behave. How many of us – birds, fish, migratory mammals? – are born here, work elsewhere, love outside our locality, raise little half-breeds, without forgetting to return, not without some homesickness, to the childhood valley in order to put new flowers on a grave? Pantope has the blood and song of a Northern gannet, Pangloss the voice of a cetacean filling vast ocean basins with its calls.

I am waiting to hear that elementary panting which rises, in its semi-muteness, above the fresh wind, above the deep-sea swell, the crackling fires, the earthquakes, the glaciers breaking up, and which hides behind Couperin and my homesickness, Houdon and the grace of your gestures, Manet, Corneille, Ravel and the grain of your voice, beneath the underground cavern of my solitude. The grail of every inspiration, I don't want to die without having discovered the source from which the primal murmuring arises. Music raises every art, codes every science, inspires every thought, better yet, cadences every number;[10] beneath it, behind it, between it and this broad call of the things lies the mute mystery, the chest of every secret. He who discovers it speaks virtually every language: Pangloss.

The robin has a vast repertory at its command: more than a thousand different songs; between the marsh warbler and its neighbours organized polyphonies are heard that even exist between different species of winged creature. Groups of chimpanzees howl at night in choirs that band and disband. Never having had any contact, the Fulani of Niger, the Naga people of Assam and the Albanians sing in pentaphonic modes over a drone, all identical. Universal among all men, like numbers, music then extends at least to apes and birds. Equipped with such small brains, how do certain of them, who change melody with every mating season, attain such pure masterpieces? Thanks to music, we fly like birds, dance in the three dimensions of water, gambol in the trees, discover or build places and space. But we also had the idea of doing so in the intimacy of our souls or of our confessions to others.

So very few of us write and have only done so since recently; no doubt we have all been speaking for thousands of years. But, before this speech, music, a million years old, dates from a colossal antiquity. Perhaps we came down from the trees the way our cousins the apes did, but in these same branches where we used to leap about, certain birds would flit around. Our plaintive modulations of desire or mourning still to this day reach deep neurons we share in our reptilian brain with chaffinches, titmice and hummingbirds. We must have first communicated by means of threnodies, inflections and melodic curves, dances and vocalizes in volutes imitating gestures and situations. This is how, with exquisite art, the Aborigines of Australia still describe the geography of their vast desert. In these pre-threnodies, in which certain inflections had to serve as prepositions, the workers of meaning, the modulations modulated space and time. Societies held together by means of these orchestras, occupied the surrounding expanse, acted, predicted, remembered by means of these music scores that never left the body and sufficed for survival. Before the adoption, contingent, non-necessary and all in all recent, of articulated language, these premusics lasted millions of years, during which, plunged in the winged polyphony of certain expressive cousins, we would continuously carry out their excellence.

Like many peasants, the troubadour Saint Francis knew this, who spoke to birds; Ronsard also suspected it, whose *Amours* invokes the nightingale chirping amid the willows for the one he loves and who returns his love; the poet's melancholy, a spurned lover, comes from the fact that he, for his part, only uses words endowed with meaning to charm, 'even though both of us have the same music'. Does the Holy Spirit descend upon us in the form of a dove so that a gusting wind and roaring fire, inert vibrating waves, plus the living musical inspiration lying, burning, beneath all language can come and so that its murmuring can become understood by all the people present? The bird of Pentecost still sings in certain branches.

We all know this: why are we scandalized by the fact that our conversations so rarely exchange meaning since, for millions of years, the only things that gathered us together were tonalities, whether arrogant or clear, pitches, sustained notes and modulations, *crescendo*, *andante*? Exceptional and precious, meaning is embedded in a flow of murmuring which alone moves our relations, whether sour or coalescent. Certain piano pieces stir, with the left hand, the dark masses of this clamour of wind, river or volcano, while the right one, high and clear, pins a few rare precious stones of meaning on this velvet cushion. This call, issuing but barely freed from the background noise of the world, leads the world, the collectives and history. It lodges us together in space. Yes, Pantope proceeds from Pangloss. Mass migration is dependent on the modulation of signals.

At the time of the new catastrophe in which meaning was invented, what we gained in precision, we lost in affinity. This is why the philosophy mountain rises, unique, amid the archipelagos of recited evocations, themselves having emerged from an ocean of panting. We all know this: a text that only states, whose sonority or rhythm doesn't descend to this depth, towards these millions of years, towards these avian neurons in us, sounds wordy and worthless, bores to tears and puts to sleep. Writing or saying only takes place by suddenly seizing, by dint of listening, the entire layer of language, whose thickness is measured starting from the rare deposited meaning, at the top, above the acoustic flesh, vowels, rhythms, numbers and movements, all the way down to the low base where this clamour touches on the stem music from which the set of languages bifurcates into branches. Look, likewise, at the surface of mountains and lakes, shores, churches and roads; dig into the ground, below, like a peasant ploughs, then like a miner towards the coal beds, lastly like those physicists who descend to the plates whose minuscule movements determine the eruptive flares and the collapses of cities in the earthquakes of the historical surface. Reaching, below the recent signification and the subtle song that sculpts it, this compact and archaic magma magnifies every singularity, the Frenchness of French, the Lusitanity of Portuguese, the Latin sum of the Romance languages, but opens on to the shadowy mouth out of which the *ur-musik* comes. From every great work emanates, as though from this dark pocket, a kind of sonorous melancholy, a calm breeze over a lake of tears, the vast space of meaning. Whoever lets its murmuring be heard not only writes or says, but begins to speak, like an angel, the compactness of language.

I am finally reaching the top of the dune from which I will see the ocean. As I climb, the chaos of the breakers, invisible behind the crest, grows. When, at a distance from the final slope and protected by this high barrier, life and time begin, the crash of this surf isn't heard. Irregular, its noise fills our hearing when we move forward, to the point of extinguishing distinct voices, reasonable words, rare confessions, subtle melodies; at some point this tremendous disorder will replace every separate signal, will drown out every wave.

Yet I believe I have formerly heard, well before coming to the foot of the dune, the dispersion of the numerous things pant; but the familiar calls, the beautiful proofs, a few rare pieces of music and even more extremely rare confessions of love distracted my ears from this murmuring. With age, the eardrums become damaged, they say, to explain its rise; no, for even solitary deafness keenly perceives this natural tinnitus, whose swell rises before the body's temporal advance like a high wave, a wall with broken and jagged crests, facing the prow of a ship.

Some morning, reaching the top of the dune, open to the horizon, I will see this vertical wave arrive, high in the sky and upright over me; I will hear only its wave. Then the minute will come when this crackling of God's fire will cover over the last of my laments – yours.

Pantope and Pangnose

Neither Abbé Huc nor M. de Bougainville had travelled every sea or every continent of the globe. Even Pico della Mirandola didn't claim to know everything. We changed all that the day the cosmonauts made us admire the round planet the way our ancestors never saw the Moon since it's half hidden. If, on the one hand, our local journeys multiply over the surface of the Earth like airports, on the other, this ascent integrates them into an actual and completed map of the world, one which closes the puzzle before we have assembled, one by one, its pieces. The day we saw, even as an image, the global vessel on which our lives are embarked, a relation of the whole to its parts was born, one far removed from Descartes' fourth rule requiring complete enumerations and general reviews in order to be assured that nothing was omitted. A little like integral calculus, we no longer had any need to go into each place or to memorize them one after another since even before the closing of this list, we enjoyed the use of totalization. Better still, this cavalier perspective was coupled with perspectives so sharp that never have we discovered any others that were as precise. So have we attained the geometral of the world?

So the same new thing occurred in our relations to knowledge. Of course, no one can prove every mathematical theorem, do every physics experiment or observe every galaxy, but each of us can acquire in specialized journals – at a minimum through results, images, graphics or estimations – what I would readily call the new scientific culture. This new culture even has a tendency to supplant the former one having a 'literary' foundation or horizon. At the very moment when everyone is declaring that the synthesis of all the sciences is surpassing every expectation, another totalization is seeing the light of day, a totalization that's almost easy, at least available.

There's more. Epistemology, the old meditation of highly rare experts, becomes multiplied today into several professions plugged into the sciences: administrators, financiers seeking to invest in private or public research, moralists and jurists preoccupied with ethics, journalists from the general or specialized press, each of them obliged to decide the fates of knowledge, the division of its disciplines, the salary or morals of its researchers and therefore holding a discourse on the sciences – hence the word epistemology – whose content and form depends, precisely, on different heights of observation. While scientific labourers – who like workers long ago and recently rarely decide their own fate – don't leave the level of their pointed specialty, the others enjoy medium or large perspectival distances. Far from laughing at their validity, I note their existence. It takes lots of deafness not to hear everything spoken about, from astronomy to biochemistry, by the entire media, journals, books and museums, political decisions, public panics, dashed hopes, humanitarian indignations, ethics of all stripes, the internet lastly and vague rumours. In a differential and gradated way, everyone today lays their hands on the encyclopedia, even if it can be deplored that, more than Enlightenment, strange shadows cover it. Formerly solitary, the epistemologist is surprised to find himself being jostled about in the middle of such a crowd. Everyone, more or less, poorly or well, practises his profession, formerly so rare.

Panepistemologists

High or medium, these new approaches have their disadvantages and their advantages. To understand them better, here is an image intermediate between humble labour at ground level and the astronautic image from flying high above, still heroic: being deposited by helicopter. Those afraid of mountains, people in a hurry, enfeebled old men, ministers and journalists can, without climbing, have themselves deposited on the most dangerous of summits by means of these expensive machines. So, the scientist resembles that magnificent guide who exposes himself roped up with a male and female client, all three sweating for dozens of hours to climb cracks and chimneys on the side of an imposing face, sometimes surprised to find, straddling the summit, a television team, ignorant of the mountains, whose cameras show the public, while flying over it for a hundred seconds, the whole of the mountain chain; better, this sequence will bring more glory to the presenter, who didn't leave the studio, than to these unknown climbers judged to be masochists or even to those photographers drunk with vertigo. A rapid roaring hoists up high, without crampon or ice axe, whoever pays for it. The next day, the same team, at ease in the same noisy elevator, will pass in review a thousand other walls, even more difficult.

So here is a new question: at the end of his career, who will know the questions regarding the mountain better? The guide or the cameraman, the one who has put up several smooth and airy routes by means of holds and pitons or the one who has flown over every chain in the world and shows everyone local images of the entire planet? This question isn't settled so easily. The photographer can be judged to be without merit and the serious guide to be a knowledgeable expert for having put his hide at risk, but conversely the images can be judged to be instructive and the specialist mountaineer to be too limited. Who likewise will know the questions of science better: the university president who has knocked about at a hundred meetings of specialists, the minister, more jurist than algebraist, but who negotiates international contracts, his principal private secretary who draws them up, the magistrate who has to make rulings in trials in which life and death are at stake, the majority stockholder of some company including research laboratories, the radio or TV commentator who has questioned all the Nobel Prize winners as well as all the preceding in the above list, each one having flown over each file, sometimes without knowing how to distinguish between two numbers, each one having benefited from being deposited by helicopter, or the humble inventor of some device, to whom most often none of the others have ever given anything but a few seconds to answer their hurried questions? Point out, if you dare, the knowledgeable expert or the best of the epistemologists. I don't know if I can.

Of course, what type of knowledge of the Alps do I draw from traversing them by Airbus at an altitude of eleven thousand metres while drinking bland orange juice and leafing through a stupid illustrated magazine? Thanks to a thousand possibilities of flight, to these depositings or passages, anybody today, as far as possible from knowledge, can write fairly long books in several days, well documented by the way, for example by means of the internet, on subjects of high sophistication, while benefiting from his ignorance besides since it brilliantly serves to explain to buyers why we don't understand … Clarity increases, according to what the media says, from this imbecilic inexpertise. The difficulty of the route inclines us more to the condemnation of the supposed abuses of science than to enthusiasm for what knowledge it has acquired. When knowledge becomes a total social fact, everyone more or less talks about it, judges it and – a democratic marvel – becomes responsible for it. We see high moral consciences with zero knowledge of the sciences they judge rise up everywhere. So here we find knowledge at the centre of a collective game that's as difficult, but also as crude, as politics since finance, insurance, law, the media, administration, public opinion, ethics, religions, in short, the entire society debates it. Who could have guessed, several decades ago, that a universal Green Party would be founded based on reflections about theories and their technological applications?

Everyone knows everything about everything. What seemed or seems impossible – I will repeat it since it has to do with a highly new event – becomes the most widely shared thing in the world. Henceforth this knowledge of knowledge spreads in the collective as the atmosphere it breathes. Pangnose becomes a common name and as though everyone's first name or prename. A curious and new answer to one of the famous Kantian questions, so easy to resolve today: 'what can I know?' Everything, of course, and not only me, but what's more, everyone. But in what form and how do we know? From what distance, from what angle of obliquity, in dispensing with what obstacles do we still know something, then little, lastly nothing anymore? This question isn't resolved so easily. The distances and angles thus measured define at least social space. While, an easy thing, being deposited by helicopter replaces training, the fact remains that astronautic flight, and perhaps each of the other kinds, also demands a training that's more or less demanding in its turn. In only having to know knowledge it hadn't invented, the old epistemology only devoted itself to work as easy, repetitive and parasitical as university commentary; the new one has this new knowledge before it, unexpected, unknown, globalized, with gradated hues, an object that's more difficult to construct and observe. Lastly, when knowledge melts in this way into the masses, a democracy of science is born, a highly bad form but the best, to this day, of the political forms available.

The wave of expansion

In spreading in this way, knowledge forms a continuous gradation, from science to information, without our being able to decide on any border between the cognitive, the economic, the juridical and the political. As a result, knowledge changes status and origin. Our language formerly lauded rigorous knowledge and despised the vague and confused, associating, in its metaphors, the crystalline solid with the precise and the liquid with the vague. During the corresponding eras, from antiquity up until yesterday morning, knowledge was concentrated in institutional sites, in the hands of specifically designated experts: schools and universities, chairs and the learned; corporations, master craftsmen, architects or engineers; churches and dogmas; palaces, kings, financiers or magistrates. Institutions, stable as the name indicates, and their servants imparted knowledge stamped with a brand. In short, knowledge had an address. Today we are moving from these lighthouse rocks overlooking the waves of ignorance, cut across with routes, to the sea itself. *Hominescence* thus talks about the end of the era of networks. We are now sailing on an ocean of information. He who teaches finds learners in front of him who know more than he does on some point; he who rules isn't able to satisfy a thousand experts in new political questions he hasn't yet mastered; administration decides according to the file and the president decides after deliberation by the board instead of a crowd who, close to revolt, laughs, often rightly, at the unfathomable ignorance of these administrators. The crisis of the author and of authority comes from the new status of the expansion of knowledge.

Everything can be found on the internet and in the atmosphere of the times, which can give anyone a cognitive point of view – true and false mixed up – that's superior to the one possessed by the old-fashioned teachers he or she can no longer endure. Thus the political and the economic are immersed in the cognitive, each of the three plunging into the two others.

The new fluid state of knowledge doesn't merely overturn knowledge, its schools and researchers, the economy, its workers and experts, the state, its masters and citizens, but in all overturns the social bond and the relation to things, the world and society, ethics and religions. In this sense and as a general equivalent, the cognitive has just acquired the capacity of money. In a thousand forms of genuine or counterfeit currency, it circulates like it, enjoying ubiquity.[11]

Panthrope

Likewise, who can profess to know, in his country, the social classes, in his climatic zone, the cultures, on the five continents, the bodies, faces and customs, the crews of the ships on the seven oceans and of all the planes on the ground or in the air, priests and warriors, scientists and workers, the Andean mountaineers and the Himalayan Sherpas, the Chinese and European peasants, the Amerindian and Mongolian herdsmen, the non-agricultural Aborigines …? Give me one anthropologist per village, one monograph per family, one linguist per tribe, one doctor per individual, not forgetting the infinity of interpreters for every behaviour.

I remember our islands from before the Second World War. The news from the villages arrived at the farm distorted; who left the hamlet for the city and the city for the capital or abroad? A few young conscripts, who didn't come back for a long time, cod fishermen over the Banks of Newfoundland, with their fiancées waiting for them on the shore. What did they bring back from this other than canteen and shipboard stories, different archipelagos? These isolates are vanishing; we no longer depart from them, if depart, according to the language, signifies separation. Even cosmonauts, from their spacesuits, never cease educating us with their gestures, showing us what they see, as if we were flying weightlessly with them. We remain on-line, if we like, with the entirety of absence. The world coagulates, curdles, solidifies. We change at leisure the very idea of distance in a space with a thousand topologies, ceaselessly recomposed.

Consequently, Panthrope's announcement goes round the networks. We have nothing but neighbours. Here, hunting the muskox, the Eskimo was visiting my living room; beneath the floor was permafrost; let me zap or click, and the Indian or Patagonian will replace the Laplander; beneath the carpet was the Pampas. The intellectual and the reporter who dealt with everything and everyone are disappearing because the virtualities they unfolded are becoming the most widely shared banality. Nothing about humanity seems strange to us any longer.

The impossibility we love to speak about, that man, too multiple, cannot be understood globally, resembles the obstacle from just now regarding knowledge. At the very moment we are making it into a mountain of difficulties, it disappears into a common molehill. Go out to the furthest reaches of the Landes forest or the swamps of Sologne, and you will always find a woman or a man who knows as much, although in a different way, about the Inuits as a PhD student in the *Musée de l'Homme*.

Here, Panthrope unites with Pangnose. Human knowledge, like the knowledge of the world of things, becomes the most widely shared thing in the world.

Homo humilis

These names that all prefix the totality, Pantope, Pangloss ... for space, knowledge, languages or humanity, don't testify to a divine, demoniacal, insane pride. No, they name the 'one'. And this 'one' that reduces the name human quite the contrary echoes its humility. Earthy, humus forms the texture of its flesh and the root of its name. Pride, as we have overabundantly learned, consists in placing the vain person's local, his language, his specialized knowledge, his technical expertise above all the others; he always comes from some navel someone made a mountain out of. The laying flat of everything, the multicoloured teeming of multiplicities, the limited number of our genes, the brownish colour of clay teach to remain humble, while laughing at those locals vaunting the height of their mediocre hillocks. One is acquainted with a thousand figures, profiles and avatars of this. I will choose one of them at random. For it remains to explain not the manifestly low quality of Rostand's *Cyrano* but its universal favour. In every part of the world – understand by this those parts where theatres open – a director in distress puts it on, certain that success will come back his way. Why is it so effective everywhere?

Because Cyrano de Bergerac reveals a secret about males. Even the handsomest men, blessed with a Grecian profile, know, without admitting it to themselves, that this nose, which they always have doubts about, makes Roxanne inaccessible to them. Who among them, when readying to get down to the business of love, has confidence in his face, in his language and launches his person ahead with self-assurance? Which of them isn't afraid of not getting hard when the time comes? Ah, the nose monologue! A peak, a cape, a peninsula? No, fiasco, the scissors box.[12] Braving death on some battlefield requires less courage. At public dances, the boys get drunk before approaching their dance partners; or they wait, sometimes their entire lives, for advances that never come. The girls know this, who, without showing it, are often the first to make a move.

Thus we know La Rochefoucauld's mistake. Far from having generality, his self-love only reflects the noble honour of the Grand Siècle, the rooster feather worn by some aristocrats, even though this rare plant needed to be encouraged, watered and perfumed in order that it might try to ignore its fragility. The *Maxims* weaves with difficulty a penis sheath for M. de Bergerac's nose, his contemporary. No, *monseigneur le duc*, self-hate triumphs most often over self-love, derived, to offset this self-hate, from this essential humility. In his spring, Narcissus himself discovers he has an ugly nose.

So understand it, this nose, an exaggerated promontory, a penis erected with difficulty. Like a theatre mask, it conceals the flat and malleable clay the face and the universal self are made of. We all come from the earth, yes, from that boulbènes to be modelled; few languages don't say this; myths and religions announce it; even philosophers acknowledge it, sometimes; Plato called it the *khôra*. We like to distinguish ourselves by some relief erected on this ground, a clod, a small peak, a mediocre hill or grandiose Everest, political power, the Olympic Games, a Nobel Prize, the kit and the caboodle. But however high and proudly it may hold its shoulders, any Matterhorn knows well that it contains the same dust as a molehill. We all come from the same earth, from the same mother, from the same universal matter. Not only does the height of the topography not change anything in the essence of this matter, but such height is also only seen in the theatre, in appearances, representations, for laughs, and everyone knows it. We only distinguish ourselves by masks. The universal earth forms us, carbon, hydrogen, nitrogen and a few rare earths. Everyone rushes to admire his plume and his nose, but who dares to say: Cyrano is me, 'one' and good clay. 'One', human; *humus*, the earth, the human Pangea.

Conclusion as Panurgy

The Greek word *ergon* signifies action or labour, energy and technology, work or practice, clever method and device. The French language uses it in *chir-urgie* [surgery]. So we ought to call plants and animals, programmed as they are, Monurge. Deprogrammed, as I've said, therefore open to every trick, we merit calling ourselves Panurge, skilled, industrious, in short, intelligent.

So this panurgy moves from biological deprogramming to practical activities that are free or imposed by needs and the environment. As technologies 'advance', the list, for example, of energies we propose to exploit grows longer: muscular, animal, mechanical, solar, wind, hydraulic, electrical, nuclear, computing and, again, biological. Will this list one day be closed? We don't know. But we can't be unaware that we search for energy far and wide incessantly and that this multiple opening characterizes us, a multiple opening from which Rabelais created the figure of Panurge by generalizing the gifts and ruses of Ulysses, still merely named Polytrope for having more than one trick up his sleeve and as many ruses and devices. The sailor has several of them; Panurge or Pantrope has all of them. He is so named because he adds up, integrates or sums up all the past, present and unpredictably contingent skills of every tradesman.

The Homeric and Renaissance times were unaware of the distinction between a moving force and the outline of the machine by which this force transmits the movements it produces. *Ergon* was taken in both senses. Thus, by distinguishing them, we became Panurge twice: in the search for basic sources of energy and in their exploitation and distribution, in motricity itself and in machines. For what do we do with these forces and why? First, from tools to the entropic scale, from the hammer to the thermonuclear bomb, in order to renew the face of the earth and change human destiny. But, since the origin of writing, we have supplemented them with other types of machines intended to store, receive and transmit information: hardware and software. These were foreseen by us so little that even the philosophers who despised or praised technology didn't suspect that in reading, in writing, they were manipulating real machines suitable for storing or transmitting soft energy. While the *ergon* eased the body's labour, it has come, already for thousands of years, to the assistance of the works of the mind. Let's not hesitate to call these machines universal, these machines said to be Turing machines, with as many programmes as you like, therefore as open as we are.

Who can, now, foresee other developments? Can we conceive a technology or general science of motors and machines, of means and media? I don't know, but, I repeat, whether it's a question of motive energy, of the machines it moves, of the uses for which we mobilize these forces and means, we tend towards the Universal: every energy, every machine, every possible use. Like knowledge and music, technology places us before the horizon of our universality. Pantope wanders in the white space of possibility; his 'advances' contingently bifurcate in this several-dimension space-time in which Panchrone also wanders; Pangnose descends the white space of the chronopedia; Pangloss rectifies the commotion into slight signals; Panurge, today, puts universal machines between the genetic universality of his corporal possibilities and the distributed universality of the world.

Even in conceiving these new machines, we don't always know how to connect the last two of these universals: our body's white universal and the world's universal, both of them in a state of becoming; we are only wagering that they are of the same order, as though equipotent. All thought, science, action, all hope is founded on this wager. The open play of connections between these two universals imposes technological intervention and cultural customs, languages and knowledge on us. Every other living thing, world-poor or Monurge, has no need of these mediations since its programme excuses it from them. Our deprogramming, free, subjects us to these indirect intermediaries with their universal play – languages, sciences and technologies. This fluidity permits lie and truth, arouses terror and enthusiasm. For we don't know whether our universality surpasses the Universe, pits itself against it or will bow before its power. Is there any danger for it, for them, for us, if we exceed our own universe? But what does 'to exceed' mean here?

We handled these global categories so poorly and mastered them so little that, for millennia, we expelled them into metaphysics. Now metaphysics haunts our everyday life, and we swing on the open path between these sums of ours – Pantope, Panchrone, Pangloss, Pangnose, Panthrope and Panurge, undefined integrals of our possibilities, whiteness and incandescence – and these two universalities, our universality, at the horizon of these names, and the universality of the Universe. Generating anxiety or enthusiasm, this swinging we must now negotiate characterizes the hominescent, whose panic comes, as I've already said, from this new infinitude more than from the comfortable finitude so often celebrated in books of philosophy.

For these questions concerning our universality are borne out today in daily practices that are numerous enough for us to now negotiate them with fear and trembling, if not with prudence. Everything that we call ecology – global warming, the eradication of species or protection of the environment, ethics, prudence, sustainable development – tends to ask the world itself to put limits on our enterprises: our universal exploitation of the Universe frightens us. Our new first names with their prefix *pan* gives us panic. We demand of the universe to accompany, regulate and moderate with its universality the panurgy of the human.

A new foundation for our actions, mediations, sciences and thoughts, the Natural Contract asks the environment to side with us or against us, as the active or reactive subject of our enterprising efforts. It attempts to settle the wager from just now, the open play between the universality of men and the universality of the world.[13] In the order of our immanent decisions, this contract takes the place of pre-established harmony, which presupposed that God imposes the universal rule for this play. As soon as

God goes absent, the Natural Contract replaces His eternal law. This doesn't mean that we all have to become atheists since a contract can be based either on a pure convention, consequently immanent to the present parties, or on a nature that's already there, transcendent with regard to them. Behind the contractual obligation, the religious decision remains open: either a bond is tied all alone, or it presupposes that what is tied here and now is tied again first and also outside of space-time.

Let's get back to the contract as such: in it, the Universal demands of the ancient subject and its archaic object to unite under its sole leadership. Here is the contemporary wisdom – as expert in knowledge and action as it is high in generosity – opened up by the Universal in presenting only its juridical profile: we don't exist alone or as men, or as assembled, or as living things, or as material piles of earth, or as subjects, or as objects, or passive, or independent, or commanding a ship like a pilot; we will only owe our salvation on the indefinite and free, scientific and inextricable paths of universal solidarity. Just as much as Pangnose needs sciences and Panthrope humans, Panurge needs the world, as global in his spread as the enterprises, knowledge, languages, space and time all become of the one who, rich in world, merits these names. Does a pantheism reveal itself at the horizon of this wisdom? That depends on what we want to base the contract on.

Among other universalities, whoever seeks or promotes a philosophy suitable for our time, this being a part of its portrait, encounters as well the universality of violence, of poverty and of radical evil.

From which its seventh name comes: *Panic.*

EVIL

Recent I

How long did men and women live without knowing themselves? Millions of years no doubt. The Greek philosophers, to whom the aforementioned Western culture owes its conceptual frameworks, hadn't yet invented the subject, except in a few precepts by Socrates, on the cognitive side, or Marcus Aurelius, after Epictetus, for behaviour. How and when did it appear? When the encounter of the Semitic and Greco-Latin worlds, of Roman law and Christian morality launched our era: Saint Augustine stated the *cogito* for the first time, and the anamnesis of his *Confessions* also explored the innermost recesses of a moral conscience and of an already psychological self.[14] The recommendation to save one's soul and the proclamation of the *Credo*, in which faith concerns the person himself, contributed to generalizing, by giving it a destinal dimension, the subject of law, already universal, something women and slaves could finally boast about.

Despite this entirely theoretical announcement and through a persistence history gives a thousand examples of, the idea of an individual took centuries to spread in the West; the portraits described by novels and the theatre or brushed by painting rarely show the unknown, the vulgar, the common, the peasant or passerby in the street except in crowds at Flemish festivals. Princes posed for Le Nain's *Peasants*, and Marie-Antoinette's court played at milking and haymaking on the farms of Trianon. From the seventeenth century on, bills of mortality, life insurance and the law of large numbers have counted people statistically and no longer en masse like censuses. Perhaps we have to wait for the beginnings of phrenology and photography to finally catch a glimpse, among the masses, of a few quasi anonymous visages, full-face or in profile, murderers, Thénardiers, convicts, Jean Valjean, who declared to the tribunal that the poor bore names that were as few in number as the houses they lived in, Rougons and Macquarts, words signifying the red stain, thus making their genetic epic into a cycle of original sin and bloody guilt. For a long time only kings, nobles, the wealthy Forsytes, a few heroes and martyrs attained subject status. Only a few greatnesses by birth or exceptions of genius ensured that a person could simply become someone. The Enlightenment and the rights of man didn't yet realize this potential universality. I'm ashamed of my country, whose hypocrisy has long claimed universal suffrage even though it only granted the right to vote to women, not yet subjects, after the Second World War;

the male chauvinist oligarchy subjugated female legal minors, more than half its population. We have always lived in an aristocracy: birth, money, diplomas, merit, sex.

The ancient tragic

In Roman and later 'natural' law, as in Christian theology or Zola's novels, the subject appears with a moral choice, which doesn't go without suffering, or before the tribunals, in danger of condemnation. As juridical, ethical or salvational, responsibility produces the soul, the moral conscience or the subject of law, three I's with names that are still anonymous. The first individuals, whose proper names I have just cited, only appear in authentic epics of poverty [*misère*], in both senses of this word, crime and destitution. *Les Misérables* christens the poor, and *Les Rougon-Macquart* does so for peasants, washerwomen and petit bourgeois in a chronicle of sweat and murder. Like everyone, the subject is born in pain. We come from nameless places: *inter fæces*, as living things, *inter pauperes*, as social animals, *inter reos*, as subjects of law.

Commenting on Leibniz, Christiane Frémont discovers a forgotten, although explicit, genealogy in the texts. The dogma of original sin, she says, doesn't imply going back up to the beginning of time but announces that Adam and Eve themselves are born, as free subjects, responsible and named, at the moment a choice puts them in the presence of Evil. God created us prelapsarian, without sin, but then non-subjects; through the malicious choice of sin, swept by the fall out of paradise into the valleys of history where toil, disease, tears and death were awaiting us, we created ourselves next as free subjects. When our first parents found themselves naked, they thus existed as individuals for the first time. They caught a glimpse of each other as such, you and me, singular. Therefore a choice that can reveal itself to be bad, sin, judgement, accusation, defence, tribulations, suffering, agony, in sum Evil, alone produce the subject. How would the subject not preserve a trace of it?

More or less ignored by the Greeks, the *ego* was therefore born twice: in Roman law, before the tribunals, facing the risk of condemnation; through the Christian novelty that requires it to believe in order to save itself from damnation. In both cases, you have to fight to deliver yourself from evil: the self is born from this combat, from its suffering. Neither theology nor, no doubt, philosophy, nor assuredly history separates the emergence of the subject from this malefic pregnancy. Psychology was born from psychopathology.

Angels

In the same text, Christiane Frémont gives angelology as a counterexample: incandescent, anonymous, mixed into a gentle crowd and celestial choir, angels and archangels are unaware of the ego; only three or four of them come close, who then are given a name; the prince of pride, of essential evil and this contingent world, Satan gazes at his reflection in his solitary narcissism; Michael fights the dragon, violent; Gabriel announces redemption from sin; Raphael, the patron saint of physicians, proposes a cure for physical pain to Tobias. They deserve, alas, to be distinguished from the pure white, choral and undifferentiated mass of others, to be individuated, because all of them come close to the worst. A countercheck that the subject comes from evil.

Christiane Frémont is right, otherwise Pascal would not have called the self hateful. To hold it dear would, in effect, amount to loving the malignancy from which it comes. The hatred of the self proceeds, here, from hatred of evils. Contrary to what La Rochefoucauld claims, who doesn't share this hatred? The subject has, yes, diabolicalness in it; seated alone in the centre of hell, where he breathes with sheer delight the odorous homages with which men of power and glory incense him, Satan becomes inflamed with vanity. As evidence, as well, the *ego* that was born in Descartes' stove-warmed room after he fought hand-to-hand against this malicious demon itself: you'd swear the philosopher stole it from him! As evidence, the modern subject, from Sade to Bataille, who delights in destruction. There is no consciousness except for bad consciousness; there is no psychology except for its pain.[15] As evidence, literature, in which neither the theatre nor novels create good characters with good sentiments. Against the angels, en masse and pure, phantoms stemming from the imagination, the historical, concrete, everyday self emerges distinctly: malicious. Nobody feels his body except when it's in pain. Consciousness emerges with lack and destitution.

So, in the reality of things and the annals of groups, history repeats the stagings of law, in the tribunal, of theology, in the first and last judgements, of cognition, in the decisions resolving doubt: all of them instances that launder the I, having a filthy origin, the way others do for drug money.

Origin through tragedy

Before the emergence of the individual, before the subject of law became universalized, the collective would fabricate subjects, rare, by means of war, sacrifice and a competition that was just as deadly; we would celebrate heroes and martyrs, exceptions the standard pedagogy invited us to imitate. Formerly highlighted to serve as models, violence produces them.

Recognize the scapegoats analysed by René Girard in these examples or champions who open, Bergson says, closed societies.

Gathered together upon the occasion of a crisis, the group transforms a victim into this goat thus loaded with the sins of the world; the group executes this goat, even if it means celebrating it afterwards as a god; it changes its species: of a man, it makes an animal, which it kills; by apotheosis, it lastly metamorphoses this animal into a divinity. This tragic character, in the usual sense as well as in the etymological sense of the word – *tragos*, in Greek, signifies goat – undergoes the process of individuation, whose celebrated principle reduces to this sacrifice, the simple and cruel putting to death of an emissary.[16] By fabricating this I through murder, the group becomes we.

Not yet individuated themselves, men and women assemble, unanimous, and succeed in forming a collective around the first individuals, victims of murder. Without individual, the collective individuates. The murder it commits is the principle of individuation itself: I emanate from we, and vice versa. Heroes, martyrs, kings or champions are all born from sacrificial murder. Once again, this subject is born from Evil, a subject whose root, *sub-jectus*, precisely designates someone thrown underneath, trampled, pillaged, stoned, lynched, sacrificed.

A model tragedy

A masterpiece of the seventeenth century and perhaps even of the human mind, Corneille's *Horace* describes with precision the lethal process by which the cities of Rome and Alba pushed their armies into fighting in their stead, the rest watching the representation, even if it meant that the armies would in turn push forward their champions, Curiatius and Horatius, in order to fight in their stead, the rest of the former combatants watching the representation, two brothers bringing the combat to an end in a duel, while the other four were dying. Representation is born from these continuing subtractions. Incidentally, what difference is there between pushing someone into fighting in your stead and sentencing him to death? This is why *Hominescence* defines all war as the decision made by the old men who declare it to kill their children; these depraved sociopaths watch, safe and sound, the spectacle, delighted, for it establishes their power.

Not content with founding representation itself in reason, *Horace* baptizes the first subjects born from this lethal process of selection, along with those watching, who thus produce this individuation. To this end, Livy and Corneille stage a collective war, which, stopped, gives way to an individual crime which, perpetrated against a brother-in-law, then against a sister, lastly gives way to a tribunal which, assembled, swings between condemnation and apotheosis. This interested series of representations lets be born, one after the other, the king – sacrificial, legislative and political; the hero – military, juridical, almost religious; tragic theatre, itself born first from human sacrifice; and lastly the tribunal that replaces it and is acquainted with it. The masterpiece carries within itself its own law, as well as the respective geneses of the theatre, of its representation, of the individual and legal subject, lastly the emergence of the judiciary.

Although collective and more complete, the process scarcely differs from the one followed by Descartes' *Meditations*, in which the subject of thought is born in a representation, hence theatrical, of radical doubt, in which the malicious demon battles against him and in which one indeed has to kill the other. By confronting death or the devil, two avatars of evil, the Cornelian hero and the Cartesian *ego* become individuals. The model tragedy gathers together sacrificial religious dynamism, the political process of the emergence of kingship, the birth of law and that of the subject in and by the collective; philosophy accompanies it by inventing, almost in parallel, in the court of doubt, the subject of thought. Even Kant's transcendental ego will be born in Critique, that is to say, near a tribunal, after theodicy put God Himself before his responsibility in the face of global Evil.

So from the first act, violent, to the last one, juridical, a process of transformation is unfolded in *Horace*, a process the spectator guesses lasts longer in real size and time than this model. One doesn't move so quickly nor so easily from the war of all against all to the social contract. Hobbes, for example, seems to believe, in addition, that the initial violence will vanish under this agreement. No, its sum remains, like the energy constant in a physical system. It transforms slowly and seems to come to a standstill as religious fervour, political authority and legislation: act by act, era by era, institutions after institutions, gods, kings and laws condense it and conceal it. It would be better to recognize its presence clearly, frozen beneath these appearances.

Champions fabricated by means of poisons

From seventeenth-century theatre to the contemporary stadium: prosecuted in law but tolerated in fact, doping is taken to be cheating in sports and a health risk; it rigs the fair equality between opponents and places their health in jeopardy. But whether founded on the morality of equal chances or medical protection, every anti-doping law today ends up yielding before the huge social, media and financial demand for a burning spectacle, one become global. Voice of the people and purse of tycoons, the entire society presses to let it go on. Why?

Because, in the tragic stadium, the athletes revive the gladiators. Before entering the arena, the latter hailed Caesar before dying: *Ave, Caesar, morituri te salutant.* We condemn the combat of retiarius against murmillo as barbarous because they sought to kill each other. But the heat, the fluidity and tactical details of the fight concealed from the eyes of the spectators their need for human sacrifice, which every society suppresses while giving themselves over to it, our society as well as other ones; for who today recognizes this human sacrifice in television's repeated spectacles, in the news that only announces bodies? Doping resumes these practices and conceals them as well. The athletes kill each other in the end. Of course, they don't actually kill each other, except sometimes in boxing or rugby, but they do commit suicide, either directly along the way or several years later in their beds, so that the crowd can satisfy its deep-rooted need to see, as a spectacle, a kind of god die and so that it can resurrect, around the body, the vanished social bond.

It's not enough to condemn the practices of pain and sports games as a drug that would prevent a people from taking an interest in its political matters. It must above all be seen that no one has the opportunity any longer to enjoy the social bond, destroyed by money. How can it be recreated? By the oldest of formulas: sacrifice, particularly human sacrifice, the most archaic, the most effective. Sports secretly become those spectacles where death prowls, the death of the men and women who offer themselves in spectacle during a scuffle. They do in reality what our spectacles show in virtuality. So doping with drugs becomes poison and the doper a sacrificial victim. Better yet, money sees to it that this effect is achieved and organizes it. It thus shows its similarity to drugs. Overpaid, overdosed, this is the winner, this is the champion. As in Corneille's *Horace*, the origin of tragedy and the origin of the tribunal are played out in the stadium, the languageless confrontation site.

The death of the hero, the executions of the martyrs, the mortifications, austerities and scourgings of the ascetics, the contemporary ones of the champions braving the harshest training and subjecting their bodies to a thousand privations and to the mortal risks of doping show that exceptional individuals are born from the same dynamic, in which evils of all types take up the largest part: the birth, at the same time, of the exceptional individual and of the surrounding collective we. Do said heroes open society, as Bergson claims?

The end of mythology

No, they close society again, and double-lock it, for this path gets blocked up quickly: in order for each person to be born as an individual in this single way, it would in effect be necessary for everyone to become victims. In order to henceforth institute a pedagogy by example or by the champion, it would be necessary for each person to enter into a dynamic in which all the others would assemble around him for murder or for glory. Impossible. Never-ending. Contradictory. The same reasoning holds for the Tarpeian Rock of the baseborn and for the Capitoline Hill of the glorious, two representations that mirror each other or form a series and which require the audience of the entire population of the city, today of the world. Everyone cannot become king. If each person wants fame, he can only get it from everyone; yet, since everyone wants it, no one can or wants to give it. The mythology or fabrication of exceptions dies from this contradiction in glory.

So two contemporary manias become clear and draw closer to each other to mark the upstream and downstream edges of an end with clean breaks. In order to get himself heard, in order then to ensure his publicity, each person seeks the glory of tracking down an accused man or to take, as fast as possible, the place of the victim: he shouts that everyone is attacking him. But everyone, precisely, wants everyone to attack him since this Tarpeian Rock of execution neighbours, precedes or follows the Capitoline Hill of power and glory. This tribunal before which each individual wants to be dragged and this generalized anthropodicy which replaces, in dividing it down, the theodicy in which God became God because, accused, he died throw many a collective nevertheless boasting of civilizing advances into a paranoia that's as dangerous as the mythologies of old were.

In a converse and complementary way, the media today know how to completely fabricate a champion drawn from the qualityless 'one'; neither beautiful nor brilliant, neither heroic nor holy, without any works or breaking any records, some man or woman, at leisure, becomes an envied star by showing his or her mediocre everyday life: each of us sees that we can attain this. We are scandalized by these fabrications because we remain drugged by myths demanding blood and death for an exception.

Madly tracking down the accused or racing to the victim shows the end of a process a thousand years old several times over, the disappearance of the processes by which mythology was born, still alive during Nietzsche's time, despite what he said, since he still dreamt of the superman, and to which Bergson gave its last breath; did the latter suspect that his theory of geniuses, heroes or saints expressed a final version of myth itself and the dynamic by which it produced rarities? Myth is so worn out today that we have just seen its contradictions.

Ordinary, the second fabrication on the contrary opens up a new era, about which it would be proper to be delighted. This is a real invention: I believe in the right of anyone to become a champion, to use a glory that's in the end empty and harmless, even though it was once overflowing with blood and death. At the end of a long anthropological road, we discover, without any possible mistake, the genuine falsity of the false gods and the futility of vainglory.

Formed by these processes, the consciousness of self therefore begins with the consciousness of evil. Narcissus ends up drowning in the circles of his own reflection. The self is born from evil. But, by the same processes, the collective we is also born from sacrificial violence, another form of evil.

Infinitude and definition

Leibniz said that evil was inseparable from the original limitation of creatures, proof that it had something to do with their definition. For there can be no definition without a limit, for example the one we with tragic tones call finitude. Did then this finitude imitate the ditches of our fields, the octrois of provinces, the borders of nations? Does this original barrier reproduce the one that's lowered in front of the farm so that the horses won't get out? Yes, this closure, these bounds finish and define [*finissent et définissent*] property sites, my animals, my house, my country, as though what is proper to man amounted to what he appropriated.

A new confusion between belongingnesses and identity: belonging to a subset or having the feeling that things and living beings belong to the one who is involuted in these belongingnesses. Every foreign body that approaches the border, that crosses it, becomes an enemy to be fought, driven back, killed. It would be impossible for him and another to sojourn at the same time and in the same circumstances in the same place: here we find the principles of contradiction and of the excluded middle or third, emanating, fully armed, from belongingness, finitude and limitation.[17] So yes, I understand the origin of evil such as Leibniz conceived it: it most certainly comes from the violence produced, in the vicinity of boundaries, by the exclusion of the third.

We now know how to construct the principle of identity, formerly tautological; it comes down to the discovery of a third and to his expulsion, literally, to the excluded middle or third; it therefore comes down to the invention of the scapegoat, therefore again to violence and evil. Not only does the metaphysics of the self find its foundation or at least its equivalent in anthropology but so does the purest logic. As a result, the elevated praise of finitude resembles too much a speech for the defence *pro aris et focis*, in favour of our altars and hearths, in defence of borders, for it not to be suspected of a patriotism lapsing into the fundamentalism [*intégrisme*] that protects the integrity of my tribe, my culture and my property.

The end of native soil

The modern West benefited from a rare bit of luck. Little by little, then en masse, it converted to an imported religion, born on another land than its own, the Holy Land, located elsewhere, in Palestine, where holy history unfolded, the history of the chosen people and of the redemption by the come Messiah. The decisive events for salvation took place elsewhere than in its home and concern other personages than the gods of its culture. Neither the holy geography nor the holy history unfold beneath its feet, the persons concerned not speaking its language. In no longer deifying their own soil, Western peoples thus separated the spiritual from their native roots. Thus they left the *pagus* of paganism, the little gods of their fields. The West has carried out said deterritorialization from its origin. Or rather: it owes its sudden bifurcation to this coming unstuck with respect to the soil.

Begun with the Exodus of the Hebrew people to the Promised Land, the holy adventure, drawn out to the extreme limits, led the Christians to consider that land of milk and honey to be inaccessible here below: we, exiled, will not return there and now aspire to the Heavenly Jerusalem. Modernity would neither emerge nor be conceived without this abstraction from the immanent soil, without this passage from the Earthly City to the City of God described by Saint Augustine. How many deaths for the fatherland soil would this hope have saved during the times of the *pro aris et focis* wars, for the fatherland, the sacred land of the forebears, whose furrows were watered by an impure blood?[18] How many of them would it still economize today?

The end of blood ties

When a father doesn't beget, when a son only knows, here below, his adoptive father and when a mother remains virgin, the familial schema breaks in addition with the ties of blood. *Hominescence* describes the Holy Family, freed in this way from this chain. We have no definition; we are neither born from a defined place nor from a defined lineage.

The West came about from this double abandonment: of the earth and of the family line; and from two correlative abstractions: the first one leaves the native soil, its finite bounds and even the entire earth in favour of a kingdom outside of this world; the second one abandons blood in favour of adoption and of the extension of the family, now chosen by dilection, to humanity in general. Every man has the right to feel at home everywhere and with family next to everyone. The West came about from leaving the local and from bringing to birth this Universal.

The fact that it didn't always make good use of this immense discovery goes without saying. But as a result, it leaves itself and its culture. Through this double abandonment, Christianity bears the exit from religions inside itself, and the West bears its own abdication inside itself. Neither I nor we were born there, nor do we think according to it. Landless and tribeless, we are citizens of the world and brothers of men. Science came about from this new anthropology, whose double abandonment in the long run implied the end, which I have just described, of all mythology.

We don't always understand religious truths because they have an immense historical and cultural persistence in comparison to received scientific truths, which are understood and exploited almost immediately and are by this very fact often temporary. The West understands itself little by little and unfolds its history according to this long and slow clarification, which erases it in return. So it took more than two millennia for us to recognize this coming unstuck, this uprooting with respect to blood and the soil. Yes, this absence of bounds and definition, this infinitude.

Clearly expressed, this infinitude is essential today as the operation we are in need of in order to invent our behaviour in the face of the end of the old agriculture, the demographic explosion and the biotechnologies, in short, in order to assume our responsibilities towards the auto-evolution that's advancing and will characterize us. Reciprocally, the unforeseen arrival of this auto-evolution could only come about under these conditions of coming unstuck. To return to the soil and to blood, in history or even in an autobiography, would be to return to paganism, before modern science. Persistent therefore, religious truths sometimes anticipate reason, prophetically.

The archaic and contemporary tragic

Violence and life

Plural or singular, I or we, subjective consciousness therefore comes about with evil and violence. The wolf devours the lamb before any consciousness.[19]

But this simple law of the food chain is only named violence the moment this consciousness appears. Does the course of evolution bifurcate here, precisely? Did humanity appear from naming these everyday laws of life in this way? From calling this fate of killing in order to survive violence and evil? Discovering death suffered and given, this animal flees it, detests it and calls it Evil. A living being appears that loves and detests life, that suddenly hates the death entailed by life. This hatred founds its consciousness and its morality. In this point that's certainly abstract, no doubt imaginary, and assuredly so little punctual that this moment has lasted since the coming of humanity and hasn't yet managed to bring itself to a close, in short, in this in-stance full of meaning, evolution turns back; the sense and direction of living time change.

For this evil, which we try to free ourselves from, this war of all against all, this violence invariant across every collective characterize life, evolution in the Darwinian sense, that appalling struggle we have tried to leave ever since we dreamt of earthly paradise but which sticks to the skin of our bodies as it does to the duration, before history, of our Grand Narrative. The human non-species continuously emerges when it leaves, with difficulty, this war of species and falls back into a species when it doesn't do so. Evil is equivalent to life, which we don't know how and don't want to define so as not to admit that life is equivalent to this violence that kills, in the long term, by mutation, selection and adaptation, that kills, daily, for dietary survival, that kills, lastly, in order not to die by being eaten, that kills, additionally, for pleasure sometimes. How, consequently, can we free ourselves from evil without abandoning life itself since it entails death, entropy, filth and crimes?

Two-valued, at least, life

Far from knowing how to define life, we are so ignorant of its secret, if it exists, that biologists have recently decided, taking the shortest route, not to look for it any more. Blinded in this way, we can only assess, estimate or evaluate life; so it becomes the value par excellence. Yet, since we kill our enemies and sometimes our neighbours, since we sentence our children to death in wars and the poor to the scaffold, since we hunt, fish, breed or gather our food provisions, eradicate species, burn thickets, destroy forests, since we forget our health when it thrives, silent, since we commit suicide in abundance and sacrifice our existences to virtual ideals, absent loves, works of imagination, dreams and deliriums, or to frenzied schedules, absurd projects, uselessly amassed money, we evidently detest and hate it. Of course, we love it since we, sometimes, banish suffering, love our comforts and stroke our grandchildren. We don't know it in science or in reason; we only make value judgements about it. What could be more normal since this word 'value' designates, at its root, health or strength of life? At least for food, defence, preservation and reproduction, life entails death. We therefore judge it to be joyful and appalling, epiphanic and deadly, positive and negative at the same time. A supreme good, but a radical evil.

Adventure and festival

I propose two equivalents for it: adventure, first, two-valued as well, unpredictable, thrilling, risky, hard work, alert, tense, inventive and dangerous, adventure and its tribulations, but above the festival.

We don't know of any culture that doesn't have festivals. Every civilization organizes regular festivities, rites, religious celebrations, anniversaries, singular moments when one and all try to forget the everyday. Nothing could be more foreign, sometimes, and particular, in any case, than a festival; nothing could better reveal the singularities of a country and of its inhabitants; yet nothing could be more widespread on the global map of customs. A paradox: a universal and common habit shows the particularities of each place and of a day. Thus life repeats itself across the universality of kingdoms but reveals itself to be singular in each individual.

Seeing the wine flow from the casks, the couples dance in costumes, hearing the bugle sound out among the bagpipes and musettes or the speakers roar under the decibels of electric guitars, you might think that in the village square or the crowd of the stadium the joy of the event was bursting out. Yes and no, for festivals celebrate a beginning and an ending at the same time; here and now an era is ending that is being put to death: the king is dying, long live the king; a year is finishing, long live the following one; the light is no longer lowering, long live the solstice; after the entombment, long live the Resurrection. To the pleasure aroused by a beginning corresponds the sadness of a bereavement. A body remains prior, and sometimes we know it, when we have sacrificed a victim, prisoner, slave, ram, bull or matador, Host or symbol. Festivals deserve sacred names owing to this sacrifice. Birth and disappearance, hymns and threnodies, laughter and tears, flowers and ashes, everything mixes in the festive whirlwind. After the ball, jealous men come to blows; after the parade on July 14 hoodlums burn cars; with victory won in the World Cup, hooligans wreck the stadium; festivals turn bad and end up in free-for-alls. The birth of tragedy, wine turns into blood; the reversal of the tragic and good news: blood turns into wine.

Like adventure and great loves, the festival has two values like life, and every festival links two eras, an emergence and a funeral. They all straddle the same mixed time that's everyday and singular, exceptional and dismal, monotonous and exciting, a rising star and a descending star, intoxicating and pathetic, attractive, mysterious, delicious like a temptation, painful like tribulations. Wheat has to be triturated in order to be sorted, beaten for the grain to slip from the ear, crushed for flour to fly, lastly its dough has to be cooked in a hellish oven for the baguette to become golden brown.[20] Harvest festivals, field threshing festivals, the windmill's round dance, the last supper where bread is transubstantiated. Amorous and adventurous, tribulations triturate and sort.

Long experience and short reason don't see any better equivalent to life than the festival. The former lasts like the latter, in the same colours, the same cries, the same crowd, the same difficulties; the latter begins and lastly becomes choked off like the former. Through the duration remaining to us to live, every breath of the instant, every impulse of desire, lack and satiety, laughter and tears, shooting pain of suffering, thirst and intoxication, shiver and sweat, dawn and dusk, happiness and ill-being, despair and hope celebrate in real time, initiate, enthusiastically crush and kill this inauguration, this jubilee, this atonement, this fast, this immense feast of life, and never cease, in tears, to take delight in it. So successful, this revel, that it makes the heart beat.

How can we free vital energy from aggression without allowing the former to fall back into the latter? This is the foundation of morality: filtering life from death. It sometimes happens that this festival, most often ugly amid garish colours, mediocre lights, dull music, heavy words, takes a rest, silent, and rises – light, suspended and transparent – through the tree branches, the racing clouds and the flocks of starlings. Then the one contemplating his tattered and failed life no longer cries over absence or despair but rather over the beauty from which ecstasy descends.

Love and hatred of life

We hate life, and at the same time we love it. Who, we? The living. But who, once more? The individual, you, me; groups, we; our species and the other ones; these are three subjects of life. In these three senses, in order to maintain and perpetuate itself, life kills, desires and reproduces life. *Sapiens* as a species loves and detests its very own species and the other ones, eradicates and studies them. A common and grandiose force transports murder and delight.

This force carries knowledge along, which we know produces comforts and weapons and doesn't necessarily improve its practitioners, disinterested sometimes, rivals often and just as much as gangsters. Predatory, the social sciences work on humans and groups provided that those studied remain inferior to the one doing the studying. 'Life is no longer questioned in laboratories,' says the biochemist;[21] not by virtue of any habit acquired from being near physics or chemistry, sciences of the dead inert, but owing to, I believe, that properly originary force already stated by Empedocles during the fifth century BC; he intuited that a law of Love and Hate regulated our existences, public and private, our practices and our knowledge, the four elements, the rocks and living things. Don't understand his discovery as a rational rule of physics, such as the rule of attraction and repulsion; Love and Hate dominate, on the contrary, every principle and every law. Upstream, their power produces existence and science. A profound truth about nature, about life and humanity shines forth here. As much violence reigns in knowledge as in the outskirts of cities or in the hearts of primeval forests. In knowing, we haven't stopped hunting: ruses, traps, patient waiting, putting to death. Hunting and knowledge together form part of life, ensuing from its force and flowing with its current. Yes, the secret of life approaches the secret of knowledge, both secrets being tragic.

Virile, life [*vie*] and violence, *vir, vis* and *vita* symbolize the sides of a single power, of a same potentiality, the banks of a similar torrent, the variants of a single theme. I feel in myself, I experience among my fellow men and see in every living thing the same magnificent and terrible force, irrepressible and dangerous, poetic and blind, beautiful like a river and horrible like its overflowings; dazzling, my power of life risks setting afire with its sparks; I don't love it merely as close to me, internal, interior and innermost, but also as what I owe everything to, from the tension of my muscles to the speed of my legs, from the pride in my joints to the subtleties of my intellect, from the enthusiasm of the heart to the tenderness of the genitals, from the kindness of the affects to the horrors of the destructive drives; therefore I love it, and I hate it; maybe even I never love anything or anyone above this sovereign, but surely I don't abhor anything or anyone in as total a way as the deadly attractive force it carries in its flanks. And I would no doubt burn, this day, with as much Hatred as Love if the torches of war hadn't forever consumed the former; but I have preserved enough of it to be able to understand the pomps and vanities of the devil and his works with a forbearing serenity. Without anyone knowing how to separate joy from terror, life springs forth with elation and streams with anguish. Life envelops death not only in apparent existence but in this deep and secret mode. Not only does every human share this experience with me, but we live it in common with the living things of every kingdom, from infusoria to sequoias, all of them immersed and then carried along in this vast moving mass of mixed molasses. Even plants, peaceable because they only eat light, try to kill their neighbours in their little territory. We live, therefore we love; we live, therefore we hate. I love life, I hate it, therefore I exist.

Thus we became, little by little, a soft and hard, inventive and exterminating, loving and thanatocratic race, with individual variables, from Stalin to Saint Francis of Assisi, from the merciless hunter to Saint Julian the Hospitaller, from the parasite to the symbiont, from the crowd of those who love power to the rare handful of saints who devote their power to love.

Violence and knowledge

This river of Love and Hatred mixed together, productive and destructive of the global whole and the tiny facts of knowledge, shapes the evolution of species, the collective history of the human race and the behaviour of individuals. Mutations invent, kill and build; natural selection kills, destroys and, by adapting, analytically constructs the exquisite detail of organisms. This nutritive and devastating torrent includes every power that unfolds existence and cognition.

How can we escape the cost of this force? How can we negotiate its negative component? Just as life is constructed from managing it, human cultures, also fluctuating with tribulations, result from similar negotiations; we only produce works, technologies or institutions so as to deliver ourselves from this carnage and, in building them, we destroy just as much. That which protects exposes. Pockets of negentropy are formed by increasing the surrounding entropy. Fire glows, warms up and burns. Force overturns and rights again. Movement jostles and thrills. Life gives birth and murders. The happiness and misfortune of men, knowledge brings regression and progress. Everything has a price.

How does a force contain knowledge? How can this be conceived? I don't really know, but how many times have I experienced the extent to which hatred likes to go all the way to the finest detail: breaks things into tiny pieces and, exacerbated, discovers analysis. Destroying causes this detail to arise; knowing in detail requires destroying. Analysis comes from the Greek verb λυω, *luo*, to untie or to dissolve. To destroy the golden calf being worshipped by the Hebrew people, Moses, angry, turned it into a fine powder and made the idolaters drink it; prophetic wrath ended with analysis. The scene begins at the foot of the holy mountain and comes to an end with chemistry and pharmacy. Is so much fury necessary to analyse or filter the false from the true?

Self-knowledge or what is man?

To refine self-knowledge, required since Socrates by Western wisdom, we spent a wealth of intelligence in order to describe ourselves as individuals, all of us singular although similar, as cultures, exquisitely differentiated, as social classes in conflict. But didn't we leave out, in these infinite labours, the long passion of the blind actions of our species as species, become such through these acts during the last act of the Grand Narrative? Only perhaps old Aristotle and a few recent prehistorians or biologists have attempted to define us in the same way as an oak tree or a marsupial.

Let's boldly attempt to answer the question 'who are we?' by consulting the Grand Narrative or the universal legend that precedes us and the tendencies that come to light among the acts that we set down. So who are we? A species whose originality concerns its relation to life and to the world. A question therefore: what did this species do over such a long time, what is it doing today, what therefore will it probably do, this species that's so enterprising that it conquers the world, life and knows part of the Universe?

Considered over the millions of years of its slow hominization, humanity lives less and less in the world and life, space and time, follows less and less the *élan vital*, as plunged in its flow of Love and Hatred and directed by it, so that it emerges from it little by little over the course of its evolution, detaches itself from it, remains, certainly, dependent on it, but, I repeat, less and less, so as to patiently direct itself towards a state where it lives more and more independent of the world and its body, of life and its laws, towards a direction that is unpredictable with every step.

Strange leaps mark the different stages of its journey in divergence from life. First, the diversification of niches and the general omnitude of diet distinguishes it from the species it was at the start, probably herbivorous and tied to its place. Next, its travels on land and by sea detach it from its habitats. The wandering omnivore at the same time frees itself from any single source of food, which can go lacking, as well as from any resting spot, area or hiding spot it could be stripped of by circumstances. Outside a single ecological niche, it begins and continues to live in divergence from ecology. Outside place or *Horla*.[22]

The first scene of the last act of the Grand Narrative

In the course of its travels, encountering by chance a happy plain without any superior predator, it devoted itself, as before, to the extermination of many species but started to dominate the neighbouring kingdoms of flora and fauna, at first partially in agriculture and livestock farming, then progressively from the beginnings of knowledge and natural history on; this strange animal which collects animals in zoos and flora in botanical gardens named itself Lord of the kingdoms before discovering it had long lived and continues to survive as Exterminator of species. It is distinguished, once again, from carnivores, even from other omnivores, from every predator and from parasites by the fact that it leaves behind it not only the bodies of individuals devoured from the outside or inside but of entire genera; it kills and knows with the same movement of violence and collection, as though the Genesis story taught the truth that the tree of knowledge bears fall and sin. *Homo specierum exterminator.*

At the extreme limit of this violence on the living and as its ultimate project or infinite task, the knowledge itself of life appears, not speculative knowledge of course but active and practical knowledge, today's knowledge. Far from trying to discover its secret, humanity exploits its power. In making use of the industrial inventions of the past century concerning inert matter, it no longer utilized the excellence of the goose, the strength of some ox or of the horse species but the *élan vital* of every living thing in its gushing forth, thenceforth utilizable. In sum, how are we to define this animal that now deciphers the genetic code and practices genetic engineering if not by grasping it in this movement of emergence, a billionaire in years, that leaves the living little by little? It's no longer a question of a vital movement whose *élan* then only concerned us from outside; we now grasp its productive secret. And since it also concerns our lives, we find ourselves in the process of auto-evolution.

The exterminator

Reaching this threshold that's so new, we remember the Grand Narrative, over the course of which we left life, and how much we suffered, for millions of years, from perpetual war, Darwinian laws, the struggle for life, the daily obligation to kill, the daily misfortune of seeing the weak die, in particular our children. A black memory, on the nether side of the one that delights or tortures the solitary individual, an anamnesis special to the species plunges us back into the evolutionary river from which the human animal emerged. One remembers; the race enters into memory. Some pathos in me, whose intensity brings me closer to animals, teaches me their misfortune. Our misfortune. The necessity to kill. Daily murder. I remember, yes, the wolves we were, slavering dogs, hypocritical lambs, crows and tigers as well, the dry chitinous insects; I recognize them in the fetishes, the bloody horror of the *Metamorphoses* and the melancholy of the *Fables*. I can't watch a relationship of strength between men without immediately seeing two atrocious animals, the gasping neck of the one between the fangs of the other. I see them without clothes or words; I remember it like it was yesterday; their day-to-day behaviour is cruel enough for me not to have much trouble remembering it.

Who are we then? The Exterminator. The species that not only hunted to eat but kills wastefully to the point that it not only destroys individuals but entire species, gone extinct through its violence. In order to survive, every living thing hunts or parasitizes individuals; mankind eradicates species; this is a first definition of the human animal: the species that exterminates species. That devotes itself not only to murdering fathers, to murdering sons in war, to assassinating enemy brothers, to the enslavement of women – why these choices restricted to the single individual subject, I? – but also to the war of all against all, to intraspecific murder, for the collective subject, we, but, in addition, to the destruction of species and kingdoms; for a hundred years even, we have declared war on single-celled organisms; but lastly, to the destruction of everything that, even inert, moves, rises or leans; so much for the living subject, 'one'. A repugnant species of destruction. We have numerous archaeological remains of it on the world's continents and islands.

I remember this terror, the sea of hatred that forces so many species to only come out at night. We carry three memories with us. I remember my own violence, which my father drowned by throwing glasses of water in my face; but I especially remember the violence of the last wars, from Spain's war to the world conflict, from its horrors to the colonial liberations; these atrocities that set the hatred in us ablaze to the point of extreme extinction then became joined with the nightmares taught to me by written 'culture', the Old French of *The Song of Roland*, the Latin of the *Aeneid*, the Greek of the *Iliad*, the endless hostilities related in the Bible; so it's enough to read Darwin to leave the written and subjects restricted to the I and the we, by the same path, and recognize in our species, beyond our culture – agricultural then scholastic, living and then said to be artistic – an exterminator of a different stamp and of an entirely different scope than those species that would only require hunting for food and survival, crueller than the bloodiest predator, cleverer than the worst parasite. We differ from animals twice over: by this universal extermination and by the astounding event that we have recognized this.

On guilt

I also call this universal memory of mine by another name: guilt, that generic bottomless hole forever buried in our thorax and loins as well as in those of all our brothers and which still prevents us, sometimes, in the midst of the tears, from killing one another, which sometimes, too rarely, checks us in our destructive enterprises. This guilty memory doesn't belong to any individual or specify any tradition, any singular religion, but is a burden on the Exterminator's flesh. Men and women share it, universally. Does it arouse, today, our environmental anxieties? Does it likewise dictate a Natural Contract? The most widely shared thing in the world, in all latitudes and cultures, guilt remains so useful that if it is lacking, as it was with the Nazi or Stalinian executioners, their real victims pay for its disappearance with their lives. In the process that made us into humans, starting from wolves who killed lambs without asking themselves any questions, who will tell of the happy share of guilt? It holds the species over baptismal fonts.

For the first species that, suddenly, because the circumstances of its random wanderings brought it into a garden without any dangerous predators, saw, understood, I don't know how to say it, contemplated in any case the universal submission of life to this law of hatred and that could, as a result, distance it enough to feel it to be hatred or even to call it Evil become human by this event. Humanity came about, as a species, at the same time as the consciousness of this universal murder. Just as the singular individual I and the collective we were born of Evil, the generic 'one' emerged from it as well. The fourfold temporal root attached to our bodies, our writings, our genes and our vital experiences reattaches us to this event, and we recall it. We never stop remembering it. What we call guilt brings it before our eyes at the same time as the certainty of belonging to a species and of defining it. Guilt stirs in us the mad hope of a deliverance from Evil. But we fairly quickly learn that extracting the Good out of this force gives rise to a hope as mad as the one of extracting the gold lost in an alloy coin or of filtering, in a perfume, the essence from the excipient. Thus, through this inescapable bond, our guilt sometimes even rises from good things. It surrounds us and jostles us just as much as the flow of mixed Love and Hatred, which we have called, ever since, Good and Evil.

Once again: we left evolutionary life through our status and our power of extermination. The winner of the battle by superslaughtering, an unimaginable ancestor saw for the first time a plain covered with bodies. He was afraid of his fellow men and of himself. He knew where he came from. He recognized the Darwinian nightmare. Darwin's immense success, quasi religious, also came from the fact we saw him replaying this primitive scene. This ancient and recent ancestor, unimaginable and scientific, felt pity. In this ocean of hatred, a rare current of love passed. He knew. He believed he could distinguish love of life and hatred of life, peace from violence, Good from Evil. Beyond the written, we remember that first knowledge that still torments our bodies. Will we ever console ourselves for barely emerging from hatred, for plunging there again up to our necks every day, for seeing the gold lost in the base metal? For surviving free like children of Evil? For always killing as during the early days, for incessantly replaying preoriginary scenes, the ones preceding knowledge? This is how original sin is defined, transhistorical, always as well as today committed in real time: violence done to everything that lives. This is how the species expels itself from its paradises, discovered by random trips. It suffices to see the law of the human jungle practice its daily ravages to learn that this true knowledge of life, always partial and approximate, doesn't differ from the knowledge and difficult distinction of Good and Evil. And Evil, often, comes from the fact that we think we distinguish them.

This evident fact exceeds all words, written or oral; it surrounds and limits the sciences, philosophies, wisdom; its transparency flies beyond the mixed pity and joy expressed by music; its subterranean truth is revealed in the midst of emotion and sobs. Beneath the words of the mouth and tongue lie the notes of the throat and the gestures of the body; beneath these threnodies and lamentations roars the pathetic torrent of memory. In any language, no text tells true if it doesn't ring, musical; no music can be moving if it doesn't make one cry these tears, our source.

Our culture's first texts don't relate the beginning of the world or of the Earth or of the species but attempt to tell, for a culture, the beginning of human culture and how it bifurcated from Darwinian law. They certainly don't tell the Grand Narrative but how it ends and by what bifurcation history begins, the first scene of its last act, contingent both of them. They tie our genetic memory to textual history, life to culture, universal extermination to a few elective murders, the murder of a brother by his brother; this small local sin masks the global catastrophe of the universal slaughter. These texts therefore relate the birth of guilt, whose threefold memory engenders the three-subject humanity, compels the Exterminator, sometimes, to take pity, overturns the law of Hatred into the law of Love, which accompanies it in a miraculously rare way. Which is what Darwin himself wrote.

The universality of evil
and of the solution

Minimal-local solutions;
the maximal-global solution

Who are we? The Exterminator. Where do we come from? From universal tears over ourselves. The I and the we are born from sacrificial violence first, the 'one', lastly, from vital violence; all of them therefore from universal evil. Where are we going? According to our new global powers, which baptize us with names prefixed with *pan*, we find ourselves today faced with a universal horizon: the possible eradication, by us, of human cultures, of living species, of inert things and of the planet. One has this panic power.

To the universal problem of evil, we have discovered and will discover local solutions, minimal, allowing us to temporarily manage its inescapable constancy. But here, for the first time in hominization, for the first time in our part of the Grand Narrative, a global solution is presented, maximal, universal, if not discovered at least necessitated by the insistent presence of this horizon of destruction. The universality of eradication stands before the universality of our violence and of evil the way just now the Universe as such stood before Panurge's acquired infinitude. Being conscious of this maximal risk causes, today, a world public opinion to be born, even ahead of political philosophies, practices and institutions: what is one going to do before this threatening horizon, now visible and accessible? One has no choice: at most, an ethics, at least, a new contract founding another law.

Broad and vague, this solution has no immediate or concrete force because individuals can't do anything about it and those in power are still a century behind. It doesn't, here and now, obligate any individual, any person in charge or humanity in general to this or that behaviour. Its only power is regulatory, but its shadow covers over the perceptible and the thinkable.

Proof by large numbers

Let's demonstrate, by numbers, the constancy and universality of evil. Even supposing that we had never found the origin of evil, a fruitless theoretical quest, we would quite like to rid ourselves of it. An example of a struggle against it: an effective remedy for headaches, aspirin additionally thins the blood, preventing coagulation, therefore preventing at the same time embolisms and wound closure. It relieves more than a hundred million people per year in the world, but kills a few dozen. When spread into sizeable populations, there is no cure with zero risk. Large numbers prohibit thinking in black and white, true and false, good and evil; a tare is introduced into the measurements. Every gesture has a remainder whose cost appears with numerous repetitions of the gesture.

Local-global passage: Large numbers and the accursed portion

Who hasn't cooked omelettes a hundred times without breaking a single egg during the transport between the refrigerator and the skillet? A hundred thousand cordon-bleu chefs, over twenty years, will carry tonnes of them and inevitably break a few dozen. When going from small amounts to large ones, from the local to the global, from the isolated case to the multiple, finally to the universal, it's impossible to eliminate breakage. Without fail, vices, accidents, manufacturing defects, errors, catastrophes return with large numbers, even when they are concerned with remedies or benefits. Out of thousands of excellent teachers, you will always find a handful of paedophiles, ineradicably. Experts in the natural, medical and social sciences doubt and waver before these ineliminable approximate percentages, while political and judicial action wants to and has to come to a decision before the spectacle of rare and appalling cases, scandalizing the crowds gaping before the vengeful announcements. How can we avoid the black consequences of this change of scale?

The media and politicians manipulate both the large numbers and the cases, group and individual; advertising, the news and polls, the new technologies, in short a thousand ordinary occupations attain large numbers, today more so than in the past, and sometimes attain totalities, like mandatory insurance or mandatory vaccination; from which it results that the problem of evil reappears as on the first day but in a different way: through this percentage, which returns, inexorably, called back, imposed by the large numbers.

Strangely unaware of this stability, the prevailing puritanism demands an absence of bacteria right where they develop by the hundreds of billions, therefore requires asepsis, absence of defect, freedom from danger, zero risk, a smooth universe without any rough edges. Yet, when problems become universal, these large numbers leave an accursed portion. Ineliminable? I believe so. This accursed portion strongly resembles that sum of violence I compared earlier to the energy constant in a physical system. Might there exist then a kind of dynamic first principle in collectives? I don't know, but I do think so.

Panic, again

This passage from the local to the global changes our ways of reasoning. We used to speak of rigour, precision and exactitude in the sciences and use binary categories drawn from the old metaphysics, Being and Nothingness, Evil and Good, Hatred and Love. Theatrical, the war of Good against Evil, of Saint George against the Dragon, becomes ineffective and silly when legions of Georges hunt down armies of Dragons. They all lose their capital letters. These performances held for mediocre populations. Demographic growth, globalization change scales, in dimensions, power, and effectiveness. An object or a tool that grows from the size of a molehill to the size of Mount Everest no longer obeys the same laws. A frog doesn't eat, reproduce or live like an ox. Who doesn't know that a nation isn't governed the way a business is managed or the way a family is organized?

Imposed little by little by the catastrophes of Hiroshima, Seveso and genetic engineering, did scientific ethics ensue from the passage to what has been called 'big science' for a half-century or at least from the fact that technology mounted towards what I call world-objects, the atomic bomb, nuclear waste, networks? Once again, changing scales imposes the accursed percentages particular to large numbers. Leibniz sometimes said that the problem of evil depended on the dimension of our apprehension of things: some motive, viewed up close, clashes out of tune, even though, seen from afar, it enters into harmony. Instead of making use of perspective, which renders this scene subjective and particular to the point of view, why didn't the theoretician of insurance remark that starting from large numbers a simple calculation rightly predicts that there will be, in a given population, so many inevitable deaths, incurable diseases, accidents, vices and corruption? Six campers can live three days on a beach without any offence; ten thousand people transform it into a cesspool; sacking the planet, tourism changes sites of beauty into sewage fields. This unites ten contemporary scandals and predictable panics; yes, panic fits here perfectly: it signifies the access of everyone to everything. The multiple is frightening: does evil lie in large numbers?

Is evil born from the passage from few to many, from a small group to large populations, from here to the world, from the I to the we, from the we to the 'one', from the individual to the group and to the species? Does it accompany the rise to the Universal? Does it flow with the Grand Narrative because this latter carries along all things? The accursed portion particular to large numbers lies at the intersection of the singular case and the gathered collective, of the personal subject and the common subject, of the element and the set. If I and we and one are born from the encounter with evil, evil comes from the encounter between the one, the we and the I. A circle of self-begetting and feedback unites evil and the three subjects; death snatches and creates the personal subject, I; we, Westerners, brought Latin, Greek, Egyptian, Assyro-Babylonian dead back to life. This very morning, 'one' is born, as a species, from the horizon of the species' self-eradication. And today, a few I's, as one or two we's, can put the 'one' to death.

A first local solution, a practical one

Far from falling asleep to the accursed portion implied by this unstoppable growth, wisdom on the contrary awakens moralities of proximity, treats this percentage with a redoubled attention and activity, manages it with care, tenaciously brings it to an even narrower minimum.

But, in order to attain this new wisdom, it is advisable to learn that the case can invert the law. This small rock falling from the height of the planets doesn't present any danger; who then has been hit by a meteorite on the head? But the rarest exception can repudiate this frequency; we can cite this case as an example but not make it into a law. Let's accompany its rare and appalling spectacle from the statement of the often total law to its opposite; some given remedy has killed in one place, certainly, but it cures everywhere else, most often.

By deciding based on the law rather than on the case, we define democracy. For this latter is founded on elections, therefore on a law of large numbers. So, like everything, it has its defects. Conversely, should we decide based on the exception, we will restore an aristocracy or a casuistry. That said, let's bring the accursed portion down to the minimum.

Panic mixture

There can be no stainless good, but conversely there can be no radical evil either; no virtuous without vice nor sinner without some goodness. The most Abominable shows itself to be good, on a nice snowy morning, as well as the Samaritan on the road. The best morality declares the worst act to be good. The enemy of the human race sympathizes and takes pity. Thus he redeems himself. Another local solution to the problem of evil. Conversely, love sometimes reveals itself to be hateful, on a stormy evening. A person caught yesterday in flagrante delicto has nevertheless, over his life, managed most of his affairs honestly and sometimes showed generosity. Even the individual singularity, in its encounters, circumstances and happenstances, employs large numbers. Everything happens as though these numbers filtered the mixture, as though evil settled out through their growth, as though large populations acted to reveal it. Tangled up in a hundred thousand difficulties, I find myself lapsed amid years of honesty; I find myself honest amid a hundred violences. Who can flatter themselves to have, in every time and place, abided by ethics? Who must be condemned absolutely?

How can we set fire in this panic mixture?

The whitening of the incandescent

The saint blazes more than he remains white. He shines because he burns inside himself the basest fuel possible. He must therefore contain a lot of Hatred for the flames of Love to climb high, incandescent. By catching fire, these flames little by little eliminate the coal encumbering him and whiten the rest.

If I knew how to express it, morality would reveal the difficult-to-find secret of setting fire to Evil. What then is the Good if not the flame itself, the one that consumes in me, without me requiring it from anyone else, the Evil I am never lacking? Against it, it's best to start with an exercise of individual symbiosis: living with. How can we negotiate this mire? I make it into my best fuel; I draw energy from it. I burn from it, incandescent. Evil implies in itself this other solution, eminently local.

The subject begins with the problem of evil because it designates a deciding authority that's fitting to resolve it. Neither the we nor the one nor the collective nor the species can arrive at this, precisely owing to the large numbers or the constant of violence. Beyond a certain quantity, one cannot eradicate the proportion of death, perversion, suffering or disease, whatever the name you may give to men or facts, whatever the term by which you may designate cesspool, refuse or garbage, inescapable in every living phenomenon. There is always a remainder, a loss, a lapse in the productivity of the machine, a cost, a payment. Nothing is free; never is there 100 per cent or zero defects, or no tolerance.

We don't know of any site that's axenic, totally devoid of microbes, completely sterilized; supposing such a place existed, billions of bacteria would be ready to swoop down on it at the first breach; it could even serve as an emblem, a paradoxical one, for extreme danger, for the most exposed place because, to exist, it would require barriers, defences and protections that would be calculably infinite. For just this once, a metaphysical and moral question can be settled by arithmetic: the law of large numbers shows the stable existence, the ineradicable perpetuation of the sewer. Risk, danger, in sum Evil, remain ineliminable, linked with the very functioning of life, with existence itself, with the numerous collective, with the innumerable species.

The subject therefore begins with the question of Evil because this subject invents, because it promotes the person that can contribute, at least here or there, at least a little, to its appeasement, to its softening. I'm not saying to its complete solution – there isn't any, except for the horizon from just now – but to its relative amelioration, to its acculturation. For the subject can quit belongingness, disjoin itself from the subset presupposing exclusion, extract itself from the whole presupposing extermination; it can therefore try to separate itself from the we, to abstract itself from the 'one' in its individual life and in singular consciousness, to not conduct itself as exclusive or as a specific exterminator.

I can refuse to avenge myself. I can refuse violence. In this respect, violence depends on me. Collectively, it doesn't depend on me, nor specifically. The best intentioned political militants, sometimes pacifist, fight and therefore propagate in a certain manner a battle whose terrifying violence becomes revealed when they take power. More profoundly, pressure groups carry within themselves, by virtue of being groups, the very evils they seek to eradicate, with the best of intentions possible, and which they aim to eliminate during the battle; thus the 'politically committed fighters' either condemn themselves to a blind and therefore foolish fidelity, or, traitors, end up refusing the first ideals of their action. Conversely, I can burn within myself this violence, the refuse and discharge of the cesspool; I can, next, invite my neighbour … I invite you, you to whom I don't return any brutality, to the same operation, and, at least by example, I invite you to say and do so to your neighbour in turn, and so on. I'm not speaking to the collective or to humanity as to wholes, but only to my neighbour in detail, and to the neighbour of my neighbour through analytical extension. I only attain this gradual propagation from neighbour to neighbour.

Likewise, questions of scientific ethics are resolved less by decrees, general principles or collective decisions, always got around in the end, than by the individual oath, once again eminently local, I proposed at the end of the Preface to the *Dictionnaire des Sciences*.

Cheese and vaccine: On experience

The sowing of a certain rot on milk sometimes has a delicious result: cheese. Thus a certain cooking turns putrefaction to our advantage. Take this cheese or wine, the gift of the gods, as examples. Wash yourself, wash yourself well, don't wash yourself too much, and you will fall ill. Making the organism, skin and mucous membranes into axenic territories weakens them to point of exposing them to death.

Get yourself vaccinated; welcome the illness inside you in small doses so that some special defences will arise.[23] Experience violence in the playground, a reduced model; practise boxing, fencing, rugby, which contain violence in their rules; expose yourself to the miasmas of rainforests and mosquito-filled swamps; travel in space and across the social body; go to tragedy; don't be loath to frequent ghettos; consider power not to be the social pinnacle but its cesspool … . Experience fortifies: what doesn't kill makes stronger. Live with germs. Between the two prelapsarians, incandescent, Adam and Eve innocent before the sin, and humanity whitened and redeemed swarms the vast crowd with the greyish soul, us.

Another local solution: The two tolerances

Let's distinguish two tolerances. The first one, virtuous, welcomes differences: Aquitanian like Montesquieu, I stopped being astonished at my Persian friends long ago; left-handed, I live at ease under the right-handed law of the majority; at times in Bamako I considered the yellowish whiteness of my skin to be putrid; yes, it's best to move to the north, sunnier, in the southern hemisphere … Let's not exaggerate the difficulty of these senses: this is the *lectio facilis* of a tolerance to be translated by a few changes in our habits, whether climatic or cultural. Lots of inadaptation is necessary to miss this good middle meaning.

But physiology and medicine on the other hand define the aptitude of an organism to withstand without falling ill the sometimes brutal intervention of a chemical or physical agent whose noxiousness can weaken the immune system. So next to a tolerance of the other exists the tolerance of Ill, the *lectio difficilior* of this word. This corporal virtue seems fundamental to me. We never consider the other as an Ill if we acculturate the Ill as an other. As one of the others within me. As one of my symbionts. Failings, my twin brothers.

Moral experience

If moral precepts seem laughable, if the person preaching is irritating, for no one lives like an absolute angel, then vital experience matters eminently. When a philosopher tries to write a handbook of ethics, it would be better if he told some true short stories in which heroes or models brave the world as such positively. The foolish life doesn't expose itself; the good one puts itself in danger, like intelligence when it wants to invent. It dives into this experience, into this adventure, exceptional and everyday, in which destitution, suffering, failure, frustration, mistakes and sin itself teach us more than every other thing in the world.

One doesn't suppress ill, one frees oneself from it; proof that it has been experienced. Instead of killing microbes or malignant cells, therapeutics would do better by trying the techniques of symbiosis. One only proves oneself through one's trials. Substitute tribulations, difficult, for temptations, easy. Just as the sciences get out into the field, the moralist doesn't hesitate to, as they say, get to work in the coal mine.[24] He won't come back out all white. So he can burn. Don't listen to any preaching from anyone if you don't see any flames emanating from him, any incandescence.

The return to the collective

The law of large numbers of course shows the constancy of the accursed portion, of this ineliminable coal. Does a lower limit exist to this malicious gravity such that one can adapt evil or even, sometimes, as in the case of cheese or tragedy, culturize it into good or beautiful? This then is worth the trouble of working to achieve it. Like medicine, sociology as well defines, for a given community, a tolerance threshold regarding machinations dangerous to its perpetuation or its equilibrium. Now, there aren't any communities that don't experience a proportion of murderers or perverts. How many of them can a community tolerate at the maximum? They do indeed tolerate little Hitlers, despots and parasites, admen and administrators who soil them with ugliness and weigh them down with useless complications! Doesn't the best collective allow, inside it, the most risks possible? The best of all possible worlds then can be defined by this tolerance threshold. Just as the best of all lives exposes itself, the best of all societies opens the window of this threshold.

When, to resolve the question of Evil, Leibniz speaks about seventh chords, disharmonies whose rending lifts and doesn't diminish, through its divergence, the chords of the whole, he approximates musically my biochemical solution of the cheese. Making a virtue of necessity here consists in the acculturation of the ineradicable, in tolerance in the difficult sense. The entire work consists in maintaining evil within these limits of acculturation.

Experience in general

What I am calling here moral experience, as a non-violent and measured relationship to evil, quite simply resembles experience period, that experience one can have of life and of nature. For whatever praise you may hear, whatever love you may profess for the sea and mountains, the desert or marshes, plants and animals, nature doesn't behave as a friend to humans or even as their symbiont. By means of waves, fire, typhoons, poisoning or devouring, it kills as calmly as bodies fall and eagles eat lambs. It doesn't pardon any mistake.

The whole of human culture emerges from managing, as well and at the same time as those of men, the violence and devastation of nature. The recommendation to obey it in order to command it doesn't only govern scientific experimentation but holds good for the ceramic and glassmaking arts as well, gathering, hunting, fishing, technologies in general, agriculture, livestock farming, smithing, but also for medicine and lastly for morality; it holds good for experience in general. The whole of culture results from a patient, long, local and temporary management, from a comprehension and from negotiations that are as infinite as those I am recommending regarding the ineradicable accursed portion. You will suppress nature as little as you do it and suppress it as little as you do nature. However deeply your enclosure in the city and at home, in the middle of tried and proven defences, may be built, however aseptically and 'culturally' your life may unfold, the violence of the wind and of suffering always returns, through some partially open aperture, in one form or another at the same time as a third one, the one blown by human perversion. The whole of the habitat is therefore built at once and without cease. At the same time as culture, morality occurs, and with a similar movement. Of course, one doesn't protect oneself against disease the way one does against a storm, nor against a murderer the way one does against a cold snap, but culture is born from having prepared these defences at a stroke. It only emerges from this prudence, said to be characteristic of the father of the family, whose wisdom manages nature and its constraints, life and its morbid bacteria, humans and their violence; it is born from these voluntary symbioses.

The philosopher recommences building culture every day; he lives and only teaches by example this triple experience, this minimal solution to the problem of Evil.

The black box

To the demonstrable universality of Evil corresponds the vast generality, visible and experienced, of destitution on the Earth. Everything happens as though the variable vicissitudes of cultural, political and social histories were carrying, within their noisy medley of colours, a fixed and silent invariant, irreducible up to now, a brand by a red hot iron. For what group, what civilization, what moment in human time and what place in space haven't known those aggregates of slaves forced by their fellow creatures into the state of misery and destitution, a dizzying pit spiralling beneath them? What supposed democracy or science doesn't try today to make us forget this black box and this black hole? You can recognize our inhuman–human societies by this ignominious sign. Like migrants, our collectives traverse history transporting this box hidden under their bellies. A crime of humanity against humanity defines humanity. Would philosophy be worth an hour's trouble if it didn't open up the hope for a collective that would not murder a part of itself in this way?

The definition of humankind lies in this box and in this hole, both black therefore inaccessible under certain conditions. For they don't constitute ordinary objects. To know what happens inside them, you have to enter; not only open them from outside but go into them for a long time. Live there. Survive there. Have survived that death and that crime perpetrated by the collective as such.

In addition, this black box behaves like a black hole: the most swinish of men don't lay into the rich, too well protected, but burglarize, rape and exploit the poorest, without any defence. Irresistibly attracting gang-leaders, mafias, cowardly little tyrants, destitution lives in the worst violence. Punishing with the utmost severity the spineless wretches who attack those weaker than them would form the first article of a declaration of the duties of man. This article would apply to many people among the powerful.

The miserable[25]

Extermination camps or forced labour camps, prisons, shantytowns or favelas, heaping individuals together in extreme conditions strips the human condition down to the point where it appears as such without any addition or blindness: here is humankind as an individual, planed down, wounded, vaporized down to its essence; here is humankind as a collective, packed together to the point of density, both of them brought to incandescence by their short circuit.

The hospital, a factory with countless bodies, in robes, stretchers or wheelchairs, the foul-smelling dormitory of old secondary schools, the violent playground placed in the middle of the school, the crew's quarters where hammocks sway, the prison with its overcrowded cells, the overpopulated cities all pile up these heterogeneous heaps. A decisive experience: living in these cramped spaces, packed with incompatible differences, descending into these hells.

For forcing singularities as diverse as the animal species to associate in an impossible homogeneity amounts to cramming together wolves and lambs, lions and deer, rams, goats and bulls, amounts to creating a jungle in which the absence of law quickly drifts into maximal suffering and violence gone astray. This is one of the unspeakable pains of misery. For my singular suffering in the nursing home, my particular sentence in prison, my own intelligence in the schoolyard, my personal idea of war and peace while shipboard, my sleep and my inmost dreams in the dormitory differ from the others, and my body, in all, differs from my neighbour's body – to such an extent that the proximity necessitated by this piling together demands a heroism or a power of pity without which an infinite fall towards an excess of misery would ensue.

The piling together fires up, to the point of agonal conflict, the individual who, having thus emerged in a superacute way, collides with the generic. My face and my limbs, my hunger, my anxiety and my sorrow, my violence and my dreams, my odour and my excrement crash, as hard as can possibly be, into the large number. Here the inimitable individual and the common genus, two definitions, concrete and abstract, of man, are contradictorily assembled. For we exist as living beings or singular subjects, through body and perception, and yet at the same time exist as genus or species, recognizable and classifiable. Piling bodies together like this repudiates at the same time the two definitions, which telescope into each other in these places since the uniform pile represses the person, who is surprised at resembling so little, at often opposing, his fellow beings. But, conversely, he who suffers this misery experiences, the hard way, the necessity of the two definitions and the two dignities, the dignity of the singular as well as the dignity of the genus, both so cruelly repressed. An implicit experience, single and tragic, of the two human universals. Only this miserable wretch knows man itself. In addition, he knows the we, for seeing it from below. The miserable wretch knows sociology better than the sociologist knows misery.

Glory, wealth, science, power, politics, culture occult, with their softness, this fundamental knowledge misery experiences directly by razing them down. Consequently, misery has a metaphysical status, at least metahistoric, unknown to science and politics, cultures and powers, which have been set up since the beginning of the world in order to avoid its hardness, at least in order to protect themselves from it. How could they avoid blindness? Certain cultures lay stress on the individual; other ones do so on the group, invariably alone named human, but no culture, to my knowledge, pushes to understand at the same time and in the same place the thorny contradiction of individual singularity and the common genus. Only misery encounters this contradiction.

Gods and men

The process of hominescence develops a culture in which the continuous increase in life expectancy designates, at the limit horizon of this regular progress, a mythical hope of immortality. The perpetual banquet of consumerism, the ubiquity of virtual presence on the communication channels, the pharmacy of analgesics, a certain all-powerfulness in weak- or strong-energy technologies lead us to compare the exceptional Western inhabitants to the ancient gods of the Latins and the Hellenes. What the Greeks dreamt of, the end of the twentieth century did: we have just attained the polytheistic pantheon. Yet, this religion fabricated gods by means of bloody sacrifices. The perpetual crime perpetrated against the poor plus the daily representation of human sacrifice in the media, murders, wars, attacks and panics, accentuate the comparison to the point of identity; by fabricating gods every day from spilt blood, we return to the most archaic polytheism, which created divinities by means of these appalling rites. From the top of their mountain, they laughed uncontrollably at the mortals.

The division of society into classes and their struggle no longer suffice, and by far, to describe our collectives undergoing globalization. In the two preceding centuries, the adversaries defined by this division at least fought on a common terrain, that of labour and production, both today divided up differently. Between the West and the third and fourth worlds, the divide has now reached such dimensions that, to better understand them, we need to see this divide as the depths of the abyss dug by myths: the wealthy banquet on the summit of Olympus while those condemned to death wage war hand-to-hand; obese gods communicate at leisure in every point of space without losing any time and stuff themselves with ambrosial remedies against satiety while the vast crowd of mortals loses hope of living a few hours without starvation or suffering and in peace. The distance between these two worlds is measured according to new spaces, foreseen by the archaic theogonies.

Yet, the Greeks themselves had recognized that mortals and mortals alone possessed the secret of humanity, in other words, its essence. And that the gods had lost it. These Ancients therefore knew what we have forgotten, that between the destitution of the frailest condition and divine omnipotence, the human, without hesitation, joins with weakness and fragility. Perhaps, as well, they have revealed to us through this fable that collectives never write anything other than the history of the best, that they never depict anything other than the manners of those who live at altitude, but that the truth of our condition lies in the lowest valleys, where death and destitution torment human flesh. As soon as the gods stuff themselves without any hunger or thirst, as soon as they banish pain and death from themselves, men are no longer anywhere except in the third and fourth worlds, history and meaning are no longer anywhere except in them and for them. Just as, in narrow groups, humankind hides itself in barrels and shantytowns, through globalization, it conceals itself in the world, vastly in the majority, of the poorest. Having recently attained the summit of Mount Olympus, the gods have lost meaning, which now only comes from the black box of destitution, out of which an irrepressible plea arises, the authentic voice of the human. Beneath the table overloaded with delights, this box no longer receives even the crumbs from the banquet; on the contrary, the white tablecloth is loaded with imported dishes that the gods again take away from the mouths of the mortals. By ignoring this black hole, therefore by increasing its shadow, these immortals, without realizing it, fill the black hole of violence with explosives. Irritated, they are surprised when it thunders.

The two invisible hands

The black box remains so as long as no one opens it. The shepherd Gyges only became king by manipulating a ring that made him invisible; in other words, everyone is ignorant of the origin and foundation of power. Each of the three blind men of Compiègne think that one of the two others received the alms from the charitable and perfidious hand or rather from the mouth announcing the gift; in other words, everyone remains blind to the social bond or to what replaces it.[26] As old as the world, these stories show that forces only accessible with difficulty exist in the collective. Economic theories confirm these statements and myths: Adam Smith believes the hand that regulates and organizes the Market to be invisible. My images of the black box and black hole don't tell us much more than this unknown arm, which in turn doesn't know much more than this trio of blind men and this momentarily eclipsed shepherd-king. Something of the unknown remains in the collective.

The invisibility of this hand, which I have already talked about, allows everyone to refuse all responsibility; no one has the brain or arm that moves it. Who should we blame for the economic catastrophes sowing hunger among the destitute? Neither this one nor that other, rather global entities: Stock Exchange, Market, Money. Facing this active absence, the black box remains passive and dark; no one acts in it, no one controls it, so that it continuously preserves the same invisibility. Therefore it explodes unpredictably: terrorist acts are the perfect counterpart to the organ Adam Smith rightfully said was inaccessible to individuals. Equipped with invisible hands, the Market henceforth faces the black hole with invisible arms.

Formerly wars and conflicts, clear because declared, therefore legally well known, opposed defined and distinct nations or classes. Concepts of law and politics, these conflicts ended with armistices and treaties, texts also drawn up in legal terms. What new concept will permit thinking the opposition, for the time of lawlessness, of these two invisibilities, the fist of terrorism and the hand of the market?

Local solution, again

Up to now, Greek myth has been in operation: the gods impelled men to wage war on each other. From time to time, Athena or Poseidon would appear to the mortals in order for them to hate each other all the more; either the gigantomachia opposed the divinities, or, Greeks and Trojans, the mortals gave each other death. But any conflict, vertical, between immortals and mortals remained unthinkable. Today, torn to pieces at ground level, these latter hear the gods fly at the altitude of six thousand metres so as to sow a hail of bullets without any risk. The Greeks didn't follow their myths through to the end.

By a strange return, are we going to witness the end of modern polytheism, the second death of the gods? The previous centuries had put the one god of the monotheisms to death. Did they understood that, in doing so, they were reinstating the old pantheon of Olympic gods? For fifty years, drugged with ambrosia, we have been feasting the way these latter, they say, did. Are the starving mortals going to yank the tablecloth and overturn the table? Profound, is the history of religion going to catch up to common history, so superficial? This global end threatens us.

In order to avoid it, will we be able to erase this black stain under the bellies of groups someday? I don't know if there is a global solution to this problem, the worst of all. But I do know that the French language distinguishes *pauvreté, indigence* and *misère* [poverty, impoverishment and destitution]. The last one lacks food and habitat; the middle one is hungry but has a roof over its head. We must now share the first one; not wealth, abundant, but poverty, superabundant. Vast and rare wealth plus abounding destitution equals median and shared poverty. Modest and local, this solution will quickly become evident, in view of the figures. From today on, poverty will become an ethical virtue, a political necessity, the foundation of philosophy.

The preliminary work of uncovering

I called history and culture superficial. Let's dig more deeply. In the holes of mines, the public works department always begins open-pit mining with *la découverte* [excavation],[27] that is to say, the pushing by bulldozers, the extraction by cranes and the removal by truck of the plant or arable humus, of the fine sand, the tuff, the more or less thick mantle covering the ore: the profitable sand, rock or metal. In order to be ignorant of this meaning, yet common in work sites, dictionary authors must have failed to have driven the lifting machines characteristic of this work. When copper is hiding beneath rock and sand, the act of uncovering first removes these coverings.

Thus certain philosophers conduct undertakings they call radical. Descartes doubted everything, without any exception; Leibniz grasped the world at its root; Husserl undertook the phenomenological epoché. In undressing all things of their usual or deceitful appearances, in going back to a sort of pure origin that time would have stained, these good folk sought a secret hidden behind the décor the way gold prospectors rid nuggets of the gangue with which the stream, the soil and time have befouled them. What will I see, what will I think, what will I live, they say, when the real as such is unveiled beneath the uncovering and after it?

The aforementioned philosophers understood the necessity of such a preliminary work, in which a jet of compressed air or of acid dusts off these exterior layers before uncovering in truth the world, the others, thought.

Who does this in truth?

Now, difficult and most often painful, this tearing up takes place and no doubt only takes place in the extreme destitution that doesn't slip any soft mattress of money, glory, sweets or illusions between the body and the hardest things. Let's suspect these thinkers of never having had the courage, genuinely philosophical for once, to take a plunge jumped by Cynics and Franciscans. Diogenes in his barrel and Saint Francis, naked in the public square or in ecstasy in the Porziuncola, showed more uprightness [*loyauté*], understand by this word both the absence of lies and a certain legitimacy,[28] as far as radicality is concerned than Descartes, famous in the salons from a tender age and meditating nice and warm in his theatrical stove-warmed room, than Leibniz in his library and travelling all over the Europe of the great or some university professor repeated by his pressure groups and propagated through their pale little clones. Doubt, epoché, these radical undertakings certainly dissolve a few stupid customs but dispense with acts that really strip so as to keep in their possession clothes, food, lodging and social renown. As long as you haven't left behind the money that procures everything, called, for this reason, general equivalent, you have abandoned nothing. 'As long as you haven't given everything, you have given nothing.'[29]

Dressed in coarse wool and drinking water from streams, begging bread on the roads and passing for a good-for-nothing, without any fixed abode or residence, the Franciscan doesn't put on a semblance like us philosophers, who pretend to critique and to abandoning all semblance, for he rejoins the destitute one who, alone, sees men as such and the world itself, perceives the shadow of Alexander's glory even in full sunlight and understands clearly birdsong, wolf howls, clear water and the transcendent Word. The *Little Flowers* and its legendary animals reach meaning and truth more genuinely than the abovementioned *Meditations*, whether Cartesian or my own. Returning to the things themselves requires throwing one's shirt and shoes into the fire and departing towards them in this naked attire.

From this destitution, philosophy will be born.

THE UNIVERSAL

The Grand Narrative unfolds the universality of time or, more concretely, the time of the Universe. Certain places on the Earth conceal and show the marks of this global duration. Our bodys' dedifferation gives us access to the Universal. In a painting, a work, a culture, sometimes, a trace indicates its presence. I have just lamented the universality of evil.

Let's clarify the meaning of this repeated word, difficult to use, and which literally means: 'turned (*versus*) in such a way as to form a single (*unus*) whole'. A field of forces, a school of fish, a flock of ducks, a division of infantrymen head in the same direction, each element parallel to each of the others. Likewise, in a system state, everything is deduced from one principle. I think coherently or obsessively; my loves remain faithful.

There is also a distribution state in which the elements diverge: Brownian motion, a thunderstorm, the same school of fish hesitant or agitated, a flock of starlings, a panicked crowd, my scattered thoughts, your capricious feelings.

Look: the squall rises, rumbles, roars; pleated with short and then high waves and intersecting currents, the sea sparkles and varies under the angles of the sun's rays. This is the second of these states of affairs: moving, chaotic, multicoloured, traversed with a hundred murmurings. Absent breeze, the ocean – calm, without a ripple, leaden, translucent – reposes beneath the moon or the sun. This is the first state: white, stable, silent, incandescent.

What we call inert things, the sea, the Earth and the Universe, the sky and landscapes, time, living things, us and our history, cultures and knowledge, abstraction and experience, you, me and our souls, everything traverses these two states in an eddy. As does this book.

Vers [towards]: The root of the universal

Who exists before someone has said to him or her: 'I love you'? The other discovers in us powers we didn't think we possessed, as though he or she lived closer to us than we do to ourselves. Or: by addressing ourselves to another, we discover what, without this exit, we would have never known about ourselves. Lastly: have we ever discovered anything about ourselves in any other way? Yes, relation creates being.

Who am I? Why do we use, to say this, expressions like being-with or being-for? The prepositions alone, along with others, suffice, without the white verb that precedes them, to weave a network of meaning – spatial, temporal, mobile, original and fluctuating – a moving or incandescent state of affairs, which traverses and marks out the subject, sheds light on it and sets it ablaze. I add up *from* plus *to* plus *with* plus *by* and *for*, unite them and launch them in such a way that this moving combination, striped with flashes of meaning, characterizes our singularity; I equal *without-with-for-by*, in variable proportions and finenesses.

Not only do prepositions construct language by loading with signification the spatial and temporal meanings they designate, a little like the way rocks assemble a wall or atoms form inert or living objects, but these little elementary pieces of language, these atoms of signification make up subjects as well. When we say 'relation', we are needlessly substantivizing, we are abstracting the set of acts described or concretely carried out by: from, with, for … No doubt, relation creates being; but rather: prepositions create language, its meaning and the speaking subject.

Dereliction

It begins without. With the abandoned I.[30] White. It will finish in the same way, with a similar abandonment [*abandon*]. Someone, our mother or God Itself, nature or the species, someone we love beyond everything – who will name him or her? – gives us [*nous donne*], certainly, but gives us banishment [*nous donne le ban*], goodbye and freedom, solitude, in sum, abandonment. Gives us and abandons us. The without-I empties, barely born, entering into a struggle with death, surviving. Before and after all things, we think, act, write and sleep in the abiding pain of the without. I love that the English 'without' chooses to say that she or he with whom I would gladly live lives outside this hope of mine. I survive with absence, whether immanent or transcendent.[31] Before learning that we *vivons de* [live from], a phrase that's by far the most used in the French language, noble for this reason, we experience that we *survivons sans* [survive without]. And this abandonment suddenly designates the subject, hollowed out like a wound, pierced without edge, lacking relations, in the shape of a zero; without indicates the absence of all the other prepositions. Once again, indifference or deprogramming.

Conversation

So I love words like traverse or encounter that are formed simply from these prepositions.[32] Here's another one: multiplying conversions, when conversation turns vivacious, it follows along the vertigo and traverses of the exchange, including reversals, contradictions and even diverse or perverse overturnings [*bouleversements*] by nonsense, so as to finish, although rarely, by veering [*verser*] to the universal. As you may have noticed, this sentence varies on a single family of words, better, around their common root: *vers*. Like a flock of flying starlings, numerous but always united around variable and quickly undone poles, conversation unites (*cum* and *vers*) a multiplicity of attentive and voluble interlocutors, each one in turn taking on the role and function of centre.[33]

The Latin verb *vertere* signifies 'turning' or 'veering', 'changing', but also 'translating' sometimes. The French and English words[34] deriving from it designate a single direction (*avertir* [to warn], *vers* and adversary, noted by the Anglo-Latin *versus*), then its change (inversion, subversion, *versatile* [changeable], conversion), lastly every possible direction, from the diverse to the universal. Direction – spatial, temporal or semantic – is produced and organized, dispersed and concentrated, totalized or lost in conversation as well as in flocks of starlings.

Towards: The generation of direction

A vector equipped with its arrow and its angle of inclination towards the horizon, *vers* [towards] runs and turns, launches at the same time a translation and a rotation, races to the goal, in French, but by its Latin source, turns.[35] Heading in a direction but changing it at the same time seems contradictory at first. In geometry, here however are the coordinates called polar, in which directions are generated by change in direction, in which the wheel of direction produces every direction, as when a fan is opened. Here are again, but in grammar, two opposite forms, prose et verse [*vers*], whose etymology however comes from the same word, *pro-vorsus* and *versus*. Like a top, a gyroscopic compass maintains a heading the more fixedly the faster it turns.

Likewise, we say a line is vertical because, upright, it also becomes a rotational pivot in the horizontal plane; thus a vertebra erected by bearing and carriage allows the body to turn, to lean forward or to the side. A vector heads in a direction, but around it is organized a fan of vectors. It has a direction, but generates all of them. Two snakes coil around the caduceus' axis, one of Hermes' attributes; here is the straight direction of the running messenger, but it traverses the translator's tricks, the businessman's finesses and the thief's ruses. The DNA helix follows these two snakes. Do these examples, going from the formal to the real, from the inert to the living, from language to the things themselves, occupy or generate the Universe?

Voluble, the marquise starts subjects of conversation and, at the first trap, obstacle or silence, changes them with discretion and skill, develops another, delightfully unfolded but wrapped up or closed in all haste, depending. The conversation veers. A fan unfolds around the central speaker, in a sudden relation with everyone; but since, according to the repetitions and responses, this centre changes and varies, a thousand and one of these plumes fly, light, in the salon's volume. The starlings become concentrated here, then suddenly part so as to find themselves again around another bird; their flight pulses; do their chaotic movements hamper or help them to head swift-wingedly towards the end of their migration?

> 'Their instinct leads them to always to get closer to the center of the pack, whereas the speed of their flight incessantly carries them beyond; in such a way that this multitude of birds, thus united by a common tendency toward a magnetic point, incessantly coming and going, circling and crisscrossing in every direction, forms a kind of highly agitated eddy, whose entire mass, without following any very certain direction, seems to have a general motion of flowing around itself, a motion resulting from the particular circling movements belonging to each of its parts, and in which the center, perpetually tending to spread out, but incessantly compressed, pushed back by the opposing effort of the surrounding lines that weigh on it, is constantly packed tighter than any of these lines, which themselves are more and more so the closer they are to the center. Despite this singular way of eddying around, the starlings, with uncommon speed, don't cleave through the ambient air any the less and, with each second, perceptibly gain the goal of their pilgrimage'. (Lautréamont, Chants de Maldoror, Fifth Song, the beginning)

Changing the subject out of modesty or shyness, we move from idle digressions to prudent avoidances, but our conversation is blindly heading towards the strange attractor where our fate precedes us.

The conversation of philosophy

When Physics is born in Lucretius' text, the atoms fall in a close rain, from which certain ones deviate: the fall and angle's straight slope, the verticality of the water-pouring [*verseau*], the spillway [*déversoir*] of the waters, followed by the clinamen. From the two associated senses of the preposition *vers* comes the vortex, translation plus rotation, in and by which the elements collide, there, here and at uncertain times, almost at random; from this vertiginous turbulence are born the things themselves and, in total, the Universe, by changing dimensions. The genesis of the world via these eddies, inside of which scales transform, is derived in a parallel way from geometry, from fluid mechanics and from grammar: things appear in the same way as direction.

From this preposition, from the spatio-temporal situation it designates – positions and movements – from the varieties it draws – for inert atoms, the flying path of migratory birds and chatty marquises – from the variations and transformations it explains and describes, many things follow in the things themselves, life and discourse but also in the sciences and philosophy: conversion therefore *Translation*, Hermes' first profession; diversion therefore *Detachment*; warnings [*avertissements*] and *Signals*; water-pourings [*verseaux*] and multicoloured diversities, *Mixed Bodies*; this circles from *Communication* all the way to *Statues*: all stability, at least temporary – compass axis, living individual or species – retains an eddying motion combining both senses of *vers*, as though this turbulence had the effect of checking the flow of irreversible time and the increase of entropy the way a pocket of information or an island of negentropy would do. We live, exist and think like such pockets, manifestly perforated, like eddies that hold back, a little, time. Life and the subject appear the way direction and things do.

Freeze-frame: in order to simplify or stabilize the turbulence, whose movements follow laws as chaotic, unpredictable and determined as conversation, draw a highway interchange; drawn on a variety regulated by the preposition *vers*, this interchange heads and turns in three or four different directions via circular changes of direction in order lastly to ensure the perfect *Distribution* of a few of these directions, previously selected. This is how things are in general with every knot. Resumption of movement: mobilize, once again, these braids, loops, splices, and you will rediscover the eddies of flows, of living things, of flocks and conversations.

The moving whole, fan, folds and unfurlings, the integration, the sum of these towardses tends towards the Universal, just as the sunny totality of the various linear directions tends towards a smooth plane, the totality of the countless directions towards a volume, the totality of colours towards incandescence, the totality of prepositions, inclinations, inflections, declensions and conjugations towards a language, the whole of the sciences towards a Grand Narrative, the mosaic of cultures towards their geometral, all of the concrete towards abstraction: one of the two states of things I just distinguished at the start tends towards the other. But not much before this perfect totalization, before the Incandescent vibrates with every chromatic tone, arise both the route where the fringed direction never stops changing, as with the *Northwest Passage*, and the eddy, the turbulent mixture of a thousand and a thousand directions.

Like physical nature, and, better yet, the nature that wakes in the living, language hides changes of dimension in the turbulence that integrates many directions: from the small to the big or from the winged individual to the collective flock, and vice versa. Conversation turns like such an eddy, as though everyone in it was fired up to make the wheel of direction spin but also his role, site or position on this circle of fortune: the I, you, she and him pass into the we there amid the intense and rare emotions of the communal fusion, or conversely, the collective's small change explodes and expends itself there in pure noisy loss. We can get lost in this noise. We plunge into the turbulence of little atoms of direction so as to come out again reunited or separated: inversions, diversions, perversities, subversions ... the aforementioned dialectic of controversy between adversaries being cut out simplistically in the zone of this fluctuating network, like a particular situation which again repeats words derived from the same preposition; likewise the resolution of the volubility of directions into unity lets us enjoy, rarely, universal harmony.

This is a philosophy that understands Hegel and Leibniz to be singular cases, as these two latest limits, consequently better able to understand time, life and history than their own philosophies.

* * *

The process of philosophical abstraction is modelled on grammar or geometry. Plato, Descartes and Spinoza readily followed the rigorous proof of the latter, while Aristotle, for example, Hegel and Heidegger relied on language. These two ways diverged two thousand years ago.

To describe the diverse events of conversation, I have just used a fluctuating network, graph and chaotic process, both described by the invariable word: *vers*. The word preposition can be thought of as a synonym for situation – this is regarding grammar; and the phrase analysis situs formerly meant topology – this is regarding geometry. The two ways converge for language and in space. Let time bring them together, and life can appear.

I'm making use of this process of abstraction, which can be called topological and whose most important aspect consists in drawing non-metric varieties, here the network, or in describing situations on the basis of prepositions, 'towards' in this particular example. This last part of the method amounts to predicting and understanding every declension, in the sense of inflected languages, since the use of prepositions replaces cases in non-inflected languages. The usual process, by concepts, leads to a nominative or accusative abstraction, which only considers substantives – nouns or pronouns (ego, essence, existence ...) without any declensions or cases – in their subject or object functions alone or only considers verbs in the infinitive (being, becoming ...) without any conjugation and most often substantivized: traditional in philosophy, I now understand such abstraction to be a kind of telegraphic speech, to avoid the racist terms *petit-nègre* or pidgin[36] – this is regarding grammar; additionally, this idiom seriously mixes up the metric and the pure, measurement and abstraction, for geometry – this is regarding it – considers measurement to be equivalent to abstraction: usual in philosophy, it prides itself on an inflexible stiffness. Who would want to touch the piano after having put on boxing gloves? Better to play with bare hands, supplely.

Abstracting topologically lastly consists in taking these clumsy gloves off and even going beyond the piano keys, which cut the sounds up into arbitrary units, so as to plunge into a refined and continuous sonorous expanse; no longer being concerned about measurement, useless here, while redoubling concern for rigour, therefore losing all stiffness and speaking the entire language; declensions or inflections, well-named, at least in relation to stiffness, draw around the nominal situation an entire circumstantial or adverbial landscape, corollas that are variable, changing and as though metastable. So traditional abstraction would resemble an atomic table with atoms stripped of their valences, would resemble a statue without elasticity, an automaton without time, a machine without life.

The genitive and the dative – of, with and to – shed light on, for example, *parasitic* situations, and the ablative – by, starting from – can date *foundations*. Thus proliferate a thousand spatio-temporal situations different from those of for and against, a hundred positions far removed from power and subjection, logics different from those of belongingness; flexible and modal, philosophy finally embraces the real and the living.

The set of prepositions draws, in a space-time, the universal topological variety whose aspect guides my philosophy.[37]

* * *

Those who converse circle on a fluctuating network of channels connected by nodes or points that are variable and voluble; around these liquid centres labile arms bustle or vanish, the valences of the atoms being considered here; they resemble the fluctuating bayous of Louisiana; these sorts of dendrites meet in a thousand and a thousand variable synapses that form and fade with the passage of the messages. The point or node can be described as an I, a you, she or he, as though communication declined it or as though it conjugated communication: communication goes to him or her, dative; it comes from her or him, genitive or ablative; it goes through him, transitive, after or before her, future or past, across him, passive, with or against her, in front of or behind him, between him and her, without, except or according to him, as implied, for or in spite of her, always subject to the laws of substitution. Communication bends into a thousand loops, braids and lashings. In varying position, the subject fills up with prepositions. Well-named, prepositions precede and construct the subject's situations and found it.

This is a simple example, although the scene it describes is filled with folds, with what I call topological abstraction and with its marking out by mobile prepositions: I don't think I've left many of them out. Add to this near and in addition to for whispered communications or winks from afar, for the topology of the continuous, of the tear or of the neighbourhood, for the *parasite* or the new technologies, and all will be said. Consequently, does a universal exist other than the whole of the network described here in its fluctuations or than the space of situations indexed by prepositions?

How are we to describe the moving whole of these flexible situations without these inclinations, without the angles that turn around the punctual position and that, in transforming this position, end up defining it? The direction doesn't only depend on the situation, it gives the situation its position and its fluctuation in time. How are we to describe the circulation of the messages themselves without a sort of reversal that transforms points into paths and the latter into the former, as though the former subjects suddenly started circling rapidly around fixed messages, contents and markers, like skillful players around the flying ball they pass to one another? Thus certain bacteria evolve and adapt by exchanging fragments of their RNA. I send you my I; you transubstantiate me into you; they mix into us and into them. The way ek-sistence ruptures every position of equilibrium and of fixity, conversation throws subjects into mobility, exchanges and passages. It divides up our bodies and drinks our blood, transubstantiates them. Who flies? Each of the starlings, a subset of them, the entire swarm or the forces traversing the chaotic movement itself? Who, in the flock, can declare himself subject? None, each and all, by flashes and occultations.

As long as philosophy invents concepts, it constructs an infinitive and substantive language no one can speak without laughing. By recognizing the spaces and times conditioning the positions, it reconstructs, through these prepositions, a sayable language close to those real ones we speak. It reaches abstract knowledge of course but also immediate sensation, corporal behaviour, life itself, the things as such lastly. So it invents fewer concepts than personages: Hermes, the Parasite, the Hermaphrodite, the Educated-Third, Harlequin and Pierrot, Atlas, Angels and Dominations, all of them wandering in the landscapes of the world, the Hominescent, the Incandescent, which all have in common vibrating between the person and the symbol, combining the singular with the universal, eddying between the two states of things I distinguished at the start.

The pilot in his ship

Cyberneticists make the same mistake of simplification as the dialecticians when they reduce the art of piloting to a repeating spiral in which cause and effect are reversed. They must never have sailed. For the bow, keel and rudder blade of a ship plunge into a liquid chaos onto which the unexpected sows its surprises. No wave resembles the next, nor those preceding it, nor in strength, direction or height, nor by the blown fringe of its breaking. Each of them pounces on the quartermaster like a singular beast; mean, he said. The ship's position and speed, but also its angle and rocking, but the situation as well of the body leaning, gripping, attached to the helm but imposing its decisions on it depend of course on the previous gestures and on the past state of the sea; all this, of course, brings about the angle to be given, and the result becomes one of the conditions, if not the effect, the cause. But the unpredictable arises every time, disrupting this conditional. The sea doesn't just bump the left bow after the right bow but also the quarter, the stern, the topside, with varied force from a thousand different angles. During the crossing, the vessel never ceases to tip and turn.[38] It advances, rolls and pitches. None of these motions beat regularly. It's a matter of irregularly singular eddies or vortexes, chaotic all in all, like the weather we'll have and do have. So every position and angle of the helm will resemble the point around which the migratory birds temporarily assemble; they incessantly change points, the way the quartermaster invents the angle and position in real time to respond in real time to the locally summed up global demand of the moment. The turbulent data of nature enter into the eddy thus constructed. The starlings draw in a broad volume the diverse decisions the pilot makes in a more linear temporality, but the two distributions, in space and along a line, resemble each other. Does the curve of the electroencephalogram jump about in the same way? This is how the weather, inert, the sea, sneaky, the starlings, living, and thought, personal, move about. Thus I am drawing a fluctuating map of the self, an ocean Mlle de Scudéry had fixed, on the map of the Tender from her *Clélie*, on dry lands.

Flames and thought

Each sensation, a fleeting impression, each idea, temporary or profound, flits about like a single starling, nearing a provisional centre, moving away from it, returning towards another and leaving again, as independent and sometimes federated. What is called thinking? Living these rigorous and aleatory bird oscillations. Varying on the Latin *cogitare*, the French verb *agiter* describes the fluctuations from just now, the flock or conversation. I have already drawn this multiplicity of thought in *Éloge de la philosophie en langue française*. Yes, the *cogito* first describes the behaviour of multiple sheep, of assembled flocks (*cum*) and guided (*agere*) by the shepherd; numerous and moving, they in effect bustle about [*s'agitent*], occupying the mountainside in such a way that the outside observer who doesn't see the shepherd, hidden, can't really predict in which direction they will head.[39] He who truly thinks ends up at a surprising result. The profession of being a philosopher consists in telling oneself a story in the morning one didn't know the day before. *Cogitare*: no word says the activity of thinking better than this pastoral verb, except that ancient breeding practices assign a guide to it. In open-housed herding, where the fixed point varies chaotically, our sheep do without any shepherd; thus the Latin *agere* transforms into an *agitare*, single behaviour into an agitation in large numbers. A bird or a thought takes on at an unexpected time the first role or the reference so as to immediately lose this. Does the entire flock pounce on the central winged creature, here and now, as though on the sacrificial goat from just now? Sorry, I was dreaming. So whoever holds on to a stable centre is not so much thinking as becoming fixed in a true system or becoming frozen into an opinion. What is called thinking? Taking up this shepherdless chaos, resigning oneself to absence or stochastic presence, to the flickering of the subject. From the same family, the verb *ex-agere* engendered ten words of exaggeration or exactitude, among them the word *essaim* [swarm]. But again the bees fly and group themselves around a definitive, genetic and programmed queen. You are exaggerating if you believe some fixed position plays the role of subject. The multitude of flying thoughts only knows temporary programmes or schemas; we freeze-frame them by taking their picture at this or that moment: this then is called a piece of knowledge or a discovery, but also a stupidity, an opinion or a stubbornness. Let them go, and you will think anew. But who thinks? Which bee, absent, mobile, lone or plunged into the multiple, steers the swarm? Which subset, which well of moving thoughts? The living eddy, the flock itself, the network of fluctuating prepositions.

These fluctuations are seen in a burning hearth. I have described its flaming dance on page 84 of *Atlas*, using every preposition. The network of their sudden spatio-temporal bifurcations traverses the flashing and glimmering I. The *Incandescent* lives and thinks in these flames.

History

Let's generalize: who would deny that the history of humankind unfolds like this devouring blaze? Since we have only come to know history, at least vaguely, since the invention of writing, we see it, afterwards, densify around certain capitals, variable according to their power, wealth and cruelty or according to the happenstance of their position, like the temporarily central starling. I have in the past described the fate of Rome by means of the Brownian motion of termites. Ur, Karnak or Babylon, Athens or Constantinople, Paris, London or Washington attracted, from time to time, a few Western birds or insects, the others remaining indifferent to this sudden density. The word politics, come from the city, no doubt refers to these temporary concentrations. It takes a lot of optimism and naiveté to place them along a line and watch it progress towards the reign of the mind. For who will ever know why the turbulent winged creatures all of a sudden rush towards this or that part of the map of the world? Why, suddenly, what a few people call the news diverges from Argentina or Afghanistan, Tokyo or Sydney? Why the volume of the flock unites part of its effort towards some locality, as though the field of its forces was guiding some of its lines towards some pole? Quickly left for other ones, these centres suddenly believe themselves to be the masters, oblivious to the fact that this zone, denser in the vicinity, fluctuates quickly and that the guide or the middle of the global flock is lacking. Thus, a curtain of sparks traverses the subject who believes he directs the organization of my thoughts.

The stupidity of these temporary tyrants is measured, spatially, by the decentred position of the attractor they occupy in relation to the flock, and, according to time, by the capricious pulsation of its localization. Mastery and possession of the world reduces to diverse facts. Better: perverse. History then shows a constant: the direction of the global flock has nothing to do with the one who is attracting it, here and now, towards such-and-such a local attractor. We can't infer that direction, single and long-range, from any of the local attractors, fractal, the way we can't know where a chaotic curve is heading starting from one of its segments. Pull the thread of this thought: does this thread break, or does it lead of itself to a truth? Here are ten differential equations without any integral. Talking about the direction or the end of history, even perhaps talking about history, according to our always temporary, bifurcating and decentred experience, doesn't have any determinable meaning. Who thinks and observes outside the flock of history? God?

Likewise, can we predict far in advance why anticyclones group themselves around this or that centre and why depressions turn around here or there? Let's move from time to weather, from duration to climate: weather maps, once again, resemble these flocks in their global form, their turbulence, the mobile distribution of their poles and unpredictability. I have just transited twice from the I-bird to considering the flock: from singularity to historical time, first, and to the spatio-temporal world map of bad weather, next, therefore from the local to the global twice. I conclude with our incapacity, sometimes, to totalize in this way and to predict, in any case.

And yet, the migratory birds reach their destination. They would vanish by not arriving since they are going to make love, eat and reproduce over there. So are they guided by the Earth's magnetic field, the movement of the Sun, the layout of the stars? These hypotheses make them seem like sailors equipped with compasses and sextants. Yet, in the past, cod fishermen plotted their route to Newfoundland without any sophisticated gear or devices but rather by relying on colours, slaps of breeze and local ice. Forward.

Dances

The Aborigines dance the environment. Their positions and their wanderings are embodied in the gestures of their limbs and the modulations of their choirs; wouldn't you say that the map of this global space the whites named Australia connects or unites, tribe by tribe, the whole of their choreographic collectives? In each person and in these ballets is inscribed the memory of places and journeys. See, in every direction, the preposed bodies dance.

When the starlings eddy around a point so as to quickly leave it and assemble again in the vicinity of another, can I dream that in the absence of writing for the sake of remembering this, they too dance their environment, local niches, temporary stops, global map? If we knew how to decipher the fluctuations of their flock or our brothers' dances, we could read like an open book what we call and they don't name their hesitant and voluntary route, one plunged into the world map, and the network of their resting places. Our gazes are closed to these corporal and collective decodings by learning drawing and acquiring the habit of writing. Choreography ('politics', 'sociology' and 'geography' at muscle- and joint-level), by its gestures and positions, makes us go from here to elsewhere (therefore draws the map), from now to tomorrow (projects and remembers), and from the individual to the collective; choreography dances or flies over the space-time of prepositions. If I knew how to read the fluctuating dances of my flying thoughts, I would write with more honesty, more precision and more fully.

Diverse, we hesitate towards the universal. Our cogitations agitate towards the truth the way the birds flit about in a whirlwind towards their destination. They arrive there, since they survive, the way we sometimes reach the true. How are we to go towards the Universal?

Towards the Universal

How are we to dance together [*ensemble*]? By plunging or drowning among those who resemble us? This then is for grammar – it is indeed a matter of the same word; its repetition draws the flatness of a plane – this is for geometry. From the passion for belonging, merciless in its rigour – this is for logic – therefore from imitation, all the evil in the world and the crimes of history – this is for anthropology – are born. The crowd of the identical judge and kill the different. We never leave violence – this is for us humans. There is no prior method; intelligence suffices. Where do its tremblings lead?

Living together, with (*apud hoc*) others or next to them, presupposes passing through the same turbulence as Lucretius' atoms, Lautréamont's birds or the flying thoughts: leaving the parallelism and imitation of 'our own people', therefore inclining or experiencing, in uncertain times and places, a hundred inclinations for a thousand different objects. So we leave the rigorous disciplines I just cited. Living together therefore: incessantly passing, by changing positions, sites, movements or languages, from the neighbouring to the distant, from the close to the foreign, from the unknown to the familiar, from those who speak in elegant language to squawking barbarians, from hatred to love and from parasitism to exchange, experiencing the friendship of those you know well and the repulsion of those you meet by chance, an abstract and infinite fondness for those who are farthest away but a permanent resentment for those who live right nearby. The precept to love one another corrects the custom – unavoidable, delicious and cruel to the point of murder – of only loving those inside one's group, of never loving anyone but those who are the same, and the law of loving one's neighbour as oneself corrects the sublime theories that allow loving the human race universally while terrorizing those close by with one's loathing; and being able to live together begins with the generous attempt at self-love, even if who in truth it is a question of is only vaguely known. Poor dancers imitate the mobile gestures of their neighbours stupidly and only reproduce them with a mechanical stiffness, whereas those whose lightness almost leaves the ground let themselves go with the music, exterior to the ballet, so as to divinely encounter, different but attuned in rhythm, tempo and melodic profile, coryphées who are just as floating and sylphlike, carried by the same exterior harmonies.

Living together therefore requires keen hearing and a velvet touch regarding distance and nearness, extensions and ruptures, forgetting and memory, regarding the continuous and regarding tears, regarding separation and excessive familiarity, distance and proximity, silence or abandonment, all the displayed or secret splendours of what scientists call topology, the subtle science of the neighbourhood and intervals, of roads that are blocked off or that can be extended, of the open and the closed. Opening, certainly, one's arms, but in what direction, at what distance and for how long? Living together therefore presupposes without and with at the same time, attentive presence and frenzied distraction, active tenderness and abrupt ruptures in the same minute, piloting close to the wind, keeping a watch on the horizon, flying towards a centre of the flock and moving away from it at leisure, not taking your eyes off the mountain, the colour of this face and the jagged outline of those seracs, the sea and the iridescence downwind from some given waters, the insects and other species that surround you. The collective of men and the world of things. Engagement and detachment. While dancing, I find you again because I listen to nature. The outside, transcendence.

Living together sometimes creates great joys when the choir, bent beneath an unexpected inspiration, resumes this music in unison, with several voices, in several languages or dialects, in fugue or in canon, no matter, except that, suddenly, the noise flees and vanishes, except that the harmony merges and fuses the symphony of voices together: then God descends Itself into the midst of the faces and pacified hearts, or better, among the fused bodies, when the person who is close comes close all the way to the innermost of the innermost, and the first precept of loving God above all else corrects the unavoidable and vital, imbecilic and savage custom of only loving oneself; yes, we know God perfectly, God who transcends or follows this harmony of differences, makes it possible or is born from it, produces or is produced by it – who will ever know the secret of this genesis? – inspires us to it or composes it via a metre so scientific and so subtle it leads precisely the most distant into our vicinity and leads the neighbour so far away he enters into the bosom of God Himself, the beyond us, the creator of us and his little child, the Father, Son and Spirit of Love. Genitor, it creates Him, engendered, it is born of Him; and burns like a flame and bends our necks beneath its hurricane so as to give wisdom, intelligence, counsel, strength, science, fear and piety.[40] Improbable, rare, precious, fertile, unknown, unheard of since ordinarily buried beneath our noises, hidden because distorted, most often put to death, appearing in the glory of these joys.

Living together: the centre of this measureless whole lies everywhere and the circumference nowhere. Finally easy to understand, God's omnipresence – as well as his eternity – is clarified by the sum of the situations indicated by prepositions, a space into which, in particular, the we plunges. Always, everywhere, that is to say, at the infinite as well as in the vicinity, in the distances and in the site occupied by the neighbour, closed up in secrecy but travelling up and down the open, and also right away, if we really wanted, but in its death throes since the beginning of history and out of our reach all the way up to forever and ever.

Per ipsum et cum ipso et in ipso est tibi Deo patri omnipotenti in unitate spiritus sancti omnis honor et gloria, per omnia sæcula sæculorum: said three times, universal totality shoots up from the network of prepositions.[41]

* * *

And what if we lived and thought in the flames, the wind, the breath, the incandescent tongues of fire? And what if conversation celebrated the Pentecost's birthday, when – in extremely rare encounters – it attained harmony?

> They were all together in the same place. Suddenly a noise like that of a raging wind, coming from the sky, occurred, and it filled the house where they were sitting. And they saw tongues separating from each other, which were as of fire, and which set down on each of them. And they were all filled with the Holy Spirit, and they began to speak different languages, according as the Holy Spirit gave them this ability to express themselves. (Acts of the Apostles 2.1-4)

Listen now to all these Galileans speaking in tongues and therefore – oh, miracle – being understood by the Parthians and the Medes, Elamites, Mesopotamians, inhabitants of Judea or Cappadocia, of Pontus and Asia or coming from Phrygia and Pamphylia, from Egypt and Libya, foreigners from Cyrene, Romans, Jews and proselytes, Cretans and Arabs; what does this fusional mixture mean if not that, for these peoples stemming from twenty positions or sites on the portulan chart and from as many directions or angles on the compass rose, the distant comes near and the foreign neighbours, if not that measure and distance disappear – no more geometry or grammar – if not that the universal diversity converts?

Dazzling, shooting out, agitated, eddying, extinguished, rekindled, short, long, coruscating, close and distant, neighbouring and sometimes universal, these tongues set the incandescents afire.

Physical culture

The precession of human relations

Entirely given over to the pleasure of describing influences and rivalries between pressure groups, the admirable Saint-Simon excels at criticizing breaches in precedence. Exclusively plunged in the network of bickering and envy in which the conversation of marquises holds first rank amid Court dances, he doesn't leave the fluctuating turbulence into which we have just plunged ourselves. He never talks about the cold, the rain, the stars or vegetables. His *Memoirs* evokes nobles and the city, never the peasant sky.

I also don't know whether the Attic orators, the Roman rhetors or comic playwrights, Proust, Céline or Sartre had ever invited these natural things into their pages except as the setting for their vague schemes. The one only mentions the wind if it prevents the start of a combat, drowns out the sacrifice of a daughter or hinders returning to Ithaca; the other vomits on a chance root. Shaken by earthquakes, the orphan of a civilization swallowed up under a marine caldera, Ancient Greece expressed itself in a language in which the word volcano never appears; by this term, the Romans understood a god. The sea and climate are reduced to advantageous or restrictive parameters, and animals are divided into useful and pests, the most important thing remaining human relations. What is a good story and what, in the end, is History?[42] Avatars of these relations. With rare exceptions – the Aristotelians and Lucretius, La Fontaine, Montesquieu, Conrad or Giono – my culture ignores nature, even when it celebrates it as a lover or a harsh mother, this prosopopoeia expressing precisely this forgetfulness.

The difficulty of getting a Physics accepted by the Greek jurists of antiquity, of showing Niagara Falls yesterday to French intellectuals passing through, intoxicated with politics, of explaining today the greenhouse effect to rulers and philosophers shows that clarity in the social sciences often blinds to physical knowledge. I'm not unaware of the reverse blindness. Lasting like our history and ennobled by law, politics and high culture, the collective narcissism declares: 'In an assembly without any earth, in a city without any outside, the crowd and I live alone in the world.' It asks: 'What interests us?,' and answers: 'Our neighbors, our rivals, superiors and slaves. Since, having no intentions, it intervenes little in our affairs, the Universe is of no interest.' Acosmist, our culture ignores life and the things.

I care about making nature enter into culture. Traditionally hard, enslaved, indifferent, today nature is becoming, under the influence of our global actions, ally, threatening, symbiont, interesting. The I ignored it. I care about introducing a subject in which objects take part into philosophy. Here it is.

The 'subject' of this book

One doesn't make love like donkeys nor like crabs; one doesn't reproduce like algae. For each living thing, these behaviours depend on its species; so in this first sentence, I used 'one', indeterminate. More concretely, these women and these males, still deprived of proper names, are part of a group, speak a language, participate in a culture and therefore say of themselves instead: we. We, the Arapesh, don't live like they do, the Gascons, nor like you, the Ainu. Seen from even closer up, these good people became, fairly recently, individuals. Saint Paul says: 'I believe'; Descartes: 'I think'; my neighbour cries out: 'I suffer.' Here are three subjects: personal, social, biological. Me, the signatory of these lines, I write a language and am part of the human race.

When I say 'I think', 'I exist', I mix these first subjects. I wouldn't have signed the preceding pages if I didn't think their content was new. But I quite willingly admit that expressing myself in French gives me advantages and raises obstacles in front of me that I would meet with in a different way were I writing in Cantonese or Guarani. In me, behind me or next to me, language speaks as much as I do and inflects what I say with its singular obliquity. My ethnology, my culture, my social provenance, my parents' religion do so just as much: I wouldn't say this or that if birth, my adolescence or my training had torn me away from Gascony, from mathematics and the war so as to plunge me elsewhere, into another environment, different disciplines and other historical moments. Agriculture, inland water transportation, Christianity and the second world conflict write and think in my stead without me always realizing it. Next my university corporation and the scientific community impose their norms and a revolt on me such that I obligate myself to strict checking of documentation and syntax but try to make myself independent of their dreary format. Plus the circumstances, the trips, loves and attachments, encounters, happpenstances, in short, the temporal chaos of the vital adventure.

For a half a century, the social sciences have detailed Montaigne's changeable and diverse self and have honestly debated the respective statuses of the observer and observed; as a result, the social sciences plunge the subject into such conditions that they cloud its purity. With the help of the cognitive sciences, they mix the sharp ego, which Descartes compared to the fulcrum of a lever, with you's and thou's, in a floating ring, several them's, numerous we's, not counting several this's, the objective, biological and living body, gestures and genes, neurons and synapses, the unconscious, if it exists, language and the environment. Organism, company, social class, professional corporation, party or trade union, denomination, family, city, country, these identifiable subsets overlap each other in this fuzzy ring so that I have doubts about the original newness of what I think and say. Therefore a several-variabled function-subject exists.

Furthermore, the grammar rules of my language obligate me to a narcissus hierarchy: just as elsewhere the masculine prevails over the feminine, so, in number agreement, the first person prevails over the second person and these two over the third person: you and me, we like mustard; you and he, you go to the seaside.[43] Male chauvinism and vanity go hand in hand.

Trained to crush rocks from my childhood and for the sciences from adolescence, I humbly obey the injunction of things. I don't invent primary numbers or falling bodies; the bargeman doesn't produce the percolation of the flows. However cleverly some technician may take part in an experiment, however intelligent we may judge the creator of a method to be, the fact nevertheless remains that the object presents itself first, although at the limit, to intuitive attention and that an intention that doesn't lift it up to this dignity is of little worth except for letting one's mind wander, boasting or blowing hot air through loudspeakers. Whatever language may say, whatever rule may be imposed by grammar, I write what the things dictate; we think on their command; the community of scientists speaks under their control. Shamelessly I admit, we admit, they admit that in a way things think in our stead more effectively than my class, my family, my childhood or even my language in the preceding subjective equation. In things reside the best of my aids and of my thoughts. The objective equation commences and commands.

As familiarity with the aforesaid objects grows, several of their properties, as I've said, never fail to astonish whoever thinks that only human subjects devote themselves to thought. The wind forms waves on the sea as though it were a matter of lines on a page; the river traces its route along the thalweg and the glacier does so in the valley; the axis projects the exact latitude of a place onto its sundial; the stylus scarifies the wax, and the diamond point engraves its mark on the window pane. Let's not claim we alone write. Oil and water don't mix; bodies select partners for their combinations to the exclusion of other elements; crystals endowed with impurities rectify the direction of certain flows. The act of choosing doesn't concern us alone. Ice sheets, cliffs, radioactive bodies engram memories. Let's not claim we alone remember. In short, the things themselves, inert, as well as the living things exchange elements, energy and information, preserve this latter, spread it, select it. Let's not claim we alone devote ourselves to exchange. This writing, these decisions, these memory storages, these codings, among other examples, endow objects with quasi cognitive properties. 'It thinks' in the sense of 'it rains' exists as much as 'I think' or 'we think'.

Furthermore, a new subject of a troubling strangeness seems to have appeared today throughout the world. Polluting the seas, spewing effluents into the atmosphere, our global technologies are more or less intervening in the environment in such a way that the climate, the events of which didn't depend on us and were taken by our parents to be the very image of chance or fate, is starting to depend on us and so that, by a backlash, we depend on what is starting to depend on us. In other words, rainfall and temperature come from an inextricable mixture of laws and happenstances, of course, but no doubt also from acts for which we are responsible. So do you think that from now on we should say: 'we are raining' instead of 'it is raining', or 'one is hot' instead of 'it is hot'?[44] A new alloy of subjects, which doesn't go without saying.

Landscape

This book therefore has posed this problem of form to me: how should the verbs I use in it be conjugated and what subject should be attributed to them? For do I know what I owe to my species, to my cultural group, to those my life has visited, to my original language and to the languages I have learnt, to my work objects, to the landscapes and to the things of the world? Who am I, me who thinks? You, he, them, this, we, these things? Who can recognize himself in such a state, one where the clouds and rain mix with the neighbour and with oneself? What philosophy calls subject and what everyday language names man alloy, in variable finenesses, all these pronouns, whose declensions, I and me, you and you, he and him, fluctuate in time or space and according to circumstances.[45]

The question of the subject therefore not having any fixed answer, I didn't know how to write this book, grammatically speaking. Who wrote it? Me, I'm inclined to believe. But us, assuredly, so much do the subsets of my belongingness that I evoked just now plus the infinite and open set of my ignorance impel me. And 'one' just as well, so much do my two legs, my genitals, mouth and brain, skin and tears bring me closer to all those who, on this planet, admit to being human. Here is, in the first person, my subjective equation, without any determinate solution, without any defined integral. Moving around in a three-dimensional ball, the subject never finds anything but a fuzzy position there, sometimes closer to the I, sometimes closer to the 'one' or the we. But as soon as love – you, to whom these pages are addressed and without whom no one would have written them – work, knowledge, dialogues and the social bond cause, in the second and third persons, you, him and them to intervene, these others hold the pen just as much as the first ones do. The ball extends to several dimensions.

Plus another dimension, decisive, as soon as the objective equation of knowledge and work, once again, of perception, obstacles or ecstasy puts the ball of these 'subjects' into the presence of the things of the world, which write, decide, remember, exchange, taking up more than half of the aforementioned 'third person', which was formerly enslaved by language and philosophy. Are we living in a time when objects are attaining the dignity of subjects? I repeat: we are starting to depend on these things, which in the past didn't depend on us and which for several years have depended on us. Transmitting, active, quasi cognitive, they enter into this subject ball, into this pronominal landscape, into this moving state of affairs and thus pass from grammar to philosophy. Hence my problem of style and composition: since all these subjects overflow me or us in this multidimensional pronominal volume, I get lost in the conjugations.

Worse still, I no longer know how or where to place objects, former style, as well as subjects, former way, since they each sometimes play the role and function of the other. Fractal and fluid, the boundary between the world and me, us and things gets lost. If things write, exchange, decide and remember in some way, the murmuring of a *præ-cogitat* travels the Universe while, in parallel, I lose much of my consciousness and freedom in organic life, language and community. The subject falls asleep, the objects wake up. So when the world's background noise contributes to life, languages and societies so as to weaken the *cogito* in the first person, the old borders of the in itself and the for itself disappear.

The former philosophical and grammatical divisions melt, divisions whose unambiguous borders established clear-cut zones between the personal subject, the collectives, their languages, the living species, bodies and the things themselves, inert or abstract, and for which maps of the world, on which one recognized continents, oceans and nations, could provide a model. The landscape of this lost subject forms one of the subjects of this book.

Maps

How are we to see or describe the landscape of this new world? How are we to describe the subject of this book or the strange object it evokes? This new nature requires a different cartography.

It fluctuates between the noisy state and the other one, incandescent. So the reader has found, exhibited here, a few pictures whose composite chaos evokes this volume-landscape's muddled-up state: the crisscrossed, multiple and bifurcating bouquet of the time of the Grand Narrative, from which the Universe ensues and from which we come; the spectrum of mixed colours in Frenhofer's painting, *The Noisy Beauty*; a passport-chip that's even bushier than a thumbprint; cultures so porous that each one mixes and extends towards the others; foreign names declining several times the name Pan, the old god of panic and totalities; flocks of starlings twirling around so as to migrate towards distant shores ..., all of them mosaics in which elementary pieces can be distinguished that are nonetheless continuously exceeded by the design.

Pointillist and many-shaded, these map-landscapes resemble my soul, in which the I unites with you, her and him, with this place, this time, this group and this corner of the world, with us, you, them, with the weather, the plants, the animals, the surrounding objects, to the point of sometimes overflowing towards the global whole of the things of the Universe. Identity cards [*cartes d'identité*], of course, but at the same time cartographies of the world and of the Tender, without any division appearing between the objects we in the past threw into the world and the subjects we formerly withdrew from it.

Nothing is apprehended, neither me nor the world, neither life nor knowledge, without this leafy landscape, but also without the smooth state I just evoked, without the eddies uniting them. Who am I if not a set of operators that transform into each other? Vibrating therefore between these two landscapes, between these two states, incandescence and iridescence, this book draws white maps and historiated medleys of colour. The chaotic there tends towards the invariant and vice versa; silence tends towards background noise; the mutually encroaching signals melt away towards muteness; white there breaks down into the coloured, the multicoloured adds up into the translucent; the former goes towards the opaque, the fluid towards the solid, and the burning cools down. Either the continuous mixture renders its components – algorithmic and discontinuous – apparent, or it confuses them together into transparency. Do we attain the Universal in this way?

We are all destined to this universality, maximally full and as empty, at the limit, as the principle of identity. Without any surname, *Nemo-Panonym* bears every name in the world. What shall we name him? I just now convoked all the pronouns as well as, above, all the prepositions in order to account for our relations.[46] What am I called, what are you called, reader, if not this convoking of every subject, indistinct from every object in the Universe?

The fine arts

Here are some magnificent ones, universally liked: African masks, Homeric texts, statues of Buddha, Etruscan jewellery, Italian or Flemish paintings, Chinese scrolls, Saxon porcelain, Boulle furniture, musical scores …; the art venerated by the dominant cultures produces works in keeping with the canonical relation to the human, works which therefore celebrate the body, face, bearing, movements, and personal or collective relations as well as amorous, warring or festive ones. They sleep in museums, which preserve them.

Andy Goldsworthy conversely creates forms that are as close as possible to the flows generated by rivers, tides, breaths of air and liquid puddles. The work doesn't remain: leaves and petals sewn together descend the torrent while being twisted by the turbulence sent into spirals by the chaos of rocks sown in its winding bed; strands of fleece vibrate in the North wind at the top of low walls; a structure of small branches collapses and gets strewn about with the ebbing tide; a breezy gust carries off small interlaced branches or an aerosol of red particles. During the Enlightenment, Parisian marquises would deal with sublime fugacities in the art of conversation in this way; nothing remained of these fireworks. In the straight current of Western culture, these women of course followed the most refined human relations, but, precisely here, caused the most precious of them to vanish in the fluctuation of inspired moments. In diverging from this exclusively collective current, Andy Goldsworthy convokes the things themselves into these flutterings and perhaps rediscovers the objective and enduring intention of Celtic art, which constructed shaky cairns at the crossroads and gathered mistletoe in the branches of trees: before signifying war between priests, the golden bough exists, lives and grows, as such.

While armies were ravaging their country, the Flemish masters were painting landscapes and calm cows. Better, the blue stained-glass windows of the Chartres Cathedral or the red ones of the Bourges Cathedral make the refined skills of the chemist and the natural rays of the sun, dawns and dusks, collaborate in splendour; the nuclear star and the glass worker's furnace combine their flames in them. Does the stained-glass window reconstruct the chromatic range of the solar spectrum, or the does daystar detail the Bible, the Gospels and the lives of the saints?

Art joins the time, regular or turbulent, of the things themselves. Through a literally revolutionary thanking, the work designates them and accompanies them as works.

Physical culture

For a long time I have sought to construct a culture in which philosophy, also a work of art, would move away a little from the black hole, unavoidable and relatively stable, into which social relations attract, in order to rejoin, at the cost of an ill-understood effort, literally superhuman, the very formation of things, world time, the chaos of the planet, the quivering of living things, in short, our forgotten global habitat as well as its Grand Narrative. We live in the world; our life varies with the instants that make the hearts of animals vibrate and trees grow. Our duration beats the spatial night and the dense day, the floodtide and the low tide, the dry and rainy seasons, the ice that stiffens the courses of rivers and the plaintive debacle, the floods; our duration rejoins, in the silence of the organs, the Earth's billions of years. Our species dates from millions of years ago; our bodies, acts and affects also come from vastly distant sources.

Urban and political, polite and refined, our culture, short, forgets the physical world and the time of the living. By redressing and readdressing them, our culture obliterates them.[47] Not that nature, in turn, would have to forget culture, not that the animals, rocks and plants would have to supplant, by right and dignity, men and women – who ever wrote such a stupidity? why would one abuse supplant a symmetrical abuse? – but rather that men and women should at least consent to live with the former in a reciprocal symbiosis. A hundred major risks today invite us to such a contract. Therefore I am trying to construct a physical culture.

Thus I'm reconstructing the self, shot through with things. Here is another effort, selected from a difficult case: evolution or the processual. In descending the torrents that scatter, I'm trying to follow Goldsworthy's flows. How are we to think becoming?

Becoming

Our predecessors substituted a trajectory for it. Launched from here, a moving body arrived there, a few minutes later, along a line, its orbit, and without any notable transformation. Consequently, only the initial conditions mattered: depending on whether the launching took place here or there, at this or that moment, with this or that force, the projectile, inevitably, would have to behave in this or that way, barring a few minor bits of friction. The differential equations that described its course in effect revealed, after integration, that the moving body did behave in this manner. Whether it's a question of the classic systems of General Mechanics or even of the more recent chaos theory, these starting conditions always return. Hence the idea, spread all the way to the social sciences and now popular, that these conditions determine everything that follows: infrastructures, sociocultural origins, traumas from early childhood. But this only holds if becoming amounts to the ballistic trajectory of a solid. Who wouldn't judge such a presupposition to be simplistic? A technological process, the launching of a projectile by an artillery shot is substituted for the phenomenon to be described and, in a way, redresses it. No more flocks of starlings, a bomb. Once more, nature disappears behind culture.

So we have to go back over becoming. Assume a given state of a changing system; I shall make no hypothesis about its matter: whether solid or fluid, liquid or gaseous, living or cultural, social or linguistic, virtual, mythical or artistic is of no importance, subjective even. It changes, it evolves according to duration. The processual rarely follows a single line but rather develops in a space-time with several dimensions. It can encounter there a circumstance that makes it bifurcate: a hard barrier, a viscous tributary, electrical tension, heat, cold, a microbe, an unexpected obstacle or adjuvant, a transformation of the environment, the occasion the Greeks called *kairos*, a lightning strike, thunder or love, Cleopatra's nose. The circumstance in question restructures the current state. How?

Hard: Circumstance to the maximum

Here is an example whose two extreme edges I have experienced. Can you imagine a peasant's life before electricity went on, the winter nights without any candles, his gestures in the dark, his clothing in the cold, his wandering thoughts? No one has these long empty moments anymore. Do we live the same states of mind in the same society? How did society evolve?

Here it's only a matter of an isolated technological invention, the lamp. Add to this mononeism paved roads, cars, planes, refrigerators, telephones. Equipped with a culture, fixed in its traditions, a collective invents and at first receives the multiplicity of these innovations, this polyneism, without a single shudder, like a vessel being loaded. For several decades, France, for example, was covered with these new things while remaining Catholic and rural, secular and anticlerical, patriotic and devoted to cooking, patois and centralized, all the way up to the precise moment when, under the impact of a single new contribution, we didn't see which, the entire ship capsized, keel in the air: the stevedores had piled too many containers on its topside. Around 1970, we changed Frances. The aforementioned new things had surpassed the threshold of tolerance for the former culture and the old collective; everything had to be changed. The final circumstance matters little; another one can be imagined that could replace it; it suffices that, by its means, this cargo load exceeds the centre of gravity below which navigation is still possible; to transport a tiny additional bit of load, the cargo ship must be changed. We will no longer pilot in the same way a ship that's been entirely rebuilt, whose steadiness at sea we don't yet know. So the final circumstance restructures the whole of the hull, of the machines and tackle; I mean of the social body, customs, religion, politics, relationships, schedules. As the final event, this circumstance sways the decision because, completing a series above its maximum, it starts a completely different one, in a direction no one could predict. You might think a single fish, suddenly placed in the centre of the school, had made the decision. Thus, the circumstance merits its name: the edge of the circle it designates measures an extremum where stability totters.

The sea, ice sheets or certain glaciers show, in their evolutions, such threshold and time effects, sometimes high, such loading-response effects, as though this capacity for piling up before reversal designated a different – subjacent – memory. Thus the new thing, endowed with its forgetfulnesses, seems to occur all of a sudden. Yet subject to the same conditions of latitude and climate, why do Canada and Siberia stay free of the vast thickness of ice shown by Greenland? The physicists of the globe answer this question in such a subtle and composite way that I shall borrow precious models from them in order to understand how culture and history abound in cases that are so strongly differentiated.

Thus rocks abruptly break under the continuous fall and wearing away of an ancient water; thus cyclones howl after the calm; thus a stone thrown into cold water precipitates the crystallization of the pack ice or the solidification of the soul in love; thus winged creatures rise above reptiles; thus, on winter nights, our children drug themselves with fast and noisy electronic games, forgetful of themselves and of their bundled-up ancestor, alone in the cold darkness, pensive, silent, sometimes attentive to the voice of his soul.

Soft: The coded circumstance

The circumstance or the thing doesn't only cause, it also codes. Look: like a share from fate, you received some hand at birth, as with cards being dealt; if, during the game, a new card comes to you, one of two things results: either it brings you nothing new, or it transforms your mediocre hand into four aces. Thus, at every moment of your life, you receive or do not receive a new dealt card and, in the first case, the series of them that follows transforms your hand little by little to the point that the original hand becomes unrecognizable. You lose, you erase, life incessantly wears away and forgets the initial conditions. Assume again that you have a series of zeros; you encounter the number one; if it stands at the end, you don't win much; if it falls, on the contrary, at the beginning, you find yourself a millionaire. A single letter, a single number, the slightest coding completely changes the initial deal: you will no longer follow the same sequence nor read the same sentence. You have just changed childhoods; the conditions transform. By means of this rocking, minuscule sometimes, a cyclonic situation, a flooding by the Garonne or the Mississippi tip into catastrophe or lull; a new living species, fortune, true love, a resounding success or failure don't happen in any other way. The circumstance or the thing in question no longer appears as a cause, hard, but as a code, soft. The first one, heavy, weighs down; the second, weightless, indicates an address.

An example: during my maritime youth, at the time of the Cold War, trawlers from the East disembarked, before our eyes, at night, in the port of Djibouti, in order to affix a gigantic stamp on the parcels of food and medicine with which American freighters had flooded the wharfs free of charge; at dawn, the Somalis read on the crates: A gift from the Soviet people. The origin changed without the cargo being transformed. The circumstance I'm talking about imprints and codes in this way and thus changes the address, sender or recipient. Even if the state of the system doesn't vary much, the deviance of its address is often enough to render the previous state unrecognizable. And everything becomes reoriented. Some thing sent on the part of some person or other no longer passes for the same thing; thus the code, soft, transforms, without any force, the things in a different way but just as much as causes do, hard or endowed, for their part, with force. Did the maize from the Corn Belt seem to have a taste of the Ukraine to the Somalis?

In the becoming of the evolution of living things, the theory of bricolage seems less relevant to me than this change of codes or addresses. That fleshy tongue at the back of the thorax, the fold of which was used for thermal equilibrium, becomes readdressed as a wing under conditions where flight gives decisive advantages. Consequently, everyone forgets the former state, the first function, the origin: the exchange of heat. This holds for love, invention, the direction taken by the flock of starlings and so many other unexpected new things. Origins rock, oscillate, grope, stutter, remain at a standstill. According to the circumstances, the address hesitates.

Thus, after the catch of the hunt, I imagine we kept a few animals in order to offer them to the gods in sacrifice; the stay-at-home women then noticed that, fenced-in, certain species adapted better than others to their new habitat; so keeping, milking and sheering them improved food and clothing. Who, in the end, remembered the sacrificial origin of domestication once its function had become readdressed? Beneath this overcoding or this redressing, every bifurcation forgets its angle, its turning, therefore the previous state, its function, its pertinence, its use. Under way in a direction, we think, when we turn around, that we couldn't have come from another one. Depending on what happens in adolescence or in middle age, some misfortune undergone in childhood throws one into illness or becomes readdressed and redressed into a vital triumph. Who doesn't, depending, make a virtue out of necessity or a catastrophe out of advantage?

Tomorrow, your childhood

Thus the initial conditions, malleable at leisure, in their turn depend today on the *kairos* encountered, whose circumstance reorganizes the former state into a thousand strange and unpredictable profiles. In fact, the difficulty of reading the first state in return makes thinking becoming difficult, especially as, by turning around towards the past, what had in fact only presented itself as a contingent event that could have never occurred, over time rearranging a thousand times the series that follows it, suddenly transforms into a determined fate.

If then some seer, journalist or psychologist questions you as an adult or a sprightly old man about your childhood, answer boldly that you don't yet know what it will become tomorrow. Like the starlings and my flying thoughts, it ceaselessly rearranges its sequences, its wholes, overcodes its elements. You will only discover it in its truth at the moment it will no longer do you any good: at the point of death, when the past will exist, when the future will be nullified, when, for some, eternity will continue on. The beginning only exists at the end. All your life, the willings and chances taken merrily take charge of an old history they distort at leisure. You will have always had the youth you are suffering from today, that tomorrow you will decide, will deserve; you will have always had the misfortunes of your adventures and the tribulations of your luck. No determination stifles our incandescent present. It shimmers like the flow of a descending stream.

Words redress the things

Like the self and becoming, thus nature becomes acculturated and culture becomes naturalized. We reimprint them, each by the other. Do they redress each other?

Thus cooking codes wheat, corn, rice, grapes, hops, meats and transforms their flavour. History filters and colours the sea, the bird, the mountain and an insect called *farfalla*, *mariposa*, *Schmetterling*, *fluture*, *papillon* … without any common root, an extremely rare thing in the Indo-European zone, a nice butterfly effect across linguistic boundaries. Each culture, in all, makes nature bifurcate through the whole of these address changes. It codes it, affixing a thousand signs on to it. In addition, it never stops doing so. While using the same coded word, I don't designate or see the same river as Du Bartas, Montaigne, La Fontaine or Apollinaire. Here too, the initial conditions depend on circumstances to come. Cultivated, we lose nature the way we postpone our childhood till tomorrow.

Extremely effective, this coding leads to the forgetting described by this book, as you will remember, at its beginning. Once the phenomenon is imprinted, nothing more than the impression is seen or read. Has the self-attractive power of language ever been estimated? Its strength can't be exaggerated: it tends to refer only to itself. Consequently, language and text, in designating the thing itself, conceal it. Literally, they obliterate it. The sign self-references to its own functions. Advertising – that's all we see anymore – masks and soils the landscape; a story fascinates more told than lived and suffered through; a project fills with enthusiasm and its completion bores; the American dream inflames those who have never lived in the place; and in the planes flying over magnificent and divinely illuminated landscapes, passengers draw the window curtains shut so as to dull their minds in the dark in front of an idiotic movie, watching the distress of its images and hearing the inanity of its words, thus falling from on high into the pit of the figure[48] that no longer represents anything but the universe of figures and into the hole of words that no longer talk about anything but language. On the boxes of milk for sale in the supermarket, you can read the seller's brand and a thousand boastful lies about the product's excellence, and even sometimes search in vain for the word: milk. Speak, and some word always remains, stuck to the inextricable spider's web of words. So gestures, tastes, eloquence and dialogues fill the world and empty its things. Incarnate word, our body forgets its flesh. It took, at least, a God and science for us to remember it. Coded, obliterated of body, my granddaughter playing in front of the alpine-pastured farm and me riveted to the Narrative, we were misjudging our age. As self-attractive as their languages, cultures tend to close over themselves. Naming our states of mind causes states of language to be born and exist in the place of the emotions we are already experiencing less or no longer feel. Words spray an anaesthetic cloud over things and drug us to spare us the terror of the real. Armoured with language, our bodies advance into the world, dampened with ether and wrapped with bandages. Soft, words erase the hard thing's spines. Toxic, they wrap the thing with cotton. And humans get drunk on words.

Here is some strong proof of it: let this person and that person battle [*se battre*], and the arbiters will propose that they de-bate [*dé-battre*]. Impassioned, discussion quells the aggression of fists. The tribunal will no longer deal with anything but defence speeches and pronouncements. No, violence doesn't move into language, rather language anaesthetizes it. Language ought to be sold in drugstores. We invented it to cool down our pugnacity, therefore to avoid our eradication. We inhabit it so as not to catch cold, and we remain there among ourselves by putting the things between brackets with words. Here is some strong proof of it: in order to rediscover the world as such and the things themselves, we must go through another language, that of mathematics.

Educated in cosmology, the physics of the globe and biochemistry, who still perceives the world the way Michelet, Bergson or Heidegger did? If all culture, original, redresses nature and buries it, the sciences give it a common and direct address in universal language. Can a different culture arise from this? Will it be given the same name?

The second physical culture: Bioculture

The bacterial world

In the enterprise of making nature enter into culture, I have tried to reconstruct the subject, proposed rethinking becoming, discoursed on language. In addition, I am lucky: in the precise sense where life is born, living nature is entering today into knowledge, technology, morality and the universal anxiety. It is entering into culture.

Pasteur taught us that we were living with microbes, which were inhabiting us, living off us and sometimes killed us. After the 1950s, the first antibiotics cured certain infectious diseases. A temporary victory of course but so decisive in comparison to the powerlessness that preceded it that these curings and the weight of their triumph still today prevent us from thinking the event. For we must distinguish the history of medicine and the anthropology of the body from a different evolution, important in a different way. Here it is.

Ever since Van Leeuwenhoek and Swammerdam observed the bustling of spermatozoa and other single-celled organisms under the lenses of the first microscopes and ever since Pasteur, to mention him again, two centuries later, and then others after him, identified certain microbes as pathogenic agents, we have confused enemies and bacteria. Putting the 'harmful pests' [*nuisibles*] to death,[49] as was said in the schoolbooks of old, and returning so suddenly to health made us blind to the evident fact that we had in fact discovered a new kingdom of living creature, preceding even the plant, animal, mushroom and algal kingdoms, the vast bacterial world, the one archaic practices had vaguely reached with beer brewing and the practices of wine-making. Within this invisible and elementary world, a world older than any visible living thing by at least two billion years, 'useful' and 'harmful' are mixed, to the point that science puts this division into doubt. Now, and here is the point: whether we were using, for our delight, ferments or diastases, or conversely combatting *Mycobacterium tuberculosis* and *Treponema pallidum*, we were making this new kingdom of 'natural' living things enter into culture. So understand this latter word in the noble sense of philosophers as well as in the modest sense of cultivators and farmers; for profound thought, only the second one counts.

For agriculture and livestock farming exercise, with respect to certain plants and animal species selected in other kingdoms of living thing, the same operations as those engaged in by this new knowledge and this new practice. Here as there, it's a matter, as we have seen, of favouring the growth and development of certain varieties to the detriment of other ones. This ploughed plot protects the wheat from the weeds; this farmyard defends the hen from the fox and the lamb from the wolf: we separate the domestic in general from the wild species; likewise, the penicillin-sheepdog keeps off the pestiferous parasite. Hence the strange resemblance of the harrowed field, the wine press and medicine. From Pasteur to Fleming, we have therefore been witness to an event surpassing by far the merely historical victory of recovered health or the appearance of a new body, so as to reconnect with the very origin of agriculture even before history began. Just as back then species of flora and fauna entered into culture, in the two senses of this word, during the 1950s the bacterial kingdom entered into the human.

The first of these origins made our condition and even the condition of every living thing, whether affected by this invention or not, bifurcate globally. Wandering hunter-gathers who had become rural, we governed species on the basis of fixed farms. Dealing with this proliferating invisible thing, we have just lived through the beginning of a new agriculture. A farmer twice over, Pasteur took on the rank of the being the last agrarian scientist, in the tradition's sense, for dog slaver and pressed grapes, when he dealt with rabies and tartrates, but when he discovered microbes, he ranked as the first contemporary cultivator, archaic and revolutionary. After him, both therapies and agricultural implements have tended to be replaced by laboratories.

Bioculture

So the past century gave rise to the advent of a bioculture, understand by this word the sciences and practices of the living thing, all kingdoms taken together, visible and invisible, algae, mushrooms, plants, animals and bacteria. Now a single profession is being created, a variable one, which deals with life in general and for which naturalists, biochemists, doctors and peasants are becoming particular cases. In the past, we only knew and practised one part of this profession; life in its totality is entering into our action and our responsibility. Here is a new universal. Must we, again, call ourselves Panbiota?

Blinded by an unhoped-for solution to the problem of evil, we were only thinking curing in historical time, whereas an event of the order of hominization was in play. Adam had only named the visible living things; through agriculture or hunting, *sapiens* had only humanized certain of them. In generalizing this act to the totality of life, we are passing through the origin again. This event, literally founding, affects two of the oldest professions in the world, the peasant and the doctor, apparently divested of their traditional practices not only by financial, juridical or administrative parasites but especially by this evolutionary shock. The crisis in medicine therefore refers to an immense duration and thus accompanies the biggest event of the century, the end of traditional agriculture.

The new domestication

It's not merely a matter of this bacterial world's entry into 'culture'. We had up to now only domesticated a small part of the species of flora and fauna: dogs, wheat, sheep or guinea fowl. We still remained hunter-gathers of another part, no less small, hare, deer or boletuses, cod, herring and whales. We sometimes put the rest on show in zoos and botanical gardens. This picture remains valid up until the Second World War, before the hominescent movement.

Yet, at the very moment we were starting to negotiate, not without anxiety, the effective aid or the virulence of the bacterial world, another anxious movement concerning the survival of the other living things suddenly impelled us to want to manage them. Up until the nineteenth century, two driving components impelled biology forward: the one, utilitarian, sought to perfect agriculture and so fought against hunger; the other, more aesthetic, went from Buffon's style to the expression of the emotions in animals, according to Darwin's words. We have recently changed all that. We administer. At the very moment when we are no longer living anywhere but in cities, deeply ignorant of life, we are discovering its original dynamism and managing it.

We open up conservation parks said to be natural without admitting to ourselves that in supervising them we humanize them, by removing them from savagery, from the savagery of our fellows of course, but also from 'nature', I mean from life and the death implied by it; hence the increase in bears, elephants, deer and wolves as soon as we 'protect' them; we calculate the number of species missing from the classifications; we restrict net size; we impose fishing quotas, so much are the schools of cod, turtles and scallops dwindling; we leave the sperm whale, penguins and tigers alone, all endangered species; we prohibit going in search of ivory and pelts; we suspend observation posts in the canopies of tropical forests; we dive, practically naked like Cousteau or on board bathyscaphes, into the silence of the depths; we follow certain migratory birds crossing the Himalayas at the altitude of nine thousand metres; we know the exploitation plans of space on the part of ant colonies and the highways connecting them; we estimate biomasses … In another conflict between rich and poor, we oppose the global demands of conservation and the climate to hungry people.

A certain knowledge of itself has taken hold of the human species, which from now on recognizes itself to be *Homo populator*. At the same time as he is universalizing his relationship to living things, global man is becoming conscious of himself and his acts. He finally admits his rage; he rediscovers in prehistory vanished species he himself had already eradicated; he comes to a prudence that replaces the power fantasy; he little by little abolishes the death penalty with which he punished every genus; he no longer recognizes this sovereign right to slaughter; should he have to do so, he now has to justify himself; he therefore tries to behave like a *bonus pater familias*, who doesn't waste his house. While economics still impels him to the mastery and possession of the world, a certain ecology demands a mastery of this mastery.

Consequently, our relationship to living things is tending towards a horizon of universal integration. Just as geophysicists study the whole of the planet, so the sciences and politics of life are heading towards the total management of the living, towards their acculturation. Virtually every species is gradually becoming, if not domesticated, at least culturized: not only on the farm but in the parks and laboratories, in the game reserves and under the canopies, on the computer screens and via the conservation laws. Television images introduce venomous snakes and unpredictable bears into our living rooms. Oxen and hens used to sleep in the barn or the farmyard, sometimes close to the beds of our slumbering families; the lions and hyenas of the Ngorongoro, hunting gazelles, pass by in our dining rooms, where we travel all over the Australian Outback, with the dingoes and feral camels, where we brave strangely shaped reptiles and insects in the dry desert of Namibia.

Three events then contribute to this new bioculture: the consciousness, specific and new, of the exterminator; the project of administering all the species; lastly this virtual farm our house becomes. The Museum of Natural History's stuffed species multiply into the coloured forms hunting and copulating amid the pixels of our screens. The peasants who were filled with wonder during Cuvier's time before the skeletons of fossils have begotten grandchildren, forgetful of ploughing, but viewing on television Chilean condors and austral jellyfish.

So the habitat changed. From the day we saw our ship through the eyes of the cosmonauts, the whole of living things has commonly inhabited the vessel. The human species became conscious of itself at the same time as of its niche and its occupants. We inhabit their home, who inhabit ours, with a common destiny. There is no outside, for the moment at least, to this house where Darwinism is becoming culturized. Managing the biological diversity, protecting the endangered species, requires us to intervene in the struggle for life. Inventing agriculture and livestock farming even consisted in stopping this struggle since we separated the scrawny plants and animals from the strong predators that remained in the forest. Conserving nature changes nature. By cultivating it, do we denature it? Not only does it become human, but, once again, we tend to make it follow our laws. But our laws removed us from evolution. Are we going to extract ourselves from it entirely?

This then is what I call bioculture: the entry of every living thing into culture, that is, the humanization of all the species, from the sequence of acids, soon to be an 'artificial' medium for information, to the rhesus monkey, not long ago a test for blood groups. Divide and continuity, this bioculture generalizes agriculture: distant ancestors brought forth the latter; we are witnessing the beginning of the former, which completes it. I don't hail it as progress or as something to be feared: we can no longer do anything about it; our prehistory has brought us here.

The stem species enters into relation with every living thing

Why? Because, again, we are without programme, because one day we became a stem species, because we maintain an incandescent relation with life, because, genetically and virtually, we haunted the Universal and are little by little inhabiting it in fact. Everything happens as though we were – oh, paradox – carrying out our non-programme.

It's not a question of another kind of domination but of another kind of domestication, of a new symbiosis. *Hominescence* recalled our omnivorous ways and ran, from there, in reproduction and knowledge as well, towards a totipotency. Occupying this entire sphere of course changes the environment but transforms us just as much. Just as every living thing, little by little, becomes humanized, so we become, little by little, every living thing. *Hominescence* says that our bodies become a *biosom*, a body that's common to everything that lives. In other words, we become the subjects but also the objects of this bioculture. We weren't aware of it, but, composed of thousands of billions of cells, occupied by as many bacteria, taking on, in the embryonic state, forms resembling so much so many closely related living things, this bioculture had already invaded us. We realize it, in both senses of this verb, knowledge and act.

Bioculture and biotechnologies

The one always accompanying the other, culture is born at the same time as technology. Biotechnologies are part of this bioculture. In becoming acculturated, all living things enter into our practices. We change them, reinvent them and, by the same act, we become transformed; genetic engineering affects plants, animals, single-celled organisms as well as humans.

Generating fear, this dazzling new thing conceals its immense ancientness poorly. Just as, with the Pasteurian revolution or the arrival of penicillin, we caused the demographic balance sheets to climb vertically, so the domestication of cattle or wheat changed our dietary patterns, our customs, our bodies and our numbers. These living things, like us, changed life expectancy, health, weight, height and appearance. The recent mastery of the genotype has ensued from this successive managing of the phenotype.

These new bits of engineering have caught us unawares, but neither more nor less than any event in our chaotic Grand Narrative: bifurcations where the possible touches the impossible, and which are unpredictable before their emergence, but which, after their contingent appearance, come to necessity. Ever since we ploughed the pulsing boulbènes and set up stud farms, we ought to have thought that it would inevitably happen that we would one day transform the species and ourselves. It was enough to go from one of the operations of evolution to the other, from selection, which Darwin observed among livestock farmers before applying it to 'nature', to mutation, which we knew in 'nature' before practising it in the laboratory. We selected; we cause mutation. We hold both of evolution's operators in our hands. The changes in agriculture can to my eyes be thought of as the most important event of the twentieth century because they resume the inventive act of the Neolithic. Bioculture completes and finishes it for the universal of the living. The Neolithic is coming to completion today.

Auto-evolution or incarnation

Failures

Because we almost always find a living thing endowed with a quality we had been specifically attributing to ourselves, we doubt every definition of the human. We now say that man has no properties; I myself have recently said he has no faculties. A contemporary failure: negative philosophy or critique, having no risk, thus gives itself up to ease. Thinking remains difficult.

In addition, man changes so much that we can't settle on a definition, which he always exceeds or falls short of. Now, the direction of a movement is seen better when it bifurcates and inflects. Now again, we have just witnessed, these last fifty years, a transformation so important that observers haven't seen it. How did this metamorphic animal metamorphose during these recent times? In *Hominescence*, I told of the new death, a global one; a change of body in height, life expectancy, relation to pain; the end of the Neolithic for livestock farming and agriculture; biotechnologies that reduce duration scales; telecommunications and the relation to others in space and across time; I have added to this, here, the sharing and expansion of knowledge.

Humanity in the process of auto-evolution

Therefore a part of humanity has changed so much in a half-century that this leads one to believe the human is at least a capacity for rapid metamorphoses. While he hasn't changed genetically, his relation to the world, to his own body and to others has mutated. None of these transformations resulted from circumstances due to the environment, about which there was nothing we could have done. On the contrary, they came from processes that were economic and social, ultimately cognitive, from that collective understanding and collective will we call science.

Since the beginning of history, and as soon as we invented tools, we have in large part become the active subjects of our changes. By means of a self-perpetuating circle whose speed is accelerating, tools come from us and which we constantly change through exo-Darwinism, transform us in turn. In an era of bioculture, this affects us eminently.

How should we define the human? As a living thing in the process of an auto-evolution that's cultural and rational into the bargain. *Homo sapiens* seems to me to be less rational and richer than the evolution it seeks to produce. Nothing could be more 'natural' than evolution; we are evolving towards its acculturation. Man tends to transform his own evolutionary nature into culture or evolution's time into historical time. He goes towards his auto-incarnation.

Modern philosophy began with this precept from Bacon: 'commanding nature by obeying it'. Up until a recent time, this nature was limited to local inert things and the laws of physics. But nature, as I've said from the beginning, also means: 'in the nascent state'. We are beginning to cause the living to be born, soon to cause ourselves to be born, and to cause ourselves to survive in a global environment we give rise to: so nature takes on its third meaning, a global, meteorological and world one. So nature enters into the old precept twice, in the sense of the birth of living things and in the sense of totality. We are posing global questions today – concerning our influence on an environment that took millions of years to form – when our biotechnologies are trying to immediately master mutation which, left to itself, takes an unpredictable amount of time.

The age of incarnation

By thus projecting the Grand Narrative's gigantically long time onto our extremely short existence and history, through projected selection, mutation and environment, we are increasingly and rationally mastering the principle elements of a contingent evolution which, for billions of years, happened without us: this is why I claim humans are the only living thing running towards auto-evolution. By imitating the laws of evolution, we are attempting to master it. Once again, the Grand Narrative bifurcates. What, from Kant to Sartre, we called personal autonomy or the creation of oneself by oneself moves from morality to fate, from short time to long time, from the I, formal and abstract, to living flesh, from the individual to the world and to humanity: from history to evolution, from mind to incarnation.

Who can deny that this fate, long announced but newly appearing and now present to our vision of the world and especially to our practices, causes us anxiety or elates us, that it faces us with unexpected responsibilities whose scope shakes habits, moralities and religions, politics and timid philosophies, the social sciences lastly? We made it happen; let's confront it. No, we made ourselves happen, let's confront ourselves.

What are we afraid of? Of the human? Of ourselves?

Panorama

Who is afraid of this Universal in labour? We sometimes call it globalization. We fear living in a uniform space and a uniform time, human desert or human pack ice. To be sure, when strength imposes its singular exception on other cultures, it vaporizes the environment. But does the Universal reduce to this uniformity?

Here are a few counterexamples.

The inert universal produces the singular everywhere

At the summit of Irazú Volcano in Costa Rica, one of the most moving panoramas in the world is unveiled: on one side, the waters of the Pacific, where the El Niño current sometimes flows, on the other, the Gulf of Mexico or Caribbean Sea, two of the radiating cradles of world meteorology. Climate's chaotic turbulence, globally predictable and locally unpredictable, its tremendous variations in space and in short time (seasons, years, centuries) or long duration (thousands of years or millions of years) fluctuate on the basis of simple and universal laws of mechanics, physics and thermodynamics.

Nowhere on the Earth today does the weather repeat itself, everywhere different in space and always various across time. These local differences without any uniformity are produced by the global climate system. So there exists at least one universal model with highly singularized local variants; better still, a kind of global equilibrium across variations that are peaceful or catastrophic, cyclones and hurricanes.

Even though governed by a highly restricted number of laws, those for example of attraction and entropy, the inert Universe exploded, billions of years before the climate was born, into a luxurious marquetry that's far from the monotonous homogeneous. Contemplate the deep sky: black holes, quasars, neutron stars, spiral galaxies, red supergiants, yellow dwarves, suns ... populate it with a hundred and a thousand forms, colours, velocities, explosions and heats, all of them singular and differentiated. Nothing could be less uniform than the Universe.

What could be easier than distinguishing this mosaic Universal from the aforementioned globalization, an invasion of space (thereby rendered monotonous) by a strong particularism – a globalization hardly different from the old colonization.

The universality of living things and of their destructions

Here are other universal advances that are productive of a bursting forth of differences. As soon as an RNA formed, unicellular organisms exploded on the basis of a single code formed from only four elements and their combinations; with time, countless species, individuals and varieties appeared according to selections, mutations, climates and latitudes. A life with a universal code, the seat of transcription errors, spread everywhere on the surface of the Earth by adapting to local conditions and thus endured more than four billions years all the way up to today; its differentiated niches teem with lines, families and genera in which, even more than in climate, an iridescent mosaic of differences explodes. To this vast set of contingent emergences add five catastrophic circumstances – also universal for their part, and whose dates we know how to document – during which most living things disappeared. We find ourselves inheritors of explosions followed by eradications.

Stemming from the universality of the genetic code, nevertheless no species resembles any other, and every individual can be distinguished from its closest relative. Even twins, natural clones, can be differentiated.

Nature and culture: Waves of expansion

This is how the Grand Narrative goes on, from the inert to living things, from living things to the emergence of man. When, having left Africa, *Homo sapiens sapiens* crossed Suez, in several attempts no doubt, and bifurcated first towards Europe, to the west, and towards Asia, to the east, where they bifurcated a second time to invade Australia and a third time to cross into America by the Bering Strait, it accomplished its first occupation of the world. Few species, like its own or that of the mosquito, have adapted in this way and to every climate on the globe as well: *Homo universalis*. Whence the emergence of a thousand different cultures.

Universal for every living thing, microbes, algae, plants and animals, the genetic code includes the universality of human DNA. And yet no woman or man resembles any other. From the cut of the continents to the climate, from the night sky to delta swamps, from living species to human cultures, from these latter to individuals never does homogeneity or monotony make an appearance even though physical laws reign universally, as well as the genetic code for the whole of living things and the African unicity of the point of departure. These universals produce differences more than they erase them.

Narrative and declaration

If certain of our friends, formerly enslaved or colonized, are suspicious of universality, in particular of the universality of the rights of man, as of a new Western and imperialistic conquest, all the more pernicious for being concealed beneath abstract words, this fear comes less from rights or from man than from the Declaration. Like a bugle, a declared text departs from a blaring broadcast source: some particular group, puffed up with glory, declaims and signs it in order to get itself heard in every horizon.

Here, the Universal has its source in the Universe. Far from someone declaring it, it recites itself. No one recounts the Grand Narrative. The lead of meteorites, fallen from the sky at random, air turbulence, the aperiodic crystal buried in abundance in living things give themselves to be read.

Humans don't become universal of themselves, but by seeking evidence from the things of the world. Nature universalizes cultures.

Corn, wheat, sheep, oxen, fruit, vegetables and microbes

Having departed South America with the invention of corn, derived from teosinte, and from the Middle East with the invention of wheat; agriculture and then livestock farming, with the domestication of the sheep and the ox, became generalized; the only populations that didn't adopt them came up against insurmountable constraints; lacking grasses or mammals and especially ruminants, the Australian Aborigines for example couldn't practise this second occupation of the world. Today, more than nine-tenths of our food comes from agrarian practices. And yet no culture has the same table manners nor the same cuisine, nor above all the same tastes.

The later spread of fruits and vegetables saved populations from famine. Stemming from America, the potato feeds Scandinavia and Northern Europe, which used to be deprived of subsistence by their harsh winters. If Parisians today eat plums, cherries, tomatoes, citrus fruit, avocados and kiwis, come from everywhere else, they owe it to this third expansion. To *sapiens'* journeys are added the journeys of the species it transports, voluntarily or unbeknownst to it: spices, fruits, grains and germs, to its benefit or its detriment. The advance of herds and flocks was accompanied, it is said, by epidemics brought about by microbes carried by these newly domesticated animals.

Begun with our first travels and increased in fact by the transfer of animals in symbiosis with their breeders into different environments, this other, parallel, expansion, the expansion of microbes and diseases, still continues today. Invisible in the past and now well documented, their history teaches that the plague, spread by armies in the field or disembarked, with the rats, from ships, killed more than the bloody and boastful declared wars. The Romans conquered the world, I believe, because they inhabited foul swamps and transported miasmas everywhere which their organisms have resisted for generations; their enemies died more from infection than from their defeats before the lines of legions.

The non-globalization of writing

Here I need to enlarge upon a tragic digression regarding a subject that has already been evoked several times in this book. We don't know whether language came to us from 'nature' or from 'culture'. For my part, I lean towards a natural music, like the music of birds, linked to now recognized neurons, which was followed by a language that's articulated, learnt afterwards, then differentiated. As with the natural case of climate, there is a human system of language that produces locally the mosaic diversity of languages. Proof again that the Universal doesn't necessarily result in uniformity; only stupid force does this. The cousins who remained in Africa and the brothers who left it thus produced a vast and multiply coloured spectrum of cultures; from almost infinitely close DNA, phenotypes are produced in which beauty explodes and scatters; agriculture and livestock farming, universals, produce rural ways differentiated according to the climate and the species. If globalization is opposed to differences, the Universal on the contrary encourages them. But since we lack information and proof about the origin of language, I can't classify this process under the same occupation of the globe.

But with regard to writing, we know from experience that the majority of the languages spoken in the world today, having remained at the oral stage, haven't attained graphic technologies. I have no doubt that the Romans, around the Mediterranean, in Gaul or Great Britain, that the Spanish in the New World, that the French in Africa destroyed a hundred oral cultures with these instruments which ensured their domination, as many as today seem to be threatened by the new technologies through the same process. So when a few Western scholars decided to have history start with writing, they excluded from it these peoples deprived of any writing system, the most numerous on the planet. When they talk about the Assyrians, the Latins or the Renaissance figures, these scholars are doing history; but if other people than them describe the customs of the Arapesh or the Kwakiutl, these people are indulging in ethnology. This appalling division condemns us. A racist category, perhaps even the mother category of all racism, history therefore consecrates the written's failure to expand into the Universe. Attached to history, often as to our court of final appeal, we Westerners have to become aware of this primary apartheid in our ways of thinking. We expel without compunction the objects of ethnology or anthropology into reservations or specialties. All the more pernicious for being concealed beneath verified knowledge, this racism stems, quite precisely, from a lack of globalization! There is no history of everything. Local, history doesn't attain the universality of the Grand Narrative.

It would have been better to have had it start with the acquisition of technology: carved stones, copper or bronze, scrapers; these practices, like that of agriculture, spread without any difficulty, fourthly. No culture lacks tools. Those tools that write but don't plough or grind flour thus reserve for us – for us Westerners – the scandalous privilege of participating in a chronology that denies living as our contemporaries to the majority of humans.

Universal culture: The expansion of abstract science

Having departed from the Greeks and, to my knowledge, spread without any imperialism or bloodshed, geometry taught humanity for the first time – oh, marvel – universal truths. As differentiated as cultures may be said to be, as strong as language barriers may appear, as insincere as a subject may appear, no one can deny that the square of the hypotenuse equals the sum of the squares of the two other sides in the case of a right triangle. Thus, from Pythagoras and the sixth century BC on, without any weapons or money, without any dogma or power, rigorous science has spread, fifthly. Mathematics functions in every place as a universal language thrice over: it applies to everything in the world and allows access to laws, universal in turn, such as the law of attraction, or to constants, such as the constant of energy; it brings us all into agreement through demonstration's necessity; it lastly ensures that the message broadcast thousands of years ago remains the same as the one we transmit to our successors: thus I often ask myself whether there is truly any other history than the history of mathematics.

Three hardware universalizations, three software universalizations

Legend has it that the first coins were struck near the Pactolus River in Lydia, the kingdom of Midas. As for me, I don't know whether other regions invented them before the Lydians or at the same time. As soon as this general equivalent appeared, abstract in some way, it became universalized by often replacing the social bond. Starting five centuries before Jesus Christ, this final globalization fascinates us more than the other ones do no doubt because, voluntary slaves, we live under the reign of the infrastructures of Mammon.

The latter three expansions began at about the same time; writing, science and money were born together, say Western historians, in a little enclosure, amid the islands and shores of the eastern Mediterranean: Samos, Ephesus, Miletus, Knidos, Patmos. Invoked by Pythagoras the arithmetician, Thales the geometer, Heraclitus the Physicist, Eudoxus the Algebraist and Saint John the Evangelist, *logos* became universalized by being diversified into account and calculating, proof, reason, proportion, revelation, into thought in general.

These expansions are distinguished from the first three globalizations having to do with the entropic technologies of the inert and of life –

agriculture, livestock farming, fruits, animals and vegetables – the first expansions being material or hard(ware), the later ones logos-based and soft(ware).[50] It goes without saying that the logos-based software can, in return, organize the material hardware: knowledge and thought comprehend the Universe.

Hermes and the angels everywhere

More recent, does the expansion of the communication networks organize, synthesize and erase all the preceding expansions? For Hermes, an image of every transmission and one of the gods of Olympus, or the angels of the monotheisms, countless, get mixed up, as translators, in human relations and, as intermediaries, sponsor exchanges of every type and, parasites sometimes, pillage and steal, fallen.

An excellent image of networks: the Acadians call channels bayous. Why have another word for an ordinary thing? Because these waterways change: according to the season, the rainfall, the water level, they appear here or there, form, dry up, disappear. And following the spots where aquatic masses fall, they flow from left to right but can reverse their course. To the south of Lake Pontchartrain and towards the mouth of the Mississippi, said bayous therefore form an inextricable network that's stable and unstable, in all, metastable. Winds, breezes and hurricanes, the trickles of air in the atmosphere, transparent for their part, conceal a similar web, with variable beds, with reversible directions, with capricious intensities. Caught there or here, now or tomorrow, in an unexpected thunderstorm or flood, you find yourself safe or carried off. Turbulent and mixed, these two fluctuating fabrics therefore never present the same outline nor the same flow nor produce the same local configurations. And yet, a universal law of the equilibrium of fluids shapes them. Instead of imagining our modern messaging system as networks crossing roads or solid electric wires, images as false as spider webs, it would be better to think it according to these aerial or aqueous volubilities.

Have we truly opened or read the messages this system transports today? The expansion of what type of new knowledge are we witnessing today? Maybe we don't understand anything about the contemporary world because we lack an epistemology of this new expanded knowledge, which Pangnose spoke to us about earlier, a knowledge that's universal by right, at everyone's disposal, always and everywhere in principle, and yet variously concretized for each of us according to one's language.

An Indian from France talks to you about languages

I'm returning to it. My parents commonly spoke Occitan, particular and scorned in France, using it at the table, in the fields, at the fair, in their small business, without any need to go to the city, much less to Paris or abroad. During the First World War, an expression that shows, like it or not, the violence of globalization, infantrymen of the same patois were often grouped together by regiment.[51] A direct descendant of these peasants, my development took place in and through a local ethnology, a singular culture. Happily unaware of political correctness, my teacher taught me a more or less acceptable French, the language of communication across the provinces. Today in favour of regionalization, Parisians, politicians and administrators like to promote the vernaculars, of which they understand nary a word, even though these vernaculars no longer have the favour of the people; since this Gascon is only spoken in a small group of communes, it prohibits its speakers from travelling across the world, in knowledge and the social body. Learning all knowledge in Cantonese, Malay or Navajo would prohibit the Indians and the immigrants access to universities in the United States. Become counterproductive, political correctness isolates the weak and poor, prohibited from travel, in their weakness and poverty. This is one of the lessons of my life.

Conversely, the history of science shows ten changes in the languages of communication that allow exchanges of wealth, information and singularities. Without such languages, universals would lack any path and cultures would lack porosity. The Mediterranean spoke Greek since the Egyptians say pyramid and the Jews still meet in synagogues; then Latin spread into the cities and ports; next astronomers, doctors, algebraists and algorithmicians, even Iranians, wrote their sciences in Arabic; but Latin recovered and persisted up until the end of the nineteenth century; the classical ages of the seventeenth century were expressed in French; we all now speak some sort of English. The demographic decline of Westerners and the dynamism of Spanish or of the two Chineses, Mandarin and Cantonese, make predicting which language will be used tomorrow difficult.

Cultures and sciences of nature

The fact remains that one or several languages are necessary. Gaze again at the constellations. Admire the estival Sirius, Latin; the lovely Aldebaran, red Betelgeuse and blue Rigel, Arab; Antares and Arcturus, at the tail of Ursa

Major, Greek. Every language of communication in the history of science mixes in the firmament. Universal, the marquetry of celestial names teaches tolerance. It would be better of course to generalize this mosaic and also invite the Aztecs and the Bearnese into the vault of the night.

For how would sailors, aviators, shopkeepers, chemists and naturalists understand one another without a common decision about their idiolect? Some of them invented semaphore and signals, Morse or Scott, by dots and dashes, the way musical notation has notes and numeration numbers. Lavoisier, then Linnaeus and lastly Mendeleev proposed naming chemical molecules, the living things of flora and fauna, atoms lastly, without any risk of omission or repetition, common mistakes when you go no further than vernaculars: for who isn't aware that several terms are used, here and there, to designate the same fish and a single word, there and here, for several varieties of wild animal? Who now then, if he doesn't wish to make a mistake, rejects chlorides and tartrates, *Quercus robur* and *Canis latrans*, manganese and uranium? Like the language of mathematics, these languages of the inert and of the living are spoken universally. Do they hamper the gardeners, sailors, miners or hunters of every country in the world? They make exchange and occupation easy for them; they unite them without crushing them. If we failed in our attempts at Esperanto and Volapük, these vocabularies of physics, chemistry and natural history have succeeded in their passage to the Universal, even though, in every parish or on every small island, we continue to say wood pigeon or mahi-mahi.

Metre, gram, litre

So if you want to fight against said globalization, fight instead, it seems to me, against a particularism, the way of life of the most powerful. On to our voluntary servitude, these latter impose their money, a vision of the world and customs that are not widely followed. Today there are more English words on the walls of Paris than there were German words during the Occupation; no one forces the admen, the new collaborators, to post them up. We can fight against this new form of colonization with universality. It's not a matter of setting the local against the global but, quite the contrary, of fighting with the global against this local.

How would peasants, for example, go about selling and buying at the market without making use of weights and measures? For trading beyond one's commune, it would be better to standardize these units in space and time. Heir to the French Revolution, the metric system seems to me to be its most successful globalization. Many peoples in the world challenge human rights, the most recent fruit, they say, of European colonialism, but fewer and fewer nations oppose the metric system, fairly successfully universal. The more it is analysed, the more its qualities appear, referred to the objective and stable meridian of the world rather than to the variable and subjective sizes of the body. Its consistency and simplicity make inches and feet laughable;[52] as proof, the obligation American physicists find themselves in to adopt it in their research, even if it means returning, schizophrenic, to miles, gallons and ounces in their private lives. Everything happens as though, in order to invent a universal culture, nature itself entered into the different cultures.

How are we to define their exception, so much does their porosity live only by absorption? A man of culture goes beyond his own culture so as to cultivate himself abroad. Ought we to look down on the languages and arts of our neighbours? As long as exceptions confront globalization, the fight sets two particularisms against each other, the one strong, the other weak, the invader and the invaded. What's more, as far as these matters are concerned, fighting sterilizes creation. War sets the powerful only against the daily market of turkeys. Beauty, fragile, takes its time so as to spread alone, universally.

The Universal adapts to the scale; the uniform dies from it

The Universe via entropy, life via inadaptation, cultures via war, empires via the intention to dominate the world after their fashion, everything dies from uniformity. Consequently, beyond a certain size, the homogeneous crumbles and falls, unadapted to largeness and duration; the uniform doesn't hold up in space or persist in time.

Does this natural scale effect, in which a threshold forces inert and living systems, like the Universe, the climate and single-celled organisms, to differentiate themselves in order to be able to grow and last, also open on to the secret of the death of empires? In wanting to spread everywhere and repeat their particularism over a long time, they wear out, decline and disappear; the Napoleonic army collapsed on the other side of the Russian borders as did American power in Vietnam. Here is a structure of space that suddenly becomes a motor of historical time: in order to at least persist, the Universal promotes differences, far from erasing them. The famous saying: 'truth on this side of the Pyrenees, error on the other side' says less about differences than about the spatial distance that produces them; past the mountains, if the laws don't bifurcate, the Universal they imply collapses;

past the decade, if you don't change your customs, you will decline; past the century, if some culture doesn't budge, it becomes erased from the face of the Earth. In order to preserve itself, identity varies. This scale effect then accounts for the diversity of cultures. And for their universality.

Is there a more important principle to teach the powerful? Armed, the strong boast about spreading their peculiar ways to the farthest distances: masters in the morning but dead beat in the afternoon. The weak trust in the Universal, luxuriously varied across space and time.

A Universal that bridges nature and culture

To my knowledge, the first universal to bridge nature and culture appeared when Thales, travelling in Egypt, defined in his theorem a form that was invariant across variation of size. Enormous, the pyramid built by Khufu remains similar, that is to say, identical in respect to form, to the Pyramid of Menkaure, mediocre, to my body, small, or to a reduced model, tiny, that I can hold in my hand, all of them flanked by the shadows they cast. The Hellenic *logos* doesn't draw its incredible originality and its universality from the fact that it designates word or unveiling, standard things in every language and thereby variable, but from the fact that it defines these two simple fractions: in relation to five hundred million, a billion Euros behaves like two cents to one. So what do wealth, largeness and strength, better yet power and glory, matter in such a relation, one that, with regard to form, makes equivalent the small and the large, fortune and poverty, heaviness and lightness, the pharaoh lynched beneath this enormous lapidation and the poor fellah who cut one of these stones, the global occupying space and the local hidden behind the hedgerow? What a revolution! The first universal abstraction implies equality between men. This equality requires this abstraction.

Clever and trained in political lies, the Greeks invented democracy not in their assemblies, where their arrogance excluded women, slaves and metics, but in the geometric definition of this new relation which, like lightning, without bloodshed or the tragedy of death, became universalized.

4 THE GRAND NARRATIVE

CHRONOPEDIA

That was one of the most beautiful of the ancient wonders, and this is the contemporary wonder, integrating all the others, as though their sum or their synthesis. I will start this book again from its beginning. And try, anew, to go back up from my culture to nature, from the singular to the universal, by the contingent path of time. In the Grand Narrative, whose stages this overview has just gone back over anew but differently, who can conceive of a duration of fifteen billion years? From the accretion of the Earth or from the birth of living things up until this morning, a time stretches out that's incommensurable with my existence.

The closure of rhythms

At an unavowable age, I am returning from a short trip to the place I was born, two years after the death of my brother. Not a living soul bearing our name lives in the space where fields and roads have taken the place of the worksites traversed, once and formerly, by boats towards the bank and trucks towards the city, whose hellish noise informed everyone of the family business. Could you live there or take the road without us? For thirty kilometres around, the walls rose from the pride of our sand, and the lanes led over the sturdiness of our broken rocks. Silence now for the name, an empty house, tools that have dissolved into the ground and the weeds, did we even live here? Born at the end of the last century, my father risked his life and compromised his health in an appalling war whose stakes we don't even understand anymore and established a business, which has disappeared without a trace, on the banks of the Garonne; he rests beneath the land he loved in the company of a wife no one remembers anymore. Yet nothing has changed, not the lines of the gentle horizon, nor the paradoxical course of the river, nor the dark colour of the alluvia, nor the pink of the peach trees at the forefront of spring, nor the Gascon man with his brotherly features: despite a long absence, I recognize myself more than ever to have come from here. In this stable constancy, a period is coming to a close which didn't last.

I knew, as a child, an agriculture, a religiosity, a language: all three dead, and later a navy, a culture, ways of behaving: all three defunct. In sum, the murderous twentieth century went by in a blink of an eye. Farms with roofs caved in here and there, a few closed churches, sentences become incomprehensible, a disbanded family, this is what homecoming shows to melancholy; but elsewhere, the graveyards of rusting boats, the Greek and

Latin languages as lost as Occitan, the customs become absurd, one must have lived through the end of certain rhythms to reckon the interval they cadence to be almost nothing. If I add the life of my father to my short life, the unit of a century didn't last very long.

Measurement kills time

Modern agriculture, modern medicine and the modern recording media for information are closing other eras, thousands of years old for their part. Born in the Neolithic, livestock-farmed sheep and cultivated wheat launched hominization into the furrows and cowsheds the West is abandoning today; in pain ever since earthly paradise, the human body is changing due to effective remedies; the invention of writing already threw us into a virtuality we are inhabiting in our technologies. Genetic engineering is taking the place of the stud farm and the plant nursery; the screen is taking the place of the page. Other multi-millennial intervals are closing, other rhythms not lasting very long. That names and families have disappeared without a trace matters little; but the things themselves (tools, ploughs, boats and yokes), technical vocabularies and bodily gestures, in sum the relation to the world, the set of bonds to others and the deep and secret relationship to oneself have just melted into absence, thousands of years in a blink of an eye.

Since we measure time by recurrences, we only reckon its duration when these periods close. Having arrived there, these periods seem almost empty to us. Here is the sunset: What have I done with the day? The start of the year links up again with the preceding one, so short. At the death of this woman: Did I love her enough? When the final signature at the bottom of the work brings it to a close, at the return to the home town where the farm is crumbling, at the conjoint celebrations of the century and the millennium, before the scattered stones of an erased civilization, when GMOs appear at agriculture's end: all this ends so quickly.

So briefly that time is called the tick-tock of a clock, beating drums and the motion of the baton pointed by the conductor even though it passes between punctuations from which these muffled blows seem to expel it. Measurement kills time; timetables shorten life; in my empty city, my family has vanished; in the countryside where peach trees with modified genes are blossoming, the Neolithic has been brought to an end. Counting by centuries or millennia exhausts the intervals while only leaving their limits: consequently, I leap over the ladder of a scale I thought was inaccessible.

My perception inhabits the rhythm of the circadian light; my memory haunts the year or the century; then, I think with my neurons and my head. If my knowledge settles into the metabolic equilibrium of nutrition, therefore into the agrarian labours of crossbreeding species, in brief, if I think with my body, then I live at ease in the millennia, and the ruins of my old farm match their debris with the excavation of that Sumer which rose from the agricultural dawn; my muscles work with Gilgamesh, and my heart beats in company with Sarah, the wife of Abraham, the patriarch shepherd.

For these diverse rhythms, short or long is of no importance, say nothing about the nature of time but display a few of the units that measure it. We always confuse nature and the measurement of time. From cardiac beating to the length of the day, from my father's life to the wearing away of the building's framework, from the conquest of the wheat fields over the forest in the Fertile Crescent to the contemporary ending of this agriculture, I'm changing rhythms, that's all; but have I perceived the corresponding time? Nothing could be less certain since I force it to enter into periods, whose beginning and death I know, which I therefore dominate, which I master by metricizing and which I nullify in this way. Jumping from era to era or flying over the levels of a scale, I find myself at the beginning of a process of hominization that is coming to a close today.

Rhythmical measurement kills time. The duration separating the recurrence of the intervals lasts hardly the blink of an eye.

Memories and rhythms

And yet what do we remember when we manage to do so? We remember rhythms, for the processual rhesis traverses us and, in passing, surpasses us, without ever returning over itself or over us. This irreversibility doesn't heap up any treasure; on the contrary, a bank has to exist for this irreversibility to force it into spending. Because it always compels into spending. Only a fortune that has already been amassed can be squandered. Thus, memory can only become attached to the reversible, to the fold formed by these two opposites, face-to-face, loss and return, current and countercurrent, the expansion that flees and the light that returns, like a relic radiation, the colours with different vibrations of light in the spectrum, anticline and syncline, the folds of the proteins, the return of the prodigal son, the repetition, da capo, of our book and our loves, the vibration of singing, the eloquence of words, the secret poetry of prose, cadences. Newton's pseudo-time, reversible, follows a rhythm; it doesn't count the duration of a flowing but describes the vibrations of a planetary system which thus puts the brakes on the irreversible. Thus, like planets, the most anxious of us try to defer their fall towards death via a timetable that leaves one gasping for breath.

Memory bends and heaps up numbers and folds, puts treasures on an island and multiplicities in a bank, seeks a pocket, like a chromosome, and fills it with negentropy, draws an island which defends its shores from the mounting entropy, amounts to rhythms, formed from numbers, heaped, folded inside the pocket. All things, vibrating, thus contain memory because they vibrate, like the screw of the celestial vault to which the Ancients and Renaissance figures gave the name Helix, like the double helix of DNA. And, obstinate and relentless, the rhesis or flow spends these treasures, undoes these folds, opens these pockets, eats away at the shores of these islands: entropy wears negentropy away grain by grain.

The rhythms of the metabolism and the arrhythmic genome

When recounting that a sage, in prison for life, finally deciphers, in proximity to death, the message buried in the secret drawing that a jaguar is wearing on its coat, Borges doesn't go back up duration very far. Caressing the hairs of the fur, at the surface of a phenotype, he doesn't plunge deeply into its flesh or into the duration of life. Of course, the old man doesn't merely think with his neurons, he decodes the carnivore's ocellated coat body to body. I guess the name of this sage: Darwin, the first one to decipher the riddles written on the bones of animals and the expression of their emotions.

But, on the nether side of the selection that gave the jaguar its special finery, we now know that the writing of the god is hidden more deeply, in the folded depths of the genome, whose musical staff we know how to read. We are beginning to take the folded strands of DNA as temporal sounders. Human only for an extremely slight percentage, the genes squeezed into these nuclear pockets combine certain of the genes that made the bonobo and the jaguar, precisely, but also birds and reptiles, in short, Metazoa and, even further back, single-celled organisms; via this list lying in the nuclei of our cells, we enter into the arcana of long time and go back up evolution, all the way back to the birth of the first prokaryote more than four billion years ago.

But what does this word 'year' mean, equipped with this laughable annual rhythm, ineffective due to its brevity, almost harmful since it designates a periodic measurement? But the new sounder abandons all rhythm so as to enter arrhythmicity: by means of an alphabet simplified to the extreme, a long message is unfolded by the strands of DNA, a message in which not only is no temporal period shown but into which enter a thousand fragments devoid of any manifest meaning or use. And since I unite a body that lasts the blink of an eye and a sounder-germ which accumulates this colossal time, a short-rhythm phenotype and a genome, part of which goes back to the first bacteria and these latter to the first atoms, a metabolism that beats like a heart and a periodless bank, does my life compose superficial cycles suitable for the rhythmic measurement of time with a stock in which its nature lies?

Chromosomes, chrono-sums?

Formed from a string of notes seemingly drawn at random, our genome, aperiodic, therefore appears to pile up either into a specific and individual summary or into one of those profiles I called scenographic above, the geometral scale of living things. Thus, through the orchestral music expressed by all the particular staffs of our genes, I silently participate in the beings surrounding me, peasant women from my city, masons and fraternal long-distance truck drivers, the bulls of the cowshed and ducks of the farmyard, shad from Garonne, the pink peach trees of the plain, wheat, corn, tomatoes and kiwi, playing their singular instruments in unequal rhythm. All together and without any measure, we plunge into the same time.

Essential to life, this aperiodicity implicates[1] several of its properties: the specificity of each text combines, in a single interlacing, the originality of life itself, plus the originality of the species, lastly the originality of the individual; in addition, the instability implicated by the rupture of all symmetry launches a divergence from equilibrium, the very time of existence. For, conversely, period and symmetry contract duration by in the end erasing what they began; stabilizing its flowing, they dissolve it. Therefore if measuring time by rhythms consists in doing away with it, breaking them, on the contrary, launches it. We then find ourselves all together thrown into the adventure of time. I am entering here into a second memory, mysterious and almost contradictory, which no longer relies on recurrences. Aperiodic therefore and universal, the genetic code adds up, sums up, totalizes the time of the biota and makes the time of each of us appear. Banks or chronic sums, will we have to call chromosomes chrono-sums? Thus, our genome contains part of evolution, the well enveloped by a part of its unfolding, from which the community of everyone and the singularity of each of us emerge. We are beginning to understand the link that unites duration deeply with individuation, myself and this colossal flow I thought I would never be able to grasp.

Combinatorics contains the secret of irreversibility

Better, the place in which this long duration is implicated, dense and motionless, combines certain elements. If measuring time requires a rhythmics, does the nature of time lie in combinatorics?

I think so, for measurement always beats a reversible time, capable, at least formally, of returning over itself. The planets revolve around the Sun, as do the hands around the circumference of a watch; the heart pounds according to regular sine waves; I count the years, centuries and millennia on side-by-side wheels: without any notable change, all this can roll backwards. But if I arrange a large number of elements together, the probability that I will soon produce the same combination as before lowers to the vicinity of zero. The sequence of these states of affairs will only return over itself at the end of an unimaginable time. With each interlacement, an originality arises. Nothing beats or revolves anymore; everything becomes other and therefore changes and transforms: so the sequence of counts and time flees, irreversible. Combinatorics thus produces an arrow: the genome contains time, endowed with its direction.

When I think or remember with my brain, I blink in fast rhythms; when I think and remember with my body, this latter slows them down; but in both cases, I do so within the very inside of periods and therefore can only attain a measurement, as in the sciences and sometimes with philosophers: all these measurements, periods or rhythms remain reversible, independent of direction, invariant if it goes in the opposite direction. But if I think in and by chromosomes, genes and DNA, I discover not a chronometer – this tool would still be used for a metrics and reversibility – but the good sounder by which I penetrate into the very nature of time, into its irreversibility, the one we always forget about.

So I rebound onto another scale. Cut up into atomic elements, dating from the formation of the world, from the big bang if it ever existed, my genome's staff combines, associates and weaves them together so as to launch other individuals locally, as unforeseeable as I am. Via these elementary notes, the musical notation of every score, I silently participate in the water of the oceans we left in an archaic form, in Garonne's currents from which I emerged long ago – when my mother was pregnant with me, she was saved from a spring flood by my bargeman father's boat – in the breaths of air I inhale, in the land that nourishes the irritable bulls and the pink peach trees, in the sand and gravel stemming from the family business and the Paleozoic Era, in the very hydrogen of the Universe, in matter, in light, in the initial fire. All of them compounds that sing, together and without any measure, disharmony and the forgetfulnesses of the world.

But this shaky harmony unfolds according to individuated combinations that are always different and therefore launches a global contingency. What is contingency? This unfolding of the irreversible, this production of singularities by the combinatory bank of time. Long ago Leibniz staged the understanding of God before the creation of the world. This strange 'organ' also contained possibilities in the form of elements. So, from time immemorial, God calculated: He combined these sorts of atoms. From each operation a world emerged. All of them were different from each other since one of these arrangements can only be repeated with an infinitely small probability. Among them, He chose the best. No, the inspired philosopher didn't claim to have slipped into the Creator's deliberations before the *fiat* that gave existence to beings and things; he merely anticipated the combinatory operations whose laws he had discovered and whose detail we are deciphering today in the nuclei of cells. What's more, by combining atoms and worlds, God created time, singularity by singularity. He created it contingently since another world could have been chosen. How can contingency and creation be brought into opposition today, two ideas that presuppose one another? Likewise, from the random arrangement of the molecular alphabet contained in DNA are born, with as many restrictions as you might like, organisms that are so diverse that their sequence follows an irreversible time; from this bank, singular times emerge by free association of elements. The old Leibnizian operation remains true for the Universe as well as for every living thing. The irreversibility of individual existence and the contingency of evolutionary time are born of combinatorics. Whose algebra or topology undoes or constructs, in effect, singularities by numbers and folds, resolving the secret that complexity, a simple word repeating folds and numbers, seems to contain. Elements and permutations form the well, the bank, the stock where time accumulates in irreversible sequences from which sometimes unfold, according to such-and-such arrangements, permutations, combinations, diverse states of affairs, always different: the physics and chemistry of the world and life.

Life links the reversibility and the irreversibility of time

Composed therefore of bodies and germs, the living thing unites the diverse phenotypic, metabolic and organic rhythms which measure time and the folded or piled aperiodic combinations hiding and unveiling its nature: rhythms plus duration, periods plus processual, reversibility plus irreversibility, measurement plus nature, memory plus forgetfulness. Again a white map on top of another – mixed – one.

What is life? The unification of a universal bank of time and the diverse reversibilities that spend its small change. By flashes and occultations, the bank of issue, microscopic and colossal, launches these strange masses into the visible, masses that burn a time which their diverse rhythms empty and destroy while the same bank jealously guards this time, a bank reproduced in its dense folds and sliding from rhythm to rhythm, silently. The nature of time produces its rhythms, therefore its measurement, therefore its spending and nullification. Through this process, our existences enter into constricted pockets in which the birth and death of the individual, the family, the city, the millennial era, the million-year-old species succeed one another in the appearance of an almost infinitely brief flash. What we take to be time and remember – work hours, the years of schooling, fleeting life and its tendernesses without hope, the short centuries and rapid civilizations, all periods during which certain states of affairs, a hidden thought, a secret love, a humble work, a visible feat, a bloody empire, traditional agriculture, ocellated fur, life and the Earth are invented, flourish and die – amounts, on the contrary, to appearances in space of a few brief symmetrical equilibria, of a few fulgurant reversibilities.

Yes, life suddenly leaves – why? sometimes out of love – the hidden sequence in which time is coiled up and launches a measurable avatar of it into the deadly entropic fall; in that case, circular beatings, periods, measurements and cycles try to slow this descent towards pure disorder as much as possible; thus strings of eddies return over themselves and create virtually stable forms across the flaming current, behind the bridge support, as though the water was delaying its course, as though the turbulence was putting off the inevitable; thus, the *clinamen* appears in the atomic rain and generates rhythms, still falling, but less so. These spirals, the measurement of time, the rhythms of music and language delay death. The time of life, the time that is forgotten in the interval of returns and cycles, slows, checks, hinders, brakes, decelerates, diverts, shifts back the entropy debacle. We stand about, procrastinate, ask for a delay while zigzagging like a ball alternately hitting two walls facing each other, two days, two years or two billion, two heartbeats or bats of an eyelash, descending to the valley, alternately grabbing handholds and footholds. Life gives alternating support in a dihedral with two facing sides thanks to which we defer falling. This rhythmic constriction delays our death. Thus timetables lengthen life as much as they ravage it. Slow it while destroying it.

What is life? These rhythmic measurements emanating from an ever-present well from which an aperiodic painting stripped of all meaning springs up. What is my life? A meaningful text, formed of books, sentences and words that, all three, begin and end, but are all three constructed from an alphabet thrown into disorder in this well. Yes, these very lines you are reading, reader, this little bit of music you will forget; this thought that seizes me upon my homecoming and will leave me. Who are we? What is our life? A rare music heading towards silence but which rises, irresistible, rhythmical, cantabile, allegro, presto, lento, triste, over an irrepressible background noise.

So eternity appears, fragile and stable, in a fulgurant phenomenal brilliance, a point held like a song – your beauty, the intuition of this dawn, luminous all three of them, the bull and the jaguar, the rooster and the pink peach trees, the granite rocks rolled in the turbulent tumult of the River Garonne and which I knew how to break in the past, these few scattered sentences, individuals, varieties, thrown into the stance, the minute, day, year, century or eras – whereas time sleeps, rolled up, folded, in a pile, as though embryonated in aperiodic sets of elements, genes and atoms deep within our bodies. Neglecting this piled-up time, kept in secrecy in these banks, we frugally live an eternity that we experience, joyful, dancing, playing according to rhythms and measures, in the brief equilibrium of our hearts, of our flesh and of the world and sometimes in the symmetry of a palindromic name.

A combiner, God plays contingent time with numbered dice. Sparkling with eternity, laughing, we shake these dice in our pockets, in cadence.

Once again, the Grand Narrative

Da capo: therefore ever since the big bang, for its part again, if it ever existed, began to construct the first atoms inert and living things are composed of; ever since the planets cooled and our Earth became a reservoir of the material, heavier still, from which our tissues and bones are formed; ever since a strange acid molecule began, four billion years ago, to replicate itself as it was, then to change by mutating; ever since the first living things began to colonize the face of the Earth by constantly evolving, leaving behind them more extinct species than we will ever know of contemporary ones; ever since a young girl, called Lucy, started to stand up in the savannah of East Africa, promising without realizing it the explosive journeys of the coming humanity into the totality of the emerged continents, into contingent and divergent cultures and languages; ever since a few tribes from South America and the Middle East invented the cultivation of corn or wheat, not to forget the worthy patriarch who planted the grapevine or the Indian hero who brewed beer, thus domesticating for the first time living things as tiny as yeast; ever since writing was in its infancy and certain tribes began to write verse in the Greek or Italic languages, then the common trunk of the grandest narrative began to grow, before our eyes, so as to give an unexpected, real and common, chronic thickness to a humanism finally worthy of the name since precisely all the languages and cultures that came from it can finally participate in it, a humanism that's single and universal since written in the encyclopedic language of all the sciences and since it can be translated into every vernacular, without particularism or imperialism.

The mosaic of cultures

But I understand you: nothing in this long epic consoles us or will protect us from not understanding one another because we don't speak the same languages, from hating one another because we don't practise the same religions, from exploiting one another so that those who don't live at the same economic levels lack defence, from persecuting one another because we don't have the same forms of government … Thus nothing can prevent us from murdering one another for all these reasons. I understand you, and you are right. Even worse, the old culture, which certain people mourn, yet founded on the horror of the Trojan War or the ban on human sacrifice under the fist of Abraham, the father of the monotheisms, has never freed us from such hellish violence, a daily occurrence in history, nor from the massacres of Gauls, Indians, Cathars or Aborigines, nor from Auschwitz or Hiroshima. With the sciences not saying the meaning, only cultures can evoke it.

We writers, sometimes humanist in every sense, have no political power or armed forces or money, and fortunately. We wouldn't make any better use of them than anyone else; we have, alas, shown this ten times over. How few men said to be of culture know that true culture, universal, would be recognized by the fact that it would allow a man of culture not to crush anyone under the weight of his culture? So we only have at our disposal language and sometimes education. So we can only work in the long term. Exactly in the long term of the Grand Narrative. How then should we answer, with our specific means, these distressing, ever-repeated questions of the problem of evil, about which we remain disconsolate? How should we work for peace, the highest of all collective goods? How should we invent another culture? Not thinking about it, not talking about it, not organizing ever useless colloquia, but really contributing to it?

I propose an appropriate action – here it is – drawn once again from the Grand Narrative.

5 AN APPEAL TO UNIVERSITIES: FOR A COMMON KNOWLEDGE

A common pedagogical trunk that would bring together, little by little, all men, beginning with students, would favour the advancement of peace. So can we imagine the universities of the world devoting the first year of instruction to a programme that would allow students of every discipline and every country to have a similar horizon of knowledge and culture? These students would, in their turn, propagate it.

This general framework is inspired by the two following points:

- The hard sciences have already attained, like a white map, universality; they follow here the evolution of the chronopedia.
- Cultures, for their part, form a mosaic map of diverse forms and colours. Pedagogy assimilates the whole of these differences.

This framework is divided into three parts, one of which is reserved for the specialty of the studies undertaken (medicine, law, sciences or humanities) and the two others for this common programme.

The Common Programme:
For the First Year of University

I. *The Standard Programme for the Specialty*

II. *The Unitary Grand Narrative of Every Science*

Elementary physics and astrophysics: the formation of the Universe from the big bang to the cooling of the planets.

Elementary geophysics, chemistry and biology: from the birth of the Earth to the appearance of life and the evolution of species.

Elementary general anthropology: the emergence and spread of the human race.

Elementary agronomy, medicine and the passage to culture: the relationship of men to the Earth, to life, to humanity itself.

III. *The Mosaic of Human Cultures*

Elementary general linguistics: the geography and history of language families.

The languages of communication: their evolution.

Elementary history of religion: polytheisms, monotheisms, pantheisms, atheisms.

Elementary political science: the different types of government. Elementary economics: the division of wealth in the world.

Selected masterpieces of the fine arts and wisdoms. Sites: the heritage of humanity according to UNESCO.

NOTES

Chapter 1

1 Grand narrative = *Le Grand Récit*. *Grand* would normally mean big, the big narrative or story, but given the tradition of translating the phrase as the grand narrative, I have followed suit. All footnotes belong to the translator.

2 Scale = *échelle*, which can also mean ladder. Serres will play with this double meaning in ways that can't be reproduced in English.

3 A reference to the legend of Ys.

4 *Maintenant, que tiens-je en main?* *Maintenant*, 'now' in English, literally means holding in one's hand.

5 *Univers bactériel* is the French title of Margulis' *Microcosmos*.

6 Defined integral = *intégrale définie*; undefined integral = *intégrale définie*, which would normally be translated respectively as definite integral and indefinite integral.

7 Ghost in French is *revenant*, which is based on the verb *revenir*, to return or come back.

8 To prevent confusion, the memory here and to follow is the faculty of memory.

9 Only used in a few French phrases, *escient* is not a common word. It basically means knowledge.

10 Fossils come out of graves = *les fossiles sortent des fosses*.

11 Agencies = *instances*, which can mean an authority with the power of decision or the agencies of the psyche in Freud's psychology. I have used both of these translations – deciding authority and agency – in this work. But 'agency' may be misleading, giving too much of a sense of activity. Serres' use of *instance* isn't always clear. In a linguistic context, it can mean an instance of discourse. So it might loosely mean an instance of something, as it seems to on pages 51 and 139. Perhaps it should be taken in its etymological sense of *instans*, standing near or in, or even being in a stance. When it clearly doesn't mean some kind of decision-making body or Freudian-style agency; or when it doesn't obviously mean an instance of something, I'll write it as 'in-stance' to differentiate it from the common English term.

12 The prefix for *connaissance* derives from the Latin *com*, with.

13 In the song *La Garonne (Si la Garonne si elle avait voulu)*, the lyrics speculate on what the river might have done if it had deviated into different directions: 'If the Garonne had wanted to … it would have melted the pole.'

Chapter 2

1 In its every species = *sous toutes les espèces*. The reference to the Eucharist is more readily apparent in the French. The basic meaning Serres is trying to convey is 'in every form'.

2 Device = *appareil*. Set sail, earlier, is *appareiller*. Dentures, a kind of prosthetic, are also referred to as *appareil* in French.

3 Serres is using the image of a staircase. The word I translate here as 'stage', *palier*, also means a landing.

4 Enclosed farm = *ferme*, which is well named due to its resemblance to the French for closed or closed off, *fermé*.

5 Hyphen = *trait d'union*, which literally reads as union line.

6 Beyond = *au-delà*; below = *en deçà*. These terms are opposites in French. For instance, beyond the mountains and on this side of the mountains. For thresholds, 'above' and 'below' would be the best translations, but given that the 'meta' of 'metaphysics' is always understood to mean beyond, I can't reproduce the opposition here.

7 Tablet = *table*, which can also mean table. The tablet here is of course the *tabula* of the *tabula rasa*.

8 Love one another only inside one's group = *aimez-vous les uns les uns* [the ones, the ones]. The French for 'love one another' is *aimez-vous les uns les autres* [the ones, the others].

9 Card = *carte*, which can also mean map. Serres will play with this double meaning at times in this work. I'll use whichever one seems more relevant to the context and occasionally both.

10 This is my translation of a 1549 French definition of 'culture'.

11 Piraeus = *Le Pirée*, which in French could be construed to be a man's name.

12 The quote is from La Fontaine's *The Cockerel, the Cat and the Young Mouse*.

13 *La belle noiseuse* means something like the quarrelsome beautiful woman, but Serres is mainly interested in noise so I shall hereafter translate it as 'the noisy beauty'.

14 The Trace of the Step = *La trace du pas*, which would normally be translated as footprint. But given the importance of trace in this passage, I've given the literal translation.

15 Noise = *noise*, which originally meant noise but now means quarrel, hence the reference to violence. White noise = *bruit blanc*; a few lines down background noise = *bruit de fond*, *bruit* being the common word for noise these days. Serres will mostly use the latter term. I will translate both terms as 'noise', except where *bruit* is paired with *fureur*, sound and fury.

16 Giraudoux's *Supplément au voyage de Cook* has been translated as *The Virtuous Island*.

17 Piece of news = *actualité*. 'News' in the following sentence is *nouvelles*.

18 Bossuet, *Sermon on Death*.

19 Reunion, Accord = *Retrouvailles, accordailles*. *Accordailles* would usually mean betrothal, but here the notion of accord or agreement seems more in line with the text.

Chapter 3

1 Attempts = *Essais*, which could also mean essays.

2 See Corneille's *Horace*, v. 1301–18.

3 This is truer in French, for which the word *viabilité* can also mean the practicability of a road.

4 One = *on*, which is an impersonal pronoun. I will hereafter put 'one' in quotes whenever there is any possible confusion with any other sense of the English word, such as the number one. Sentences with this pronoun are often translated into a passive construction. I will make of point of not doing so only when it is important for the context.

5 The etymology of *on* goes back to the Latin *homo*.

6 The ferret and woods refers to a children's game similar to 'Hunt the Slipper'. The children play it while singing about the ferret of the woods who runs: the ferret, it's running, it's running; the ferret of the woods, my ladies …

7 Re-membered = *remembré*, which in French has nothing to do with memory.

8 'Reed' is a reference to Pascal's famous 'man is but a reed'.

9 A reference to Pascal's quote 'through space the universe encompasses [*comprend*] and swallows me up like a point; through thought I comprehend the world'.

10 Number = *nombre*. Besides the numerical meaning, *nombre* also has a rhetorical one: the harmony resulting from a certain arrangement of words in prose or verse.

11 In French, 'genuine or counterfeit' reads as true or false.

12 From the monologue [my translation]: What is this oblong capsule used for? An inkpot, monsieur, or a scissors box?

13 Play = *jeu*, which can also mean game.

14 Moral conscience = *conscience morale*. *Conscience* can also mean consciousness.

15 Bad consciousness = *mauvaise conscience*, which would normally be translated as 'guilty consciousness', but I feel that would obscure Serres' point.

16 In French, scapegoat is *bouc émissaire*, literally emissary goat.

17 Excluded middle or third = *tiers-exclu*, which normally means excluded middle but in French reads as excluded third.

18 The latter part of this sentence refers to the refrain of the 'La Marseillaise'.

19 Consciousness = *conscience*, which could equally mean conscience.

20 Triturated = *triturer*, whose Latin etymology is to thresh. Beaten = *battre*, which should be translated as 'thresh' here, but that would obscure Serres' point.

21 The quote is from the French biologist François Jacob.

22 'The Horla' is a short story by Maupassant. Serres reads *hors là* in the title: outside the there.

23 Illness = *mal*, which is also the French for evil. In the following two subsections, where *mal* is used in both senses, I will render it as ill, otherwise it will be translated as evil or illness, depending on the context.

24 Get to work in the coal mine = *aller au charbon*, or go to the coal, which is an idiom for getting to work or rolling one's sleeves up.

25 The Miserable = *Miséreux*, which also and more usually means the poor or the destitute, but in this section the poor don't seem to be at issue so much as the miserable or wretched. So *miséreux, misère and misèrable* have all been rendered as some form of misery or wretchedness. Nevertheless, in the previous and following sections, these words do mean the destitute. Unfortunately, it is not possible to reproduce this double meaning in English.

26 *The Three Blind Men of Compiègne* is a medieval story in which a young mischievous cleric sees three blind men walking a little too surely asking for alms. So he decides to test them by offering them a crown, which he does not give. Of course, each of the blind men assumes one of the others received the money, which leads to problems when they go to a restaurant.

27 The French word *la découverte* evokes discovery and uncovering more than the corresponding English term, excavation. Hence hereafter and in the subsection title I'll make use of 'uncovering'.

28 *Loyauté* can mean honesty as well as fairness and uprightness in behaviour.

29 The quote is from Georges Guynemer, a top French fighter pilot who went missing during the First World War.

30 Without = *sans*; with = *par*. There is no opposition in the French between these two prepositions.

31 In French, 'to live' is *vivre*, and 'to survive' is *survivre*, so there is a stronger linguistic tie there than in English. *Vivre de* [to live from] in the following sentence has the sense of subsisting because of something, for instance, living by one's pen or intelligence, by bread alone, living on a salary or on a vegetarian diet, or living off one's savings. 'Living from' seems to summarize all these meanings best.

32 Traverse = *traverse*, which contains the French preposition *vers*, towards; encounter = *rencontre*, which contains *contre*, against.

33 Voluble = *volubiles*, which may also be intended in its Latin etymological sense of turning around, rolling. The French word once meant changing and inconstant.

34 The original French made no mention of 'and English words'.

35 *Vers* most often means towards. Interestingly, the *ward* of 'towards' derives from the same Latin root as the French *vers*. I will translate it as towards but will retain the French when that particular word is at issue.

36 *Parler petit-nègre* means to speak pidgin, however the word *nègre* has become highly offensive.

37 Topological variety = *variété topologique*, which would normally be translated as topological manifold.

38 Tip and turn = *verser*.

39 Whenever the phrase 'to bustle about' appears in this book, it translates *s'agiter*. Hereafter, I will at times render *s'agiter* as some form of agitate.

40 Genitor, it creates Him = *Géniteur, il Le crée*. It is not entirely clear what the intended referent is for the masculine pronoun here: *il*. Every noun in the preceding seven or eight lines is masculine except harmony, difference, genesis and metre. My best guess would be the Spirit of Love or perhaps the Son, probably intended as the same thing.

41 The word *Deo* was left out in the French edition. I've assumed this was a mistake and reinstated it.

42 *Qu'est-ce qu'une bonne histoire et qu'est-ce, enfin, que l'Histoire?*

43 You and me, we like mustard; you and he, you go to the seaside = *toi et moi aimons la moutarde; toi et lui allez à la mer*.

44 One is hot = *on fait chaud*, which isn't said in French. It is hot = *il fait chaud*.

45 You and you = *tu et toi*, which are the subject case and the object case.

46 Name = *nom*; pronoun = *pronom*.

47 Redressing = *redressant*, which I would usually translate as 'rectifying'. Rectification has a broader sense of correcting mistakes than 'redressing' does, not to mention the added meaning of conversion.

48 Figure = *figure*, which could also mean a figure of speech.

49 *Nuisible* means pest and literally reads as harmful.

50 Material or hard(ware) = *matérielles ou dures*; logos-based and soft(ware) = *logicielles et douces*.

51 First World War = *Première Guerre mondiale*; globalization = *mondialisation*.

52 Inches and feet = *pouces et coudées* [cubits], which refer to thumbs and elbows.

Chapter 4

1 Implicates = *implique*, which contains *pli*, the French for fold. It would usually be translated as 'implied'. But the term's archaic sense of folding or intertwining also seems to be at play here.